T0240624

Undergraduate Topics in Computer Science

Undergraduate Topics in Computer Science (UTiCS) delivers high-quality instructional content for undergraduates studying in all areas of computing and information science. From core foundational and theoretical material to final-year topics and applications, UTiCS books take a fresh, concise, and modern approach and are ideal for self-study or for a one- or two-semester course. The texts are all authored by established experts in their fields, reviewed by an international advisory board, and contain numerous examples and problems. Many include fully worked solutions.

More information about this series at http://www.springer.com/series/7592

Frank Nielsen

Introduction to HPC
with MPI for Data Science

 Springer

Frank Nielsen
École Polytechnique
Palaiseau
France

and

Sony Computer Science Laboratories, Inc.
Tokyo
Japan

Series editor
Ian Mackie

Advisory Board
Samson Abramsky, University of Oxford, Oxford, UK
Karin Breitman, Pontifical Catholic University of Rio de Janeiro, Rio de Janeiro, Brazil
Chris Hankin, Imperial College London, London, UK
Dexter Kozen, Cornell University, Ithaca, USA
Andrew Pitts, University of Cambridge, Cambridge, UK
Hanne Riis Nielson, Technical University of Denmark, Kongens Lyngby, Denmark
Steven Skiena, Stony Brook University, Stony Brook, USA
Iain Stewart, University of Durham, Durham, UK

ISSN 1863-7310   ISSN 2197-1781   (electronic)
Undergraduate Topics in Computer Science
ISBN 978-3-319-21902-8   ISBN 978-3-319-21903-5   (eBook)
DOI 10.1007/978-3-319-21903-5

Library of Congress Control Number: 2015960834

Printed on acid-free paper

This Springer imprint is published by SpringerNature
The registered company is Springer International Publishing AG Switzerland

To the memory of Reine
To Audrey Léna and Julien Léo

Preface

Welcome to the world of High Performance Computing! Welcome to the world of high performance Data Science!

In this textbook, we give an introduction to *high performance computing* (HPC for short) for *data science* (DS). Therefore, this textbook is organized into two parts: The first part (six chapters) covers the fundamentals of HPC while the second part (five chapters) describes the basics of DS and shows how to write distributed programs for the basic sequential algorithms in order to cope with large size datasets. Nowadays, many large-scale datasets are publicly available, and these datasets offer potentially a rich source of information that need to be purposely extracted.

We mainly distinguish two ways to design parallel algorithms: (1) Parallelizing algorithms on single multi-core shared memory machines using multi-threading, or (2) Parallelizing algorithms on a *cluster of machines* with distributed memory.

On the one hand, when parallelizing algorithms on shared memory architectures (like your smartphones, tablets, and very soon your smartwatches and other Internet of Things, IoTs, too!), computing hardware units (cores) are located on the same chip, and we can easily parallelize for example video decoding or rendering tasks using multi-threading. This kind of parallelism is said *fine-grained* but it is limited by the physical number of cores one can put on a chip (typically eight cores on a high-end smartphone in 2015). On the other hand, clusters of machines (that are distributed memory architectures) allow one to scale up resources on-the-fly according to the dataset size. There is a lot of flexibility when building a cluster of machines such as choosing heterogeneous computer nodes and deciding which topology is best for interconnecting those nodes. This kind of parallelism is called *coarse-grained* since bulks of local computations are performed independently on the machines before communications take place between them.

This undergraduate textbook focuses on designing parallel algorithms on distributed memory by using the standard interface called Message passing interface (MPI). MPI is the *de facto* standard to operate communications and global collaborative calculations between nodes of a cluster of machines. There exist several vendor implementations of MPI that can themselves be binded with several programming languages such as C, C++, Fortran, Python, etc. We chose to use the C++ oriented-object language for implementing data science algorithms and use the C binding application programming interface (API) of OpenMPI to write parallel programs.

The two parts of this book are described concisely as follows:

Part I   Introduction to HPC with MPI. We start by giving a quick introduction to the HPC world in Chap. 1, and describe both Amdalh's law and Gustafson's law that characterize the theoretical optimal speed-up and scaled speed-up.

Then we describe the main concepts of MPI and its programming interface: We introduce the notions of blocking/non-blocking communications, deadlocks, and the various global communication routines (like broadcast, scatter, gather, all-to-all, reduce, parallel prefix, etc.).

In Chap. 3, we emphasize on the role of the topology of the interconnection network. We shall distinguish between the *physical topology* and the *virtual topology* (or logical topology) that is considered when designing parallel algorithms. In particular, we describe communication procedures on the ring (including the optimized pipeline broadcasting) and on the hypercube. The latter one relies on a particular numbering of the nodes, called the Gray code.

In Chap. 4, we describe the main parallel algorithms for sorting on distributed memory. First, we naively parallelize the renowned Quicksort algorithm, and then introduce HyperQuicksort and the PSRS procedure (stands for parallel sorting by regular sampling) that is widely used in practice.

In Chap. 5, we study a few algorithms for multiplying matrices and vectors. We concisely explain the various techniques for computing matrix products on the topologies of the ring and of the torus.

In Chap. 6, we introduce the hot paradigm of parallel programming called "MapReduce" (that is often used with its open source counterpart called Hadoop). MapReduce allows to handle a very large number of networked computers (say, several thousands) by using programs that are built with two main user-defined functions called `map` and `reduce`. But MapReduce is also a full framework that includes a master–slave architecture that is able to take into consideration various hardware failures, or to re-route parallel computation tasks (jobs) on other machines when some machines become too slow (the so-called stragglers). We explain how to program those types of MapReduce algorithms in MPI (MPI has zero-fault tolerance) using a dedicated software library called MR-MPI.

Part II   Introduction to Data Science. This part gives both a concise introduction to data science and furthermore explains how to parallelize those algorithms using MPI.

First, we start by describing the two most fundamental data clustering techniques that are flat partition-based clustering (in Chap. 7) and hierarchical tree-like clustering (in Chap. 8). Clustering is a very fundamental notion in exploratory data science for discovering classes in datasets, groups of homogeneous data.

Then we consider supervised classification using the k-nearest neighbor rule in Chap. 9 and make the connection with k-means.

In Chap. 10, we present yet another recent paradigm in computer science that allows one to solve optimization problems approximately on large datasets (potentially high-dimensional too!): That is, we seek core-sets that are subsets of data that guarantee an overall good approximation on the full datasets. This technique has become recently popular, and allows us to scale down Big Data to Tiny Data! Since data are usually given in high-dimension spaces, we also briefly explain a powerful technique to perform effective linear dimension reduction by stating the Johnson–Lindenstrauss' theorem, and giving a short recipe to compute a low-distortion embedding of data into a lower dimensional space that preserves distances within a prescribed approximation factor. Interestingly, the dimension of the embedding is independent of the original extrinsic dimension but depends on logarithmically on the dataset size and the approximation factor.

In the last Chap. 11, we cover a few algorithms on graphs. Graphs are commonly encountered when performing social network analysis and in other application fields. We introduce both a sequential heuristic and a parallel heuristic to find a dense subgraph in a graph that is closed to the "densest" subgraph. Finally, we explain the simple task of testing graph isomorphism by branch-and-bound techniques on computer cluster. Testing graph isomorphism is a remarkable problem since its theoretical complexity is not yet settled (although some polynomial algorithms exist for some specific subclasses of graphs).

At the end of each chapter, we summarize the essential points to remember. The reader is invited to skim through these summaries for a first quick reading. Over 40+ exercises are given at the end of some of the chapters: These exercises are labeled with various difficulty degrees and allow the reader to test his/her understanding of the material covered. Sections that begin with an asterisk may be skipped and read later on.

The main goal of this textbook is to allow you to design parallel algorithms and then program your parallel algorithm using C++ with the C binding of MPI. The second goal is to expose you to the richness of the fields of HPC and DS, and hopefully to foster their interactions.

This undergraduate textbook has been written to be an introductory text on HPC and DS. Only basic knowledge of algorithmics and programming abilities are assumed. Therefore advanced notions in both HPC and DS fields are not covered nor mentioned. For example, task scheduling problems and automatic parallelization of nested loops although important in HPC are not covered. Similarly, regression techniques and kernel machine learning methods for the data science field are omitted.

Happy Reading!

December 2015   Frank Nielsen

Acknowledgments

I am grateful to the following talented colleagues who gave me their valuable feedback (list in random order) and helped me debug the textbook: Claudia d'Ambrosio, Ulysse Beaugnon, Annaël Bonneton, Jean-Baptiste Bordes, Patrice Calégari, Henri Casanova, Antoine Delignat-Lavaud, Amélie Héliou, Alice Héliou, Léo Liberti, Frédéric Magoulès, Gautier Marti, Sameh Mohamed, François Morain, Richard Nock, Pierre-Louis Poirion, Stéphane Redon, Thomas Sibut-Pinote, Benjamin Smith, Antoine Soulé, Bogdan Tomchuk, Sonia Toubaline, and Frédéric Vivien. Besides those colleagues, I also benefited from many valuable discussions with other colleagues that will recognize themselves by reading these lines. I would also like to thank all the students (promotion X13) enrolled in the INF442 curriculum of École Polytechnique (Palaiseau, France) for their fruitful comments and feedback, and to the Computer Science Department of École Polytechnique (DIX) for their support.

Book Web Page

Extra materials for this textbook (including 35+ programs in MPI/C++/ R/Scilab/Gnuplot/Processing, slides, related links, and other goodies) can be found at the book web page:

```
https://www.lix.polytechnique.fr/nielsen/HPC4DS/
```

The program source codes that are available online are indicated throughout the chapters as follows:

```
WWW source code: example.cpp
```

This book has been typeset using MikTeX (`http://miktex.org/`) with figures prepared using the Ipe drawing software (`http://ipe.otfried.org/`).

Contents

List of Figures

List of Tables

Part I
High Performance Computing (HPC) with the Message Passing Interface (MPI)

Chapter 1
A Glance at High Performance Computing (HPC)

1.1 What is High Performance Computing (HPC)?

High Performance Computing, or HPC for short, is an area encompassing among others the various paradigms of parallel programming, their related programming languages and application programming interfaces (APIs), the dedicated software tools, the international specialized conferences (ACM/IEEE Super-Computing, or SC for short), etc. Loosely speaking, HPC is both the *scientific* and *technical* fields of study of "Super-Computers" (SCs).

The list of the top 500 supercomputers (called the Top500[1]) is regularly updated and available on the Internet. In 2014, it is the supercomputer named Tianhe-2 (translated from Chinese as MilkyWay-2 in English) of the *National Super Computer Center* in Guangzhou (China) that received the top rank position. This supercomputer consists of an impressive 3.12 million cores (a core being a processing unit, PU), and delivers an amazing overall performance of 54.9 Petaflops, where a PFlops is 10^{15} floating-point operations per second. This number one supercomputer requires 17.8 MW in electrical power to work properly! Roughly speaking, the cost of 1 MW is about 100 dollars/hour, meaning that the electricity cost of this supercomputer is about 1 million dollars per year

Table 1.1 summarizes the main scale orders when referring to the processing power and memory storage capabilities of (super-)computers. Nowadays, the international community is racing to reach the Exaflop performance (10^{18} flops, 1024 Pflops) that we hope to have ready for 2017–2020, and then will come the era of zetaFlops (10^{21}), maybe around 2030 (?), and thereafter the yottaFlops (10^{24}), and so on.

This traditional rating of supercomputers is based only on peak processing performance of arithmetic operations, and completely ignores the energy cost required to obtain this performance. Another twice-yearly eco-friendly ranking called the *green HPC*[2] focuses instead on scoring supercomputers according to their performance in

---

[1]http://www.top500.org/.

[2]http://www.green500.org/.

© Springer International Publishing Switzerland 2016
F. Nielsen, *Introduction to HPC with MPI for Data Science*, Undergraduate
Topics in Computer Science, DOI 10.1007/978-3-319-21903-5_1

Table 1.1 Scale orders characterizing the overall computing and memory performance of super-computers: Super-computers are rated in FLOPs (floating-point operations per second), and the memory size in bytes (with one byte being eight packed bits)

Unit	Scale	Computing performance	Memory size (in bytes)
K (kilo)	10^3	KFLOPS	KB
M (mega)	10^6	MFLOPS	MB
G (giga)	10^9	GFLOPS	GB
T (tera)	10^{12}	TFLOPS	TB
P (peta)	10^{15}	PFLOPS	PB
E (exa)	10^{18}	EFLOPS (around 2017–2020)	EB
Z (zeta)	10^{21}	ZFLOPS	ZB
Y (yotta)	10^{24}	YFLOPS	YB
...	...	...	...
googol	10^{100}	googolFLOPS	googol bytes
...	...	...	...

When we choose $1024 = 2^{10}$ (a power of 2) instead of $1000 = 10^3$ for the gap between two consecutive orders, we get the following international units (SI): Ki (2^{10}), Mi (2^{20}), Gi (2^{30}), Ti (2^{40}), Pi (2^{50}), Eo (2^{60}), Zo (2^{70}), and Yi (2^{80})

MFlops/W. In November 2014, the L-CSC supercomputer from the GSI Helmholtz Center (Darmstadt, Germany) achieved the performance of 5.27 gigaflops per Watt. For comparison, this L-CSC supercomputer ranks 168 in the Top500, with 10,976 cores, and has a 593.6 TFlops peak performance. Although processing power is definitely an important criterion (and one that motivates us to implement HPC solutions), one also needs to take other parameters into account, like the overall memory size, the network bandwidth of the interconnection network, and so on. Finally, let us point out that the cost per GFLOPs exponentially decreases, and is estimated to cost 0.08 US$ in January 2015.

1.2   Why Do We Need HPC?

The first answer that comes to mind is that HPC is useful for being *faster* and being thus *more precise* overall (say, for simulation purposes like weather forecasting, numerical mechanics for car crash tests, or in other various complex phenomena modelings). HPC also allows one to solve *larger* problems: simulations can be carried out either on more finely-meshed domains or on bigger data sets (the Big Data trend). But what is less widely known is that HPC is very useful for *saving energy*: indeed, at constant flops performance, we prefer to use more lower-profile processors that consume less overall than high-profile processors which require more energy to work. Finally, HPC is well-suited to some kinds of algorithms that are *intrinsically* parallel in essence. Indeed, algorithms in image or video processing often compute filters that are operations that can be carried out independently in parallel for each pixel or voxel (in medical imaging). In the latter case, graphics cards (*Graphics Processing Unit*, GPU) are hardware cards that have many cores (nowadays, a few thousand). For example, the high-end NVIDIA® card has 1536 cores and deliver a performance of 2.3 TFlops. AMD® Radeon Sky 900 GPU has 3584 core and get 1.5 TFlops (in double-precision). Those GPU cards not only allows one to get stunning images, they are also useful for general computing: this is the GPGPU (*General Purpose Graphics Processing Unit*) paradigm.

Let us now more precisely mention several case studies of supercomputing:

- Use models to perform *simulations*. Otherwise, it is too difficult to build (blower or wind tunnel) or too expensive to build (car/airplane crash test), or too slow on usual computers (evolution of climate or galaxies), or too dangerous in practice (nuclear weapons, drugs, pollution, epidemics).
- Get results *fast*, and ideally without delay. That is, allow incremental results delivered by *on-line algorithms*: some results have a time-limited value, like weather conditions, which are only useful to predict in the future! Tomorrow's weather is only useful to know if we can predict it before tomorrow! Similarly, it is interesting to be the *first* to get the results in order to take decisions as soon as possible (like in the stock market, where high-frequency trading algorithms are automatically booking orders).
- Processing *big* data-sets like genome analytics or families of genomes, or even to search for extra-terrestrial intelligence (see the *SETI* project[3]).

1.3 Big Data: The Four Vs (Volume, Variety, Velocity, Value)

Big Data is a buzzword that has been extremely used in the media and encompasses many meanings. We can define it as the technologies for processing massive data-sets, or performing *large-scale data processing*. We can characterize the processing of big data-sets using the four Vs:

- Volume,
- Variety (heterogeneous data),
- Velocity (data obtained continuously from sensors),
- Value (not simulation but valuable insights).

---

[3]http://www.seti.org/.

1.4   Parallel Programming Paradigms: MPI and MapReduce

There are several paradigms for programming parallel algorithms on large/big data-sets (a sub-area of HPC). Those models depend on whether they are robust to computer or network errors (like hardware failures). Nowadays, the two main programming models that are complementary to each other are:

- Programming with MPI (*Message Passing Interface*), which has zero tolerance for hardware or network errors, but offers programmers a flexible framework, and
- Programming with *MapReduce* (or its free open source version, *Hadoop*[4]) which includes an infrastructure tolerant of errors and hardware failures, but has a rather a limited model of parallel computing compared with MPI.

1.5   Granularity: Fined-Grained Versus Coarse-Grained Parallelism

One can design and program parallel algorithms using various degrees of granularity of parallelism. Informally speaking, the granularity is the proportion of the code that can be parallelized. Granularity can also be explained as the ratio of computing time to communication time in a parallel algorithm. We classify parallel algorithms into three main categories according to their granularity:

- *Fine-grained parallelism*: at the variable level inside the same task. Data are often transferred between the computing units. It is worth noting that the instruction set of common microprocessors based on the x86 architecture (released in 1978) has been extended with various extension sets like MMX, SSE or SSE2, etc. Many of these extensions provide SIMD instructions (*Streaming SIMD Extensions*[5]). Fine-grained parallelism can also rely on GPU code snippets of the graphics card.
- *Mid-grained parallelism*: at the level of tasks of a same program using threads.
- *Coarse-grained parallelism*: Data transfers are limited, and occur after big chunks of calculations. Coarse-grained parallelism can also be done at the application level using the task scheduler, which handles tasks to be executed on the computer cluster (the "parallel machine").

---

[4]http://hadoop.apache.org/.

[5]http://fr.wikipedia.org/wiki/Streaming_SIMD_Extensions.

1.6 Architectures for Supercomputing: Memory and Network

We classify parallel computers either as parallel machines with *shared memory* or as parallel machines with *distributed memory*. Usually, on a multi-core processor, all cores use the same (shared) memory banks: this architecture, called *symmetric shared memory multiprocessor* (*SMP*), considers all cores as independent computing units. Even when we consider this shared memory model of parallel computation, we need to take into account the various types of shared memory: fast register memory located inside the processor and L1, L2, L3 cache memories ('L' for layer, emphasizing the hierarchical memory structure), hard-disk drives (*disk arrays*), *Solid-State Drives* (SSDs), magnetic tapes for backup, etc.

In practice, in order to obtain good computer performance, one needs to take into account the *spatial locality* of data when accessing memory. For example, let us compare this C/C++/Java nested loop code:

```
for (int j=0; j<n; ++j)
  {
    for (int i=0; i<n; ++i)
       {y[i] += a[i][j] * x[j];}
  }
```

with this other code:

```
for (int i=0; i<n; ++i)
  {
    for (int j=0; j<n; ++j)
       {y[i] += a[i][j] * x[j];}
  }
```

In theory, those two programs have the same complexity: quadratic time, in $O(n^2)$. However, in practice, compilers[6] carry out various optimizations (like caching variables or pipelining instructions and fetching) for fast memory access. To report a concrete example of the time difference between these two code snippets, we got 1.45 s when $n = 10,000$ for the non-optimized code, and 0.275 s for the optimized binary executable obtained after compiler optimization using the g++ -O command.

On the opposite side of shared memory architectures, we have parallel computers with distributed memory that consist of independent computers linked by an interconnection network. The chosen topology for the interconnection network affects the efficiency of communications, but also implies a corresponding hardware cost. Figure 1.1 displays common topologies for the interconnection network. We distinguish between the bus interconnection and the complete graph interconnection network. Messages can be exchanged point-to-point (for example, using the bus of the complete graph) or by being routed using intermediate nodes.

Figure 1.2 depicts schematically the evolution of computer architectures over the last decades: as manufacturing processes like lithography have improved

---

[6]See the -O option argument of g++. Other options are listed using g++ -help.

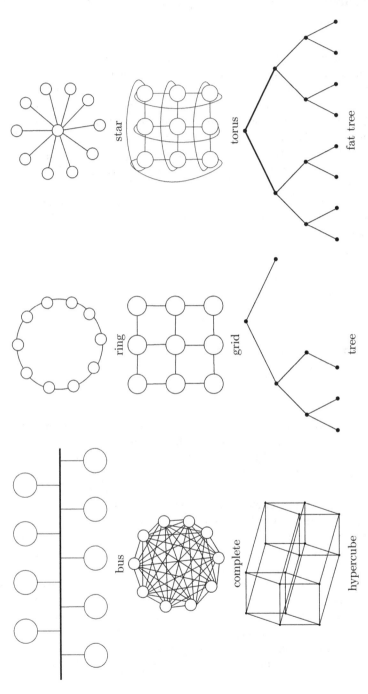

Fig. 1.1 Common topologies met in practice for the interconnection network in a distributed memory computer cluster. Communication links can be either one-way or bi-directional

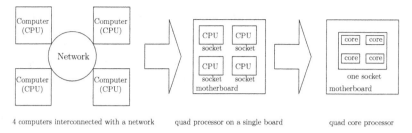

4 computers interconnected with a network   quad processor on a single board   quad core processor

Fig. 1.2 Evolution of computer architectures: from small interconnected computers to multi-processor computers and recently multi-core computers

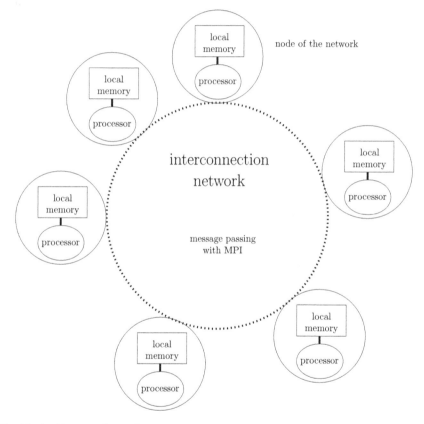

Fig. 1.3 Architecture of a parallel machine with distributed memory: nodes communicate between them using the network by message passing (that is, sending and receiving messages using the standard API: MPI)

considerably, a former small network of 4 interconnected computers has been put first on a single computer, as a quad-processor computer using a socket per processor to connect the processors to the motherboard, and recently we have a quad-core CPU that is attached by a single socket to the motherboard for communication efficiency. However, this on-chip reduction is still limited to a few cores and cannot (yet?) be scaled.

Distributed memory architecture have a local memory associated to each processor: there is no shared memory in this model. Memory access to another process is explicitly carried out by exchanging messages on the network. Figure 1.3 illustrates this model of parallel machine that we focus on in this book. It is the interconnection network that determines the speed of data access. In general, three features of the network are considered:

- *latency*: time required to initiate a communication,
- *bandwidth*: rate of data transfer over communication links,

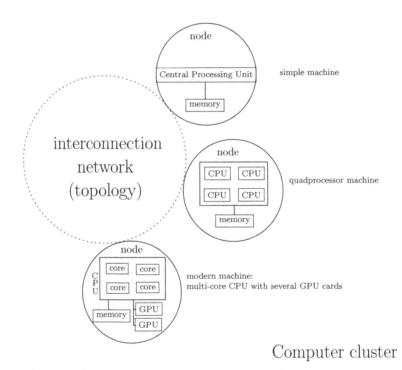

Fig. 1.4 Architecture of a computer cluster: computing resources are located in nodes that are interconnected using a network. Computers attached to the cluster (the parallel machine) can either be simple computers (a CPU), or multi-processor machines (several CPUs with sockets on the mother boards), or modern multi-core CPUs with several graphics cards (GPUs). In theory, for sake of simplicity, we assume that each process is run on a distinct node on a single processing unit (CPU or core)

- *topology*: physical architecture of the interconnection network (like the star topology or the grid topology).

There exist several models of parallel programming. On vector supercomputers (like the Cray machines), one can use the paradigm of *Single Instruction Multiple Data* (or SIMD for short). On multi-core computers with shared memory, one can use *multi-threading* and its standardized application programming interface called OpenMP[7] (*Open Multi-Platform shared-memory parallel programming*). We can also consider *hybrid models* of computation, which use the GPU for some of the computations. GPU are controlled using several possible APIs like CUDA, OpenCL or HMPP. Finally, we can use a *blended style* where each MPI process can use several threads, and both *blended and hybrid styles* where each multi-core processor node are programmed using MPI and GPU interfaces. Figure 1.4 displays the architecture of a computer cluster. For the sake of simplicity, we assume in this textbook that each process runs on its proper node on a single processing unit (CPU or core).

1.7 Speedup

Let t_{seq} denote the time spent by a *sequential program* (also called *serial* program) and t_P the time spent by an equivalent *parallel program* executed on P processors. We denote by t_1 the execution time of the parallel program ran on $P = 1$ processor.[8] We define the following three quantities:

- *speedup*: $\text{speedup}(P) = \frac{t_{\text{seq}}}{t_P}$. Often, we have $\frac{t_{\text{seq}}}{t_P} \simeq \frac{t_1}{t_P}$,
- *efficiency*: $e = \frac{\text{speedup}(P)}{P} = \frac{t_{\text{seq}}}{P \times t_P}$. Less efficiency means that there is a large parallel overhead (in contrast with linear speedup). An optimal linear speedup implies a maximal efficiency of one, and vice-versa,
- *scalability*: $\text{scalability}(O, P) = \frac{t_O}{t_P}$ with $O < P$.

1.7.1 Scalability and Iso-efficiency Analysis

Most of the time, one is often interested in characterizing how parallel algorithms scale in practice with the number of available processors P. Indeed, one would like to use resources *on the fly* as more nodes of a computer cluster are dynamically allocated to the project (for instance, once other project runs on a cluster have been completed). A *scalable* parallel algorithm is an algorithm that makes it easy to execute on P processors for any arbitrary value of P. For a given problem size n, when we increase the number of processors P, the efficiency usually tends to decrease. Thus

---

[7]http://openmp.org/.

[8]For sake of simplicity, we assume that each process runs on a distinct processor that is a node of the distributed-memory parallel machine.

in order to preserve a good speedup when P increases, it is also important to increase the data size n of its input: that is, the parameters n (data size) and P (processors) are correlated.

This is precisely the point that iso-efficiency analysis focuses on. The key question in iso-efficiency analysis is how to decide the growth rate ρ of the input size as a function of the number of processors, in order to keep the efficiency constant. The smaller the ρ value, the better! Given a problem, one tries to design good isoefficient algorithms.

1.7.2 Amdahl's Law: Characterizing the Asymptotic Speedup for Fixed Data-Size Problems

Gene M. Amdahl (IBM) first characterized in 1967 the ideal expected performance speedup [1] as follows: let α_{par} denote the proportion of the code that can be parallelized, and α_{seq} the proportion of code that is intrinsically sequential (that is, that can not be parallelized). We have $\alpha_{par} + \alpha_{seq} = 1$. Now, we can mathematically write the time t_P of a parallel implementation using P processors as

$$t_P = \alpha_{seq}t_1 + (1 - \alpha_{seq})\frac{t_1}{P}$$
$$= \alpha_{par}\frac{t_1}{P} + \alpha_{seq}t_1.$$

Assuming $t_{seq} = t_1$, we deduce that the speedup of a parallel implementation using P computers is

$$\text{speedup}(P) = \frac{t_1}{t_P}$$
$$= \frac{(\alpha_{par} + \alpha_{seq})t_1}{(\alpha_{seq} + \frac{\alpha_{par}}{P})t_1}$$
$$= \frac{1}{\alpha_{seq} + \frac{\alpha_{par}}{P}}.$$

Thus, as the number of processing elements tend to infinity ($P \to \infty$), the speedup is always *upper bounded* by the proportion $\alpha_{seq} = 1 - \alpha_{par}$ of non-parallelizable code as follows:

$$\lim_{P \to \infty} \text{speedup}(P) = \frac{1}{\alpha_{seq}} = \frac{1}{1 - \alpha_{par}}.$$

Figure 1.5 plots the graphs of the functions speedup(P) for $0 \le \alpha_{seq} \le 1$, using a logarithmic scale on the x-axis. Amdahl's law reflects the sequential bottleneck in parallelism.

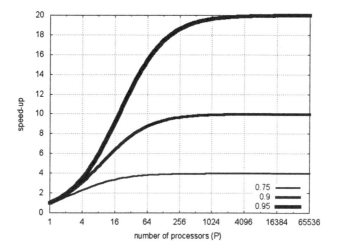

Fig. 1.5 Amdahl's law characterize the speedup as a function of the percentage of parallelizable code. We used a logarithmic scale on the x-axis. Observe that the maximum speedup is always upper-bounded by $\frac{1}{\alpha_{seq}}$, where α_{seq} denotes the proportion of serial code

Theorem 1 *Amdahl's law gives the optimal asymptotic speedup of a parallel program as* speedup $= \frac{1}{\alpha_{seq}} = \frac{1}{1-\alpha_{par}}$, *where* α_{par} *denotes the proportion of the program that can be parallelized and* $\alpha_{seq} = 1 - \alpha_{par}$ *the proportion of code that is intrinsically sequential.*

The Gnuplot[9] code for plotting the theoretical curves of Fig. 1.5 is given below:

WWW source code: `Amdahl.gnuplot`

```
set terminal png
set output 'Amdahl.png'
set encoding iso_8859_1
set logscale x 2
set xrange [1:65536]
set autoscale
set xlabel "number of processors (P)"
set ylabel "speed-up"
set key on right bottom
set pointsize 2
Amdahl(p,s) = 1/(s + ( (1-s)/p))
set grid
show grid
plot Amdahl(x,1-0.75) title "0.75"  lt -1 lw 3,\
   Amdahl(x,1-0.90) title "0.9" lt -1 lw 5, \
Amdahl(x,1-0.95)title "0.95" lt -1 lw 7
```

---

[9]A free graphing utility that can be downloaded from http://www.gnuplot.info/.

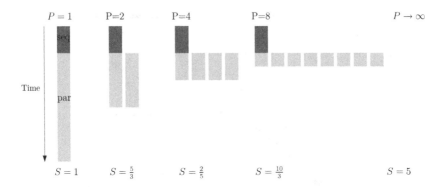

Fig. 1.6 Amdahl's law considers the speedup for a fixed data size and provides an upper bound on the maximal speedup as the inverse of the fraction of the proportion of the sequential code. Here, the maximal speedup is asymptotically $\times 5$

Note that Amdahl's law makes the assumption that the input data size is *fixed* (this is not a strong assumption, since there are many programs with constant input sizes). In other words, the workload is prescribed once and for all. It states that no matter how many processors P you have, the theoretical maximal speedup will be upper bounded asymptotically by the inverse of the proportion of serial code: speedup $= \frac{1}{\alpha_{\text{seq}}}$. This is illustrated in Fig. 1.6. Observe also that the performance to price ratio falls quickly as P increases.

Although that the speedup is theoretically upper bounded by P, one can sometimes obtain better speedups in practice! That is, one can sometimes observe *super-linear speedups*. This may seem surprising at first, but this phenomenon is simply explained by the fact that in practice there is a hierarchy of memories. For example, when one uses P computers in parallel for processing n data, we implicitly assume that each computer can store $\frac{n}{P}$ data in its local memory (the RAM). However, one computer needs to use hard disks to store the $\frac{n-1}{P}$ remaining data that it cannot store in the RAM, and disk access is far slower than RAM access. Thus super-linear speedups can be observed for large data sets, simply by allowing all data to be stored in the local memory (RAM) of the processors.

1.7.3 Gustafson's Law: Scaled Speedup, Increasing Data Size with Resources

Gustafson's law [2] characterizes the impact of *data parallelism*, challenging Amdahl's law by offering a novel viewpoint. In this setting, we no longer assume that the data size is constant, but rather that it depends on the number of processors P (the available resources). This framework is therefore different from Amdahl's law, which considers a fixed input (with incompressible running time, the critical time, due to the intrinsic serial code). Indeed, Gustafson observes that in practice program users tend to set the data size according to the available resources in order to get reasonable[10] overall execution time. Setting the data size according to the computing resources is the case for example in video processing or medical imaging, where people tend to first rescale large image data input down so that it fits into memory and yields reasonable expected running times. Similarly, in simulations the data size depends on the chosen grid resolution. As faster (multi-core) machines become available to users, the users pour more data into programs. In this scenario, data sizes are considered to be arbitrary large (for example, think of 4K videos, 8K videos, etc.).

Again, let α_{par} denote the proportion of parallelizable code and $\alpha_{seq} = 1 - \alpha_{par}$ the proportion of sequential code on all the P processors. Then the speedup is the ratio of the sequential processing time $t_{seq} + P t_{par}$ (for a workload $\alpha_{seq} n + \alpha_{par} n P$) to the time $t_{seq} + t_{par}$ achieved by the parallel algorithm:

$$\text{speedup}(P) = \frac{t_{seq} + P \times t_{par}}{t_{seq} + t_{par}}.$$

Since $\frac{t_{seq}}{t_{seq}+t_{par}} = \alpha_{seq}$ by definition, and $\frac{t_{par}}{t_{seq}+t_{par}} = \alpha_{par}$, we deduce that the speedup is given by

$$\boxed{\text{speedup}_{\text{Gustafson}}(P) = \alpha_{seq} + P \times \alpha_{par} = \alpha_{seq} + (1 - \alpha_{seq})P.}$$

Theorem 2 *Gustafson's law states that the optimal speedup is asymptotically* speedup$(P) = P \times \alpha_{par}$, *where* $\alpha_{par} > 0$ *denotes the proportion of the code that is parallelizable.*

When the problem size increases for a fixed serial portion, speedup grows as more processors are added. Therefore Gustafson called his speedup analysis *scaled speedup*. We observe that the workload is scaled up with the number of processors in order to maintain a fixed execution time. Thus Gustafson's philosophy is that the true power of a parallel system is demonstrated when large enough data problems are given in input, as depicted in Fig. 1.7.

1.7.4 Simulating Parallel Machines on Sequential Computers

One can simulate *any* parallel algorithm on a classic computer by sequentially executing the elementary instructions or pieces of code for the P processors $P_1, \ldots, P_P$ one instruction at a time. A portion of code is defined between two synchronization

---

[10]Indeed, we are not interested in running a program on a data-set that may take 100 years to complete.

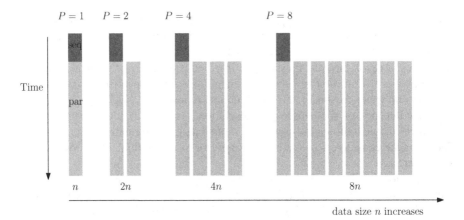

Fig. 1.7 Gustafson's speedup law considers data size being scaled up with the number of processors (or assumes constant parallel run time)

barriers, which are blocking communication primitives. Thus a parallel algorithm always yields a sequential algorithm, but not necessarily the other way around: a parallel algorithm needs to be designed, and often from scratch! One has to think purposely to design efficient parallel algorithms!

In theory, there are several conclusions that can be drawn from being able to simulate a parallel program on a sequential computer. First, the maximal speed up is in $O(P)$, where P denotes the number of processors. Second, it yields a lower bound for problems, since the time complexity to solve a problem in parallel is at best in $\Omega(\frac{c_{\text{seq}}}{P})$ (where $\Omega(c_{\text{seq}})$ denotes the sequential lower bound). Last, we note that we necessarily have $t_{\text{seq}} \leq t_1$: the time of a parallel algorithm executed on a single processor is necessarily more costly than the time of an equivalent sequential problem. (Otherwise, this single-node parallel algorithm would be better, and could replace the sequential algorithm.)

1.7.5   Big Data and Parallel Inputs/Outputs (I/O)

To process Big Data, one has to read and save huge files, or an extremely large number of small files. These operations are called *Input/Output*, or I/O for short. On a distributed memory architecture, this can be managed by explicitly programmed parallel I/O (say, using multi-collective *MPI-IO*[11]), or locally by explicit I/O on every node. Fortunately, in order to avoid this time-consuming programming task, there exist several parallel file systems that handle the complexity of those various

---

[11] Available since MPI-2.

I/O operations. For example, supercomputers may use the free software Lustre,[12] or IBM's GPFS[13] (*General Parallel File System*) for data-set sizes exceeding the petabyte (10^{15} bytes). MapReduce, the other popular system used for processing Big Data, relies on the Google file system called GFS (or HDFS for Hadoop Distributed File System).

1.8 Eight Common Fallacies on Distributed Systems

One of the very first large-scale distributed systems was the ARPANET network (1969), which yielded the Internet. Another world-wide distributed system is the SWIFT money transfer protocol[14] (SWIFT stands for *Society for Worldwide Interbank Financial Telecommunication*). After gaining half a century of experiences in distributed systems, nowadays it is still difficult to design and scale large distributed systems. There are many reasons for this, but Peter Deutsch (SUN, 1994) and James Gosling (SUN, 1997) have listed the following eight common fallacies:

1. the network is reliable,
2. the latency is zero,
3. the bandwidth is infinite (or at least large enough),
4. the network is safe,
5. the network topology does not change (meaning it is static over time),
6. there is only one network administrator,
7. the transport cost is free, and
8. the network is homogeneous.

We shall now briefly explain what those fallacies are, and why these assumptions do not hold in practice.

Fallacy 1: The network is safe.   Many critical applications need to be always available at any time of the day, and thus should be always functioning properly and have a zero-tolerance policy towards hardware/software breakdown. However, say, when a switch router becomes out of order, there can be an unexpected cascading chain reaction, which can cause an unpredictable catastrophe (think of a nuclear power plant getting out of control). In order to avoid this scenario (or at least to minimize it!), one has to introduce redundancy both in the hardware and in the software. In practice, the risks are evaluated in terms of investment (or equivalently in terms of redundancy).

Fallacy 2: The latency is zero.   Although latency in LANs (*Local Area Network*) is good enough, it becomes worse in WANs (*Wide Area Network*). In the past eleven years network bandwidth has increased by a factor of 1500, but latency

---

[12]http://lustre.opensfs.org/.

[13]http://www-03.ibm.com/systems/platformcomputing/products/gpfs/.

[14]http://www.swift.com/about_swift/company_information/swift_history.

has only been reduced by a factor of 10. Latency is intrinsically bounded by the speed of light in optic fibers. Indeed, consider the time required to ping: that is, to go to and come back between two antipodal points on the earth (*rtt, round trip time*). This requires 0.2 s (20000 km × 2 × 5 μs/km = 0.2 s, ignoring time spent in computing!), and 40 ms between New York and Los Angeles. Thus one has be extremely careful with latency problems when deploying applications worldwide beyond LANs!

Fallacy 3: The bandwidth is infinite.   Although bandwidth is steadily increasing over the years, the data size of content is too (like nowadays 4K video, and soon 8K video)! Also, routing algorithms have to deal in practice with congestion problems and packet loss in WANs that require us to *resend* data (and hence increase the network traffic).

Fallacy 4: The network is safe.   Well, nobody is fool enough to believe this anymore. Even worse, hacker attacks are increasing exponentially (sometimes, international companies have to face hundreds of attacks per week). Thus one has to plan for backing up systems and data, and design emergency and recovery procedures, etc.

Fallacy 5: The network topology is static.   Although at first one can assume a static topology when developing an application, clearly in practice one does not control the topology on WANs; and even worse, Internet topology is constantly evolving. This means that deployed applications should always consider the network topology as dynamic and make sure it is robust and adaptive to these various kinds of topologies.

Fallacy 6: There is only one network administrator.   In the best case scenario, even if we assume that the network administrator is never ill and can reply instantly to the many user requests, network administration is nowadays far too complex to be mastered by a single expert. Indeed, the variety of architectures and software to take into account requires many competencies that can be handled only by a *group* of administrators. In other words: nowadays each administrator is necessarily specialized in their field of expertise, but they can no longer cover the full spectrum of knowledge for administrating a large-scale IT structure.

Fallacy 7: The transport cost is free.   Of course, network cables and other related equipment like routers have a cost. But besides this obvious observation, in practice one has to pay to get a guaranteed *Quality of Service* (QoS) for network traffic. Also, to run an application in single-node mode and have this application executed in a distributed fashion on several nodes, one has to transfer application data on the network, thus incurring an implementation cost as well. That is, one has also to implement a *(de)serializing procedure* in bits and bytes of structured data in order to send and receive them between nodes. This latter point requires an extra software development cost.

Fallacy 8: The network is homogeneous.   In large international companies, employees use many different kinds of computers, operating software and solution software, and it then becomes critical to have *interoperability* between platforms and software in order to smoothly run the business.

1.9   Notes and References

This chapter covers the basic notions of High Performance Computing (HPC). The various concepts introduced here can be found in most textbooks dealing with parallelism. Amdahl's law has been revisited and extended by taking into account the multicore era with energy considerations [3, 4]. Both Amdahl's and Gustafson's laws can be generalized using the generic memory bound model of Sun and Ni [5]. The eight fallacies on distributed systems are detailed in the 2006 paper [6]. With the rise of the Big Data era, one seeks to process as big as possible data-sets and this as fast as possible: Big and Fast Data targets a real-time analysis of data flows (like the incoming flow of tweets) by minimizing latency to deliver results.

1.10   Summary

The main purpose of parallelizing algorithms is to obtain better performance (reducing time, increasing output throughput rate, reducing power consumption, etc.). Large-scale (or massive/big) data processing relies on supercomputers that are ranked according to their performance measured in FLOPS (*FLoating-point Operations Per Second*): that is, supercomputers are ranked according to the maximum number of elementary floating-point arithmetic operations they can carry out per second (peak performance). In high-performance computing, we distinguish between parallel multi-core computers with shared memory that use threads with shared memory, and parallel computer (cluster) with distributed memory. In the latter case, machines are modeled by nodes linked by an interconnection network. On distributed memory architectures, data transfers are explicitly executed using message passing, using a standard interface named MPI which includes all basic communication primitives. The efficiency of communication depends on the underlying topological network, the bandwidth, and the latency of uni-directional/bi-directional links. Amdahl's law rigorously demonstrates that the speedup is upper-bounded by the ratio of code that can not be parallelized. Nowadays, we are racing towards the exaflops supercomputer, which we wish to build around 2017–2020.

Notation:

n	input size
P	number of processors (or processes, nodes)
$t(n)$	sequential (or serial) time or data of size n, or $t_s(n)$
$t_P(n)$	parallel time on P processors for data of size n
$t_{\text{seq}}(n)$	sequential time for n data
$t_{\text{par}}(n)$	parallel time for n data (P implicitly assumed)
$c_P(n)$	cost: work performed by all processors: $c_P(n) = P t_P(n)$
$t_1(n)$	single-node parallel algorithm, $t_1(n) \geq t(n)$ but often $t_1(n) \approx t(n)$

$S_P(n)$ speedup: $S_P(n) = \frac{t(n)}{t_P(n)}$

$E_P(n)$ efficiency: $E_P(n) = \frac{t(n)}{C_P(n)} = \frac{S_P(n)}{P} = \frac{t(n)}{P t_P(n)}$

α_{par} proportion of parallel code ($\alpha_{par} = 1 - \alpha_{seq}$)

α_{seq} proportion of sequential code ($\alpha_{seq} = 1 - \alpha_{par}$)

$S_A(P)$ Amdahl's speedup for fixed workload: $\frac{1}{\alpha_{seq} + \frac{\alpha_{par}}{P}}$

           (upper bounded by $\frac{1}{\alpha_{seq}}$)

$S_G(P)$ Gustafson's scale speedup: $S_G(P) = \alpha_{seq} + (1 - \alpha_{seq})P$

scalability(O, P) generic scalability $\frac{t_O(n)}{t_P(n)}$ with $O < P$

1.11 Exercises

Exercise 1 (*Amdahl's law*) A program can be parallelized at 90 %. Calculate the asymptotic speedup using Amdahl's law. The serial program runs in 10 hours. What is the critical time that no parallel algorithm will be able to beat? Deduce again the maximal speedup. Same questions when only 1 % of the code can be parallelized.

Exercise 2 (*Estimating the fraction of parallelizable code for Amdahl's law*) Show that one can estimate the ratio of parallelizable code using the formula $\widehat{\alpha_{par}} = \frac{\frac{1}{S} - 1}{\frac{1}{P} - 1}$, where S is the measured speedup observed when using P processors. Deduce a formula for the maximal speedup given the measured speedup S achieved when using P processors.

Exercise 3 (*Upper bound for Amdahl's law*) Prove that for an arbitrary number of processors P, the speedup is always upper bounded by $\frac{1}{\alpha_{seq}}$ where α_{seq} is the relative proportion of serial code.

References

1. Amdahl, G.M.: Validity of the single processor approach to achieving large scale computing capabilities. In: Proceedings of Spring Joint Computer Conference, AFIPS '67 (Spring), pp. 483–485. ACM, New York (1967)
2. Gustafson, J.L.: Reevaluating Amdahl's law. Commun. ACM **31**(5), 532–533 (1988)
3. Hill, M.D., Marty, M.R.: Amdahl's law in the multicore era. Computer **41**(7), 33–38 (2008)
4. Woo, D.H., Lee, H.-H.S.: Extending Amdahl's law for energy-efficient computing in the many-core era. Computer **41**(12), 24–31 (2008)
5. Hwang, K.: Advanced Computer Architecture: Parallelism, Scalability, Programmability, 1st edn. McGraw-Hill Higher Education, New York (1992)
6. Rotem-Gal-Oz, A.: Fallacies of distributed computing explained (2006), (initially discussed by James Gosling and Peter L. Deutsch). See http://www.rgoarchitects.com/Files/fallacies.pdf

Chapter 2
Introduction to MPI: The Message Passing Interface

2.1 MPI for Parallel Programming: Communicating with Messages

Programming parallel algorithms is far more delicate than programming sequential algorithms. And so is debugging parallel programs too! Indeed, there exists several *abstract models* of "parallel machines" (parallel computations, distributed computations) with different kinds of *parallel programming paradigms*: For example, let us mention:

- *Vector super-computers* that rely on the programming model called *Single Instruction Multiple Data* (*SIMD*) with their optimized code based on pipelined operations,
- *Multi-core machines* with shared memory and their programming model using multi-threading, with all threads potentially accessing the shared memory. Programs can be easily crashing and it is difficult to debug sometimes due to potential conflicts when accessing concurrently a shared resource,
- *Clusters of computer machines* interconnected by a high-speed network that have a distributed memory.

It is precisely this last category of "parallel machines", the clusters of machines, that we are focusing on in this textbook: namely, parallel programming paradigm with distributed memory. Each computer can execute programs using its own local memory. Executed programs can be the same on all computers or can be different. Cooperation takes place by sending and receiving messages among these interconnected computers to accomplish their overall task.

Speaking on the size of these clusters, we can distinguish between:

- small-size to mid-size clusters of computers (say, dozens to hundreds, sometimes thousands, of computer nodes) that communicate with each other by sending and receiving messages, and
- large-size clusters (thousands to hundreds of thousands, sometimes millions computers) that execute rather simpler codes targeting *Big Data* processing.

© Springer International Publishing Switzerland 2016   21
F. Nielsen, *Introduction to HPC with MPI for Data Science*, Undergraduate
Topics in Computer Science, DOI 10.1007/978-3-319-21903-5_2

Usually, these large-size clusters are programmed using the MapReduce/Hadoop programming model.

The Message Passing Interface (or MPI for short) standard is a programming interface: namely, an *Application Programming Interface* (*API*) that defines properly the syntax and full semantic of a software library that provides standardized basic routines to build complex programs thereof. Thus the MPI interface allows one to code parallel programs exchanging data by sending and receiving messages encapsulating those data. Using an API has the advantage of leaving the programmer free of the many details concerning the implementation of the fine details of implementing from scratch network procedures, and allows the ecosystem (academy, industry, programmers) to benefit of interoperability and portability of source codes. It is important to emphasize the fact that the MPI API *does not depend* on the underlying programming language it uses. Thus we can use MPI commands with the most common (sequential) programming languages like C, C++, Java, Fortran, Python and so on. That is, several *language bindings* of the MPI API are available.

MPI historically got initiated from a workshop organized in 1991 on distributed memory environments. Nowadays, we use the third version of the standard, *MPI-3*, which standardization has been completed and published openly in 2008. We shall choose *OpenMPI* (http://www.open-mpi.org/) to illustrate the programming examples in this book.

Let us emphasize that the MPI interface is the dominant programming interface for parallel algorithms with distributed memory in the HPC community. The strong argument in favor of MPI is the standardization of *many* (i) global routines of communication (like broadcasting, the routine that consists in sending a message to all other machines) and (ii) many primitives to perform global calculations (like computing a cumulative sum of data distributed among all machines using an aggregation mechanism). In practice, the complexity of these global communications and calculation operations depend on the underlying topology of the interconnection network of the machines of the cluster.

2.2 Parallel Programming Models, Threads and Processes

Modern operating systems are *multi-tasks*: from the user viewpoint, several non-blocking applications seem to be executed (run) "simultaneously". This is merely an illusion since on a single Central Processing Unit (CPU) there can be only one program instruction at a time being executed. In other words, on the CPU, there is a current process being executed while the others are blocked (suspended or waiting to be waked up) and wait their turn to be executed on the CPU. It is the rôle of the *task scheduler* to allocate dynamically processes to CPU.

Modern CPUs have several *cores* that are independent *Processing Units* (PUs) that can execute truly in parallel on each core a thread. Multi-core architectures yield the multi-threading programming paradigm that allows for *concurrency*. For example, your favorite Internet WEB browser allows you to visualize simultaneously several pages in their own tabs: each HTML page is rendered using an independent thread that retrieves from the network the page contents in HTML[1]/XML and displays it. The resources allocated to a process are *shared* between the different threads, and at least one thread should have a `main` calling function.

We can characterize the threads as follows:

- Threads of a same process share the same memory area, and can therefore access both the data area but also the code area in memory. It is therefore easy to access data between the threads of a same process, but it can also raise some difficulties in case of simultaneous access to the memory: In the worst case, it yields a system crash! A theoretical abstraction of this model is the so-called *Parallel Random-Access Machine* (or *PRAM*). On the PRAM model, we can classify the various conflicts that can happen when reading or writing simultaneously on the local memory. We have the *Exclusive Read Exclusive Write* sub-model (EREW), the *Concurrent Read Exclusive Write* (CREW) and the *Concurrent Read Concurrent Write* models.
- This multi-threading programming model is very well suited to multi-core processors, and allows applications to be ran faster (for example, for encoding a MPEG4 video or a MP3 music file) or using non-blocking applications (like a web multi-tab browser with a mail application).
- Processes are different from threads because they have their own *non-overlapping* memory area. Therefore, communications between processes have to be done careful, in particular using the MPI standard.

We can also distinguish the parallel programming paradigm *Single Program Multiple Data* (SPMD) from the paradigm called Multiple Program Multiple Data (MPMD). Finally, let us notice that we can run several processes either on a same processor (in parallel when the processor is multi-core) or on a set of processors interconnected by a network. We can also program processes to use several multi-core processors (in that case, using both the MPI and OpenMP standards).

2.3 Global Communications Between Processes

By executing a MPI program on a cluster of machines, we launch a set of processes, and we have for each process traditional local computations (like ordinary sequential programs) but also:

- some data transfers: for example, some data broadcasted to all other processes using a message,
- some synchronization barriers where all processes are required to wait for each other before proceeding,

---

[1] *Hypertext Markup Language.*

$$(+\ 1\ 2\ 3\ 4)=(+\ (+\ 1\ 2)\ (+\ 3\ 4))=(+\ 3\ 7)=(10)$$

```
                          10
                          +
        ( +          3              7            )
                     +              +
        ( +     1         2      3      4      )
```

Fig. 2.1 Example of a global reduce computation: calculating the global cumulative sum of the local values of a process variable. We illustrate here the reduction tree performed when invoking the reduce primitive

- global computations: for example, a reduce operation that calculates, say, the sum or the minimum of a distributed variable x belonging to all the processes (with a local value stored on the local memory of each process). Figure 2.1 illustrates a reduce cumulative sum operation. The global computation depends on the underlying topology of the interconnected cluster machines.

Global communication primitives are carried out on all processes belonging to the same *group of communication*. By default, once MPI got initialized, all processes belong to the same group of communication called MPI_COMM_WORLD.

2.3.1   Four Basic MPI Primitives: Broadcast, Gather, Reduce, and Total Exchange

The MPI broadcasting primitive, MPI_Bcast, sends a message from a *root process* (the calling process of the communication group) to all other processes (belonging to the communication group). Conversely, the reduce operation aggregates all corresponding values of a variable into a single value that is returned to the calling process. When a different personalized message is send to each other process, we get a scatter operation called in MPI by MPI_Scatter.

Aggregating primitives can either be for communication of for computing globally: gather is the converse of the scatter operation where a calling process receives from all other processes a personalized message. In MPI, MPI_Reduce allows one to perform a *global calculation* by aggregating (reducing) the values of a variable using a commutative binary operator.[2] Typical such examples are the cumulative sum (MPI_SUM) or the cumulative product (MPI_PROD), etc. A list of such binary operators used in the reduce primitives is given in Table 2.1. Those four basic MPI primitives are illustrated in Fig. 2.2. Last but not least, we can also call a global

---

[2]An example of binary operator that is not commutative is the division since $p/q \neq q/p$.

Table 2.1 Global
calculation: predefined
(commutative) binary
operators for MPI reduce
operations

MPI name	Meaning
MPI_MAX	Maximum
MPI_MIN	Minimum
MPI_SUM	Sum
MPI_PROD	Product
MPI_LAND	Logical and
MPI_BAND	Bit-wise and
MPI_LOR	Logical or
MPI_BOR	Bit-wise or
MPI_LXOR	Logical xor
MPI_BXOR	Bit-wise xor
MPI_MAXLOC	Max value and location
MPI_MINLOC	Min value and location

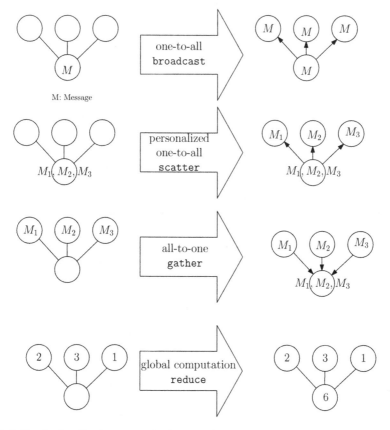

Fig. 2.2 Four basic collective communication primitives: broadcast (one to all), scatter (personalized broadcast or personalized one-to-all communication), gather (the inverse of a scatter primitive, or personalized all-to-one communication) and reduce (a global collective computation)

all-to-all communication primitive (MPI_Alltoall, also called *total exchange*) where each process sends a personalized message to all other processes.

2.3.2 Blocking Versus Non-blocking and Synchronous Versus Asynchronous Communications

MPI has several send modes depending on whether data are buffered or not and whether synchronization is required or not. First, let us start by denoting by send and receive the two basic communication primitives. We describe the syntax and semantic of these two primitives as follows:

- send(&data, n, Pdest): Send an array of n data starting at memory address &data to process Pdest
- receive(&data, n, Psrc): Receive n data from process Psrc and store them in an array which starts a local memory address &data

Now, let us examine what happens in this example below:

```
            Process P0                              Process P1
...
a=442;                                   ...
send(&a, 1, P1);                         receive(&a, 1, P0);
                                         cout << a << endl;
a=0;
```

Blocking communications (not buffered) yield a *waiting time* situation: that is, a *idling time*. Indeed, the sending process and the receiving process need to wait mutually for each other: it is the communication mode commonly termed handshaking. This mode allows one to perform synchronous communications. Figure 2.3 illustrates these synchronous communications by hand-shaking and indicates the idling periods.

The C program below gives an elementary example of blocking communication in MPI (using the *C binding* of the OpenMPI vendor implementation of MPI):

> WWW source code: MPIBlockingCommunication.cpp

```cpp
// filename: MPIBlockingCommunication.cpp
#include <stdio.h>
#include <stdlib.h>
#include <mpi.h>
#include <math.h>

int main(argc,argv)
int argc;
char *argv[];
{
    int myid, numprocs;
```

```
int tag,source,destination,count;
int buffer;
MPI_Status status;

MPI_Init(&argc,&argv);
MPI_Comm_size(MPI_COMM_WORLD,&numprocs);
MPI_Comm_rank(MPI_COMM_WORLD,&myid);
tag=2312; /* any integer to tag messages */
source=0;
destination=1;
count=1;
if(myid == source){
  buffer=2015;
  MPI_Send(&buffer,count,MPI_INT,destination,tag
     ,MPI_COMM_WORLD);
  printf("processor %d received %d \n", myid,
     buffer)
}
if(myid == destination){
    MPI_Recv(&buffer,count,MPI_INT,source,tag,
       MPI_COMM_WORLD,&status);
    printf("processor %d received %d \n",myid,
       buffer);
}
MPI_Finalize();
}
```

Clearly, for blocking communications, one seeks to minimize the overall idling time. We shall see later on how to perform this optimization using a load-balancing technique to balance fairly the local computations among the processes.

We report the syntax and describe the arguments of the send[3] primitive in MPI:

- Syntax using the C binding:

```
#include <mpi.h>
int MPI_Send(void *buf, int count, MPI_Datatype
   datatype, int dest, int tag, MPI_Comm comm)
```

- Syntax in C++ (Deprecated. That is, it is not regularly updated since MPI-2 and we do not recommend using it):

```
#include <mpi.h>
void Comm::Send(const void* buf, int count, const
   Datatype& datatype, int dest, int tag) const
```

The tag argument in send assigns an integer to a message (its label) so that processes can specify which type of message to wait for. Tags are useful in practice to filter communication operations, and ensures for example that messages sent/received are pairwise matching using blocking communications.

The C data types in MPI are summarized in Table 2.2.

---

[3]See the manual online: https://www.open-mpi.org/doc/v1.4/man3/MPI_Send.3.php.

Fig. 2.3 Blocking
communications by
hand-shaking: **a** sending
process waits for the "OK"
of the receiver and thus
provoke a waiting situation,
b one seeks to minimize this
idling time, and **c** case where
it is the receiving process
that needs to wait

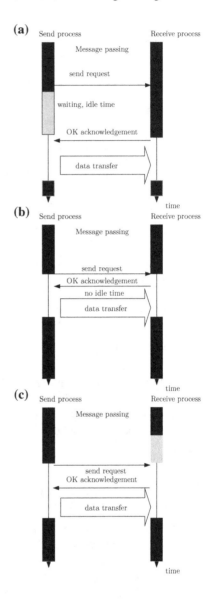

2.3.3 Deadlocks from Blocking Communications

Using blocking communications allows one to properly match "send queries" with
"receive queries", but can unfortunately also yields deadlocks.[4]

---

[4]In that case, either a time-out signal can be emitted externally to kill all the processes, or we
need to manually kill the processes using their process identity number using Shell command line
instructions.

Table 2.2 Basic data types in MPI when using the C language binding

MPI type	Corresponding type in the C language
MPI_CHAR	signed char
MPI_SHORT	signed short int
MPI_INT	signed int
MPI_LONG	signed long int
MPI_UNSIGNED_CHAR	unsigned char
MPI_UNSIGNED_SHORT	unsigned short int
MPI_UNSIGNED	unsigned int
MPI_UNSIGNED_LONG	unsigned long int
MPI_FLOAT	float
MPI_DOUBLE	double
MPI_LONG_DOUBLE	long double
MPI_BYTE	
MPI_PACKED	

Let us consider this toy example to understand whether there is a deadlock situation occurring or not:

Process P0	Process P1
send(&a, 1, P1);	send(&a, 1, P0);
receive(&b, 1, P1);	receive(&b, 1, P0);

Process $P0$ send a message and then waits the green light "OK for sending" of receiver process $P1$, but the send query of $P1$ also waits for the green light "OK for sending" of process $P0$. That is typically a *deadlock* situation. In this toy example, we have highlighted the deadlock problem when using blocking communication primitives. However in practice, it is not so easy to track them as process programs can take various execution paths.

In practice, in MPI, each send/receive operation concerns a group of communication and has a tag attribute (an integer). From an algorithmic viewpoint, blocking communications are a highly desirable feature to ensure consistency (or the semantic) of programs (for example, to avoid that messages arrive in wrong orders) but they can yield difficulties to detect deadlocks.

In order to remove (or at least minimize!) these deadlock situations, we can preallocate to each process a dedicated memory space for buffering data: the *data buffer* (bearing the acronym DB). We then send data in two steps:

- First, the send process sends a message on the data buffer, and
- Second, the receive process copies the data buffer on its local memory area indicated by the address &data.

This buffered communication can either be implemented by hardware mechanisms or by appropriate software. However, there still remains potential deadlocks when the data buffers become full (raising a "buffer overflow" exception). Even if we correctly manage the `send` primitives, there can still be remaining deadlocks, even with buffered communications, because of the blocking receive primitive. This scenario is illustrated as follows:

Process P0	Process P1
`receive(&a, 1, P1);`	`receive(&a, 1, P0);`
`send(&b, 1, P1);`	`send(&b, 1, P0);`

Each process waits for a message before being able to send its message! Again, this is a deadlock state! In summary, blocking communications are very useful when we consider global communication like broadcasting in order to ensure the correct arrival order of messages, but one has to take care of potential deadlocks when implementing these communication algorithms.

A solution to avoid deadlocks is to consider both the `send` and `receive` primitives being non-blocking. These *non-blocking communication routines* (not buffered) are denoted by `Isend` and `Ireceive` in MPI: There are *asynchronous communications*. In that case, the send process posts a message "Send authorization request" (a pending message) and continues the execution of its program. When the receiver process posts a "OK for sending" approval, data transfers are initiated. All these mechanics are internally managed using signals of the operating system. When the data transfer is completed, a check status let indicate whether processes can proceed to read/write data safely. The C program below illustrates such a non-blocking communication using the C binding of OpenMPI. Let us notice that the primitive `MPI_Wait(&request,&status);` waits until the transfer is completed (or interrupted) and indicates whether that transfer has been successful or not, using a state variable called `status`.

WWW source code: `MPINonBlockingCommunication.cpp`

```cpp
// filename: MPINonBlockingCommunication.cpp
#include <stdio.h>
#include <stdlib.h>
#include <mpi.h>
#include <math.h>

int main(argc, argv)
int argc;
char *argv[];
{
    int myid, numprocs;
    int tag, source, destination, count;
    int buffer;
    MPI_Status status;
    MPI_Request request;

    MPI_Init(&argc, &argv);
    MPI_Comm_size(MPI_COMM_WORLD, &numprocs);
    MPI_Comm_rank(MPI_COMM_WORLD, &myid);
    tag = 2312;
```

```
      source=0;
      destination=1;
      count=1;
      request=MPI_REQUEST_NULL;
      if(myid == source){
        buffer=2015;
        MPI_Isend(&buffer,count,MPI_INT,destination,
          tag,MPI_COMM_WORLD,&request);
      }
      if(myid == destination){
          MPI_Irecv(&buffer,count,MPI_INT,source,tag,
            MPI_COMM_WORLD,&request);
      }
      MPI_Wait(&request,&status);
      if(myid == source){
        printf("processor %d  sent %d\n",myid,buffer);
      }
      if(myid == destination){
        printf("processor %d  received %d\n",myid,
          buffer);
      }
      MPI_Finalize();
  }
```

We summarize the calling syntax in the C binding of the non-blocking primitives Isend and Irecv:

```
int MPI_Isend( void *buf, int count, MPI_Datatype
    datatype, int dest, int tag, MPI_Comm comm,
    MPI_Request *req )
```

```
int MPI_Irecv( void *buf, int count, MPI_Datatype
    datatype, int src, int tag, MPI_Comm comm,
    MPI_Request *req )
```

The structure MPI_Request is often used in programs: it returns *flag=1 when the operation *req has completed, and 0 otherwise.

```
int MPI_Test( MPI_Request *req, int *flag,
    MPI_Status *status )
```

The primitive MPI_Wait waits until the operation indicated by *req has been completed

```
int MPI_Wait( MPI_Request *req, MPI_Status *status )
```

We summarize the various communication protocols (blocking/non-blocking send with blocking/non-blocking receive) in Table 2.3.

Table 2.3 Comparisons of the various send/receive operation protocols

	Blocking operation	Non-blocking operation
Bufferized	send completes after data have been copied to the data buffer	send completes after having initialized DMA (*Direct Memory Access*) transfer to the data buffer. The operation is not necessarily completed after it returns
Not-bufferized	Blocking send until it meets a corresponding receive	To define
Meaning	Semantic of send and receive by matching operations	Semantic must be explicitly specified by the programmer that needs to check the operation status

The program listings so far highlighted eight common procedures of MPI (among a rich set of MPI instructions):

MPI_Init	Initialize the MPI library
MPI_Finalize	Terminate MPI
MPI_Comm_size	Return the number of processes
MPI_Comm_rank	Rank of the calling process
MPI_Send	send a message (blocking)
MPI_Recv	receive message (blocking)
MPI_Isend	send a message (non-blocking)
MPI_Irecv	receive message (non-blocking)

All these procedures return MPI_SUCCESS when they are completed with success, or otherwise an error code depending on the problems. Data types and constants are prefixed with MPI_ (we invite the reader to explore the header file mpi.h for more information).

2.3.4 Concurrency: Local Computations Can Overlap with Communications

It is usual to assume that the processors (or Processing Elements, PEs) can perform several tasks at the same time: for example, a typical scenario is to use non-blocking communications (MPI_IRecv and MPI_ISend) at the same time they perform some local computations. Thus we require that those three operations are not interferring with each other. In one stage, we can therefore not send the result of a calculation and we can not send what has been concurrently received (meaning forwarding). In parallel algorithmic, we denote by the double vertical bar || these concurrent operations:

$$\texttt{IRecv}||\texttt{ISend}||\texttt{Local\_Computation}$$

2.3.5 Unidirectional Versus Bidirectional Communications

We distinguish between *one-way communication* and *two-way communication* as follows: in one-way communication, we authorize communications over communication channels in one direction only: that is, either we send a message or we receive a message (MPI_Send/MPI_Recv) but not both at the same time. In a two-way communication setting, we can communicate using both directions: in MPI, this can be done by calling the procedure MPI_Sendrecv.[5]

2.3.6 Global Computations in MPI: Reduce and Parallel Prefix (Scan)

In MPI, one can perform global computations like the cumulative sum $V = \sum_{i=0}^{P-1} v_i$ where v_i is a local variable stored in the memory of process P_i (or the cumulative product $V = \prod_{i=0}^{P-1} v_i$). The result of this global computation V is then available in the local memory of the process that has called this reduce primitive: the calling process, also called the root process. We describe below the usage of the reduce[6] primitive using the C binding of OpenMPI:

```
#include <mpi.h>

int MPI_Reduce ( // Reduce routine
 void* sendBuffer , // Address of local val
 void* recvBuffer , // Place to receive into
 int count , // No. of elements
 MPI_Datatype datatype , // Type of each element
 MPI_OP op , // MPI operator
 int root , // Process to get result
 MPI_Comm comm // MPI communicator
 ) ;
```

Reduction operations are predefined and can be selected using one of the keywords among this list (see also Table 2.1).

---

[5]https://www.open-mpi.org/doc/v1.8/man3/MPI_Sendrecv.3.php.
[6]See manual online at https://www.open-mpi.org/doc/v1.5/man3/MPI_Reduce.3.php.

`MPI_MAX`	maximum
`MPI_MIN`	minimum
`MPI_SUM`	sum $\sum$
`MPI_PROD`	product $\prod$
`MPI_LAND`	logic AND
`MPI_BAND`	bitwise AND
`MPI_LOR`	logic OR
`MPI_BOR`	bitwise OR
`MPI_LXOR`	logic XOR
`MPI_BXOR`	bitwise COR
`MPI_MAXLOC`	maximal value and corresponding index of the maximal element
`MPI_MINLOC`	minimal value and corresponding index of the minimal element

In MPI, one can also build its own data type and define the associative and commutative binary operator for reduction.

A second kind of global computation are *parallel prefix* also called *scan*. A `scan` operation calculates all the partial reductions on the data stored locally on the processes.

Syntax in MPI is the following:

```
int MPI_Scan( void *sendbuf , void *recvbuf , int count ,
    MPI_Datatype datatype , MPI_Op op , MPI_Comm comm )
```

Calling this procedure allows one to perform a *prefix reduction* on the data located in `sendbuf` on each process with the result available in the memory address `recvbuf`. Figure 2.4 illustrates graphically the difference between these two global computation primitives: `reduce` and `scan`.

```
MPI_Scan( vals , cumsum , 4 , MPI_INT , MPI_SUM ,
    MPI_COMM_WORLD )
```

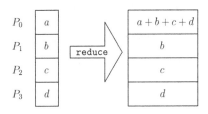

Fig. 2.4 Visualizing a reduce operation and a parallel prefix (or scan) operation

We described by syntax of `reduce` and `scan` using the C binding because the C++ binding is not any longer updated since MPI-2. In practice, we often program using the modern oriented-object C++ language and call the MPI primitives using the C interface. Recall that the C language [1] is a precursor of C++ [2] that is *not* an oriented-object language, and manipulates instead data structures defined by the keyword `struct`.

These global computations are often implemented internally using spanning trees of the underlying topology of the interconnection network.

2.3.7 Defining Communication Groups with Communicators

In MPI, communicators allow one to group processes into various groups of communications. Each process is included in a communication and is indexed by its *rank* inside this communication group. By default, `MPI_COMM_WORLD` includes all the P processes with the rank being an integer ranging from 0 to $P - 1$. To get the number of processes inside its communication group or its rank inside the communication, we use the following primitives in MPI: `int MPI_Comm_size (MPI_Comm comm, int *size)` and `int MPI_Comm_rank (MPI_Comm comm, int *size)`.

For example, we create a new communicator by removing the first process as follows:

> WWW source code: `MPICommunicatorRemoveFirstProcess.cpp`

```
// filename: MPICommunicatorRemoveFirstProcess.cpp
#include <mpi.h>

int main(int argc, char *argv[])
    {
    MPI_Comm comm_world, comm_worker;
    MPI_Group group_world, group_worker;
    comm_world = MPI_COMM_WORLD;

    MPI_Comm_group(comm_world, &group_world);
    MPI_Group_excl(group_world, 1, 0, &group_worker)
        ;

    /* process 0 is removed from the communication
        group */

    MPI_Comm_create(comm_world, group_worker, &
        comm_worker);
    }
```

In this second listing, we illustrate how to use communicators:

WWW source code: `MPICommunicatorSplitProcess.cpp`

```cpp
// filename: MPICommunicatorSplitProcess.cpp
#include <mpi.h>
#include <stdio.h>
#define NPROCS 8

int main(int argc, char *argv[])
    {
    int *ranks1[4]={0,1,2,3}, ranks2[4]={4,5,6,7};

    MPI_Group orig_group, new_group;
    MPI_Comm new_comm

    MPI_Init(&argc, &argv);
    MPI_Comm_rank(MPI_COMM_WORLD, &rank);
    sendbuf = rank;

    // Retrieve the intial group
    MPI_Comm_group(MPI_COMM_WORLD, &orig_group);

    if (rank < NPROCS/2)
        MPI_Group_incl(orig_group, NPROCS/2, ranks1,
            &new_group);
  else
     MPI_Group_incl(orig_group, NPROCS/2, ranks2, &
        new_group);

// create new communicator
MPI_Comm_create(MPI_COMM_WORLD, new_group, &new_comm
    );

// global computation primitive
MPI_Allreduce(&sendbuf, &recvbuf, 1, MPI_INT,
    MPI_SUM, new_comm);
MPI_Group_rank(new_group, &new_rank);
printf("rank= %d newrank= %d recvbuf= %d\n", rank,
    newrank, recvbuf);

MPI_Finalize();
}
```

`MPI_Comm_create` is a collective operation. All processes of the former communication group need to call it, even those who do not belong to the new communication group.

2.4 Synchronization Barriers: Meeting Points of Processes

In the coarse-grained parallelism mode, processes execute large chunks of computations independently from each other. Then they wait for each other at a *synchronization barrier* (see Fig. 2.5, `MPI_Barrier` in MPI), perform some send/receive messages, and proceed their program execution.

2.4.1 A Synchronization Example in MPI: Measuring the Execution Time

For example, let us illustrate a way to measure the parallel time of a MPI program with a synchronization barrier. We shall use the procedure `MPI_Wtime` to measure time in MPI. Consider this master/slave code:

> WWW source code: `MPISynchronizeTime.cpp`

```
// filename: MPISynchronizeTime.cpp
double start, end;

MPI_Init(&argc, &argv);
MPI_Comm_rank(MPI_COMM_WORLD, &rank);
```

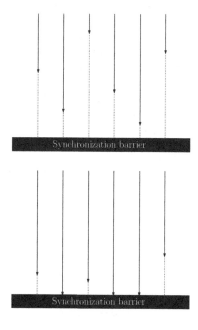

Fig. 2.5 Conceptual illustration of a synchronization barrier: processes wait for each other at a synchronization barrier before carrying on the program execution

```
MPI_Barrier(MPI_COMM_WORLD); /* IMPORTANT */
start = MPI_Wtime();    .

/* some local computations here */
LocalComputation();

MPI_Barrier(MPI_COMM_WORLD); /* IMPORTANT */
end = MPI_Wtime(); /* measure the worst-case time of
    a process */

MPI_Finalize();

if (rank == 0)
        { /* use time on master node */
        cout<< end-start <<endl; // here we use C++ syntax
        }
```

We can also use a MPI_Reduce() procedure to compute the minimum, maximum, and overall sum of all the process times. But this eventually requires to add
an extra step for perform the global computation with a reduce operation.

2.4.2 The Bulk Synchronous Parallel (BSP) Model

One of the high-level parallel programming model is called the *Bulk Synchronous
Parallel* (or *BSP* for short). This abstract model has been conceived by Leslie G.
Valiant (Turing award, 2010) and facilitates the design of parallel algorithms using
three fundamental steps that form a "super-step":

1. concurrent computation step: processes locally and asynchronously compute, and
   those local computation can overlap with communications,
2. communication step: processes exchange data between themselves,
3. synchronization barrier step: when a process reaches a synchronization barrier,
   it waits for all the other processes to reach this barrier before proceeding another
   super-step.

A parallel algorithm on the BSP model is a sequence of super-steps. A software
library, BSPonMPI,[7] allows one to use this programming model easily with MPI.

---

[7]http://bsponmpi.sourceforge.net/.

2.5 Getting Started with the MPI: Using OpenMPI

We describe several ways to use the OpenMPI implementation of the MPI standard using either the C, C++, or Boost bindings. There is also a convenient Python binding[8] that is touched upon.

2.5.1 The "Hello World" Program with MPI C++

The traditional "Hello program" reflects the minimal structure of a program displaying a simple message.

> WWW source code: `MPIHelloWorld.cpp`

```
// filename: MPIHelloWorld.cpp
# include <iostream>
using namespace std;
# include "mpi.h"
int main ( int argc, char *argv[] )
{
   int id, p, name_len;
   char processor_name[MPI_MAX_PROCESSOR_NAME];
// Initialize MPI.
   MPI::Init ( argc, argv );
// Get the number of processes.
   p = MPI::COMM_WORLD.Get_size ( );
// Get the individual process ID.
   id = MPI::COMM_WORLD.Get_rank ( );
   MPI_Get_processor_name(processor_name, &name_len);
   // Print off a hello world message
  cout << " Processor " << processor_name <<" ID="<<
      id << " Welcome to MPI!'\n";
// Terminate MPI.
   MPI::Finalize ( );
return 0;
}
```

To compile this C++ source code, we type in the terminal:

```
mpic++ welcomeMPI.cpp -o welcomeMPI
```

When the `-o` option is not set, the compiler will write the byte code in a default file called: `a.out`. Once compile, we execute this program, here on machine named `machinempi`:

```
>$ mpirun -np 4 welcomeMPI
   Processor machinempi  ID=3 Welcome MPI!'
```

---

[8]http://mpi4py.scipy.org/docs/usrman/.

```
Processor machinempi  ID=0 Welcome MPI!'
Processor machinempi  ID=1 Welcome MPI!'
Processor machinempi  ID=2 Welcome MPI!'
```

Let us note that on the console, the messages are displayed in the order of the execution time of the cout orders. Thus if we launch again this program, we order of messages on the console may be different. Therefore let us emphasize that when we invoke the mpirun command, we create *P* processes that all execute the same compiled code. Each process can take different branches of the program by identifying themselves using their rank.

We can use two machines to run the program as follows:

```
>$ mpirun -np 5 -host machineMPI1,machineMPI2 welcomeMPI
   Processor machineMPI2  ID=1 Welcome MPI!'
   Processor machineMPI2  ID=3 Welcome MPI!'
   Processor machineMPI1  ID=0 Welcome MPI!'
   Processor machineMPI1  ID=2 Welcome MPI!'
   Processor machineMPI1  ID=4 Welcome MPI!'
```

The mpirun execution command is a symbolic link to the orterun command in OpenMPI. We can list the various libraries of MPI as follows:

```
>mpic++ --showme:libs
mpi_cxx mpi open-rte open-pal dl nsl util m dl
```

And we can add a new library as follows:

```
export LIBS=${LIBS}:/usr/local/boost-1.39.0/include/boost-1_39
```

And then compile this command line in the shell:

```
mpic++ -c t.cpp -I$LIBS
```

As usual, it is better to set the shell configuration file properly by editing the .bashrc. After having done your editing, you need to re-read the configuration file by typing this built-in-shell command:

```
source ~/.bashrc
```

You are now ready to use simultaneously a large number of machines. But please keep in mind that you have to be kind when using a large number of resources: everybody shall uses the shared resource fairly!

In the Appendix B, we describe the SLURM task scheduler to launch MPI jobs on a cluster of machines.

2.5.2 Programming MPI with the C Binding

The toy program below describes a way to define a master-slave program:

> WWW source code: `MPICBindingExample.c`

```
/* filename: MPICBindingExample.c */
int main (int argc, char **argv)
{
        int myrank, size;
        MPI_Init (&argc, &argv);
        MPI_Comm_rank (MPI_COMM_WORLD, &myrank);
        MPI_Comm_size( MPI_COMM_WORLD, &size );

        if (!myrank)
          master ();
        else
                slave ();
        MPI_Finalize ();
        return (1);
}

void master()
        {printf("I am the master program\n");}

void slave()
        {printf("I am the slave program\n");}
```

Note that the MPI interface that we have used here is fairly different from our first program "Hello World". Indeed, we use the C binding of the MPI here. The C binding is the most commonly used binding of MPI and is frequently updated. It offers all functions of the MPI standard. The C++ binding is not anymore supported and offers less functions. Therefore we recommend to use the C binding, even in a C++ program (C calling style of MPI procedures inside a C++ object-oriented program). This explains why in our codes, we have C calling function style with `cout` print order to the console!

2.5.3 Using MPI with C++ Boost

Boost[9] is a C++ library that is very useful for dealing with matrices and graphs, etc. Interesting, this library also offers its own style to use MPI programs. Here is a small Boost-MPI program to showcase the library:

---

[9]http://www.boost.org/.

> WWW source code: `MPIBoostBindingExample.cpp`

```cpp
// filename: MPIBoostBindingExample.cpp
#include <boost/mpi/environment.hpp>
#include <boost/mpi/communicator.hpp>
#include <iostream>
namespace mpi = boost::mpi;

int main()
{
    mpi::environment env;
    mpi::communicator world;
    std::cout << "I am process " << world.rank() << "
        on " << world.size()
                << "." << std::endl;
    return 0;
}
```

If you are using Unix, you can compile this program as follows:

/usr/**local**/openmpi−1.8.3/bin/mpic++ −I/usr/**local**/boost−1.56.0/include/
−L/usr/**local**/boost−1.56.0/lib/ −lboost_mpi −lboost_serialization myprogram.cpp
−o myprogram

2.6   Using MPI with OpenMP

OpenMP[10] is yet another Application Programming Interface for parallel programming with shared memory. OpenMP is a cross-platform standard that offers bindings in the C/C++/Fortran imperative languages among others. OpenMP is typically used when one wants to use multi-core processors. Here is a "Hello World" program using both the MPI and OpenMP APIs:

> WWW source code: `MPIOpenMPExample.cpp`

```cpp
// filename: MPIOpenMPExample.cpp
#include <mpi.h>
#include <omp.h>
#include <stdio.h>
int main (int nargs, char** args)
{
int rank, nprocs, thread_id, nthreads;
int name_len;
char processor_name[MPI_MAX_PROCESSOR_NAME];

MPI_Init (&nargs, &args);
```

---

[10]http://openmp.org/wp/.

```
MPI_Comm_size (MPI_COMM_WORLD, &nprocs);
MPI_Comm_rank (MPI_COMM_WORLD, &rank);
MPI_Get_processor_name(processor_name, &name_len);

#pragma omp parallel private(thread_id, nthreads)
{
thread_id = omp_get_thread_num ();
nthreads = omp_get_num_threads ();
printf("Thread number %d (on %d) for the MPI process
    number %d (on %d) [%s]\n",
thread_id, nthreads, rank, nprocs,processor_name);
}
MPI_Finalize ();
return 0;
}
```

We use the option -fopenmp of the mpic++ compiler as follows:

```
mpic++ -fopenmp testmpiopenmp.cpp -o testmp.exe
```

Then we execute this program at the command line as follows:

```
mpirun -np 2 -host royce,simca testmp.exe
```

```
[royce ~]$ mpirun -np 2 -host royce,simca dmp.exe
Thread number 0 (on 8) for the MPI process number 1 (on 2) [simca.polytechnique.fr]
Thread number 1 (on 8) for the MPI process number 1 (on 2) [simca.polytechnique.fr]
Thread number 5 (on 8) for the MPI process number 1 (on 2) [simca.polytechnique.fr]
Thread number 3 (on 8) for the MPI process number 1 (on 2) [simca.polytechnique.fr]
Thread number 4 (on 8) for the MPI process number 1 (on 2) [simca.polytechnique.fr]
Thread number 7 (on 8) for the MPI process number 1 (on 2) [simca.polytechnique.fr]
Thread number 0 (on 8) for the MPI process number 0 (on 2) [royce.polytechnique.fr]
Thread number 1 (on 8) for the MPI process number 0 (on 2) [royce.polytechnique.fr]
Thread number 5 (on 8) for the MPI process number 0 (on 2) [royce.polytechnique.fr]
Thread number 4 (on 8) for the MPI process number 0 (on 2) [royce.polytechnique.fr]
Thread number 7 (on 8) for the MPI process number 0 (on 2) [royce.polytechnique.fr]
Thread number 2 (on 8) for the MPI process number 0 (on 2) [royce.polytechnique.fr]
Thread number 6 (on 8) for the MPI process number 0 (on 2) [royce.polytechnique.fr]
Thread number 2 (on 8) for the MPI process number 1 (on 2) [simca.polytechnique.fr]
Thread number 6 (on 8) for the MPI process number 1 (on 2) [simca.polytechnique.fr]
```

It can be seen that the two host machines have 8 cores each. We observe that the arrival printing order on the console depends on many system factors. Running another time the program will likely yield a different arrival order. Instead of naming explicitly the host machines, we can also use a resource scheduler like SLURM[11] that will allocate automatically all necessary resources of a cluster to MPI programs (see Appendix B).

2.6.1 Programming MPI with the Python Binding

Python[12] has become widely popular the last decade as a fast prototyping language. The Python binding is available from the following URL: http://mpi4py.scipy.org/docs/usrman/

---

[11]https://computing.llnl.gov/linux/slurm/.

[12]https://www.python.org/.

> WWW source code: `MPIHelloWorld.py`

```python
#!/usr/bin/env python
"""
MPI Hello World example
"""

from mpi4py import MPI
import sys

size = MPI.COMM_WORLD.Get_size()
rank = MPI.COMM_WORLD.Get_rank()
name = MPI.Get_processor_name()

sys.stdout.write(
    "Hello, World! I am process %d of %d on %s.\n"
    % (rank, size, name))

# mpirun -np 5 python26 hw.py
```

2.7   Main Primitives in MPI

We recall the main collective communication primitives that are global operations performed on a communicator (group of machines):

- broadcast (one-to-all) and reduce (all-to-one, that can be interpreted as the reverse operation of a broadcast primitive),
- scatter or personalized broadcast that sends different messages to all processes,
- gather or all-to-one that assembles individual messages from all processes to the calling process (inverse operation of a scatter primitive)
- global computational like reduce or scan (as known as parallel prefix),
- total communication, all-to-all, also called total exchange (personalized messages for all processes),
- etc.

2.7.1   *MPI Syntax for Broadcast, Scatter, Gather, Reduce and Allreduce*

- broadcast: `MPI_Bcast`[13]

  `int MPI_Bcast(void *buffer, int count,`

---

[13]https://www.open-mpi.org/doc/v1.5/man3/MPI_Bcast.3.php.

```
MPI_Datatype datatype,
int root, MPI_Comm comm)
```

- scatter: `MPI_Scatter`[14]

```
int MPI_Scatter(void *sendbuf, int sendcount, MPI_Datatype
sendtype,  void *recvbuf, int recvcount,
MPI_Datatype recvtype, int root,  MPI_Comm comm)
```

- gather: `MPI_Gather`[15]

```
int MPI_Gather(void *sendbuf, int sendcount, MPI_Datatype
 sendtype,     void *recvbuf, int recvcount,
MPI_Datatype recvtype, int root,    MPI_Comm comm)
```

- reduce: `MPI_Reduce`[16]

```
int MPI_Reduce(void *sendbuf, void *recvbuf, int count,
MPI_Datatype datatype, MPI_Op op, int root, MPI_Comm comm)
```

- Allreduce: `MPI_Allreduce`[17]

```
int MPI_Allreduce(void *sendbuf, void *recvbuf, int count,
    MPI_Datatype datatype, MPI_Op op, MPI_Comm comm)
```

Those operations are visually explained in Fig. 2.6.

2.7.2 Other Miscellaneous MPI Primitives

- The *prefix sum* primitive considers a binary associative operator $\oplus$ like $+$, $\times$, max, min, and computes for $0 \leq k \leq P - 1$ the "sum" stored on P_k:

$$S_k = M_0 \oplus M_1 \oplus \cdots \oplus M_k$$

The P messages $\{M_k\}_k$ are assumed to be stored on the local memory of process P_k.
- *all-to-all reduce* is defined according to a binary associative operation $\oplus$ like $+$, $\times$, max, min, and outputs:

$$M_r = \oplus_{i=0}^{P-1} M_{i,r}.$$

---

[14]https://www.open-mpi.org/doc/v1.5/man3/MPI_Scatter.3.php.

[15]https://www.open-mpi.org/doc/v1.5/man3/MPI_Gather.3.php.

[16]https://www.open-mpi.org/doc/v1.5/man3/MPI_Reduce.3.php.

[17]https://www.open-mpi.org/doc/v1.5/man3/MPI_Allreduce.3.php.

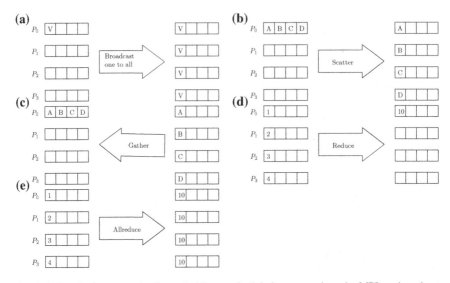

Fig. 2.6 Standard communication primitives and global computations in MPI: **a** broadcast, **b** scatter, **c** gather, **d** reduce and **e** allreduce

We have P^2 messages $M_{r,k}$ for $0 \le r, k \le P - 1$, and messages $M_{r,k}$ are stored locally on P_r.

- *Transposition*, is a personalized all-to-all primitive that carries out a transposition of messages on the processes as follows:

$$
\begin{array}{cccccccc}
P_0 & P_1 & P_2 & P_3 & P_0 & P_1 & P_2 & P_3 \\
M_{0,3} & M_{1,3} & M_{2,3} & M_{3,3} & M_{3,0} & M_{3,1} & M_{3,2} & M_{3,3} \\
M_{0,2} & M_{1,2} & M_{2,2} & M_{3,2} \rightarrow & M_{2,0} & M_{2,1} & M_{2,2} & M_{2,3} \\
M_{0,1} & M_{1,1} & M_{2,1} & M_{3,1} & M_{1,0} & M_{1,1} & M_{1,2} & M_{1,3} \\
M_{0,0} & M_{1,0} & M_{2,0} & M_{3,0} & M_{0,0} & M_{0,1} & M_{0,2} & M_{0,3}
\end{array}
$$

We have P^2 messages $M_{r,k}$ with P messages $M_{r,k}$ stored on P_r, and after the transposition, we have the $M_{r,k}$ stored on P_k for all $0 \le k \le P - 1$. This transposition primitive is very useful for inverting matrices partitioned in blocks on the grid or torus topology, for example.

- The *circular shift* operates a global shift of messages as follows:

$$
M_0 \quad M_1 \quad M_2 \quad M_3 \rightarrow M_3 \quad M_0 \quad M_1 \quad M_2
$$

The P messages M_k are stored locally and the message $M_{(k-1)\bmod P}$ is stored at P_k in the output.

2.8 Communications on the Ring Topology with MPI

In Chap. 5, we shall consider distributed algorithms for the matrix multiplication on the ring and torus topologies. Here, we illustrate a short MPI program using the blocking communication primitives `send` and `receive` to perform a broadcast operation:

> WWW source code: `MPIRingBroadcast.cpp`

```
// filename: MPIRingBroadcast.cpp
#include <mpi.h>
int main(int argc, char *argv[]) {
int rank, value, size;
MPI_Status status;
MPI_Init(&argc, &argv);
MPI_Comm_rank(MPI_COMM_WORLD, &rank);
MPI_Comm_size(MPI_COMM_WORLD, &size);

do {
if (rank == 0) {scanf("%d", &value );
/* Master node sends out the value */
MPI_Send( &value, 1, MPI_INT, rank + 1, 0,
    MPI_COMM_WORLD);
}
else {
/* Slave nodes block on receive the send on the
    value */
MPI_Recv( &value, 1, MPI_INT, rank - 1, 0,
    MPI_COMM_WORLD, &status);
if (rank < size - 1) {
MPI_Send( &value, 1, MPI_INT, rank + 1, 0,
    MPI_COMM_WORLD);
}
printf("process %d got %d\n", rank, value);
} while (value >= 0);

MPI_Finalize();
return 0;
```

2.9 Examples of MPI Programs with Their Speed-Up Analysis

Let us now present different types of parallel implementations depending on the type of data transfer and on the local computations, and let us investigate the speed-up obtained on several problems. We recall that the speed-up is defined as follows:

$$s_p = \frac{t_1 = \text{time for one process}}{t_p = \text{time for } p \text{ processes}}.$$

We aim at reaching a *linear speed-up* in $O(P)$, where P denotes the number of processes (each process ran to its own processor). In practice, one has to take care when accessing data (communication time, the different hierarchical levels of cache memories, etc.). In particular, we need to partition data when the data size are too big to hold on a single local memory of a processor (horizontal or vertical data partitioning).

Often, one can obtain a nice parallelization whenever the considered problem is said to be *decomposable*. For example, when playing chess, we need to find the best move given a configuration of the chessboard. Although the space of chess configuration is combinatorially very large, it is nevertheless finite, in $O(1)$. Thus in theory, one could explore all potential moves: at each move, we partition the space called the *configuration space*. The communication stages are for partitioning the problem into sub-problems and for combining the solutions of the sub-problems (`reduce`). Therefore, one expect to obtain a linear speed-up. In practice, the chess performance of a parallel software depends on the depth of the search tree it uses for exploring the configuration space. High Performance Computing has been instrumental in designing such a powerful chess software that won against Human: in 1997, Kasparov lost a chess play to the computer named Deeper Blue using 12 GFLOPS. Nowadays, people are focusing on the go game that offers a bigger combinatorial space. Advances in go program performance also implies progress in many other technical fields.

However, not all problems can be easily or well parallelized. For example, problems using *irregular* and *dynamic domains* like when simulating snow melting (that requires to dynamically and locally re-mesh domains, etc.). In that case, in order to obtain a good speed-up, we require to explicitly manage the load balancing among the processes. Splitting dynamically data among processes cost a lot since it requires to transfer data, and the overall speed-up is difficult to predict, because it depends on the semantic of the problem on the considered input data-sets, etc.

Let us know consider some very simple illustrative MPI programs.

2.9.1 The Matrix–Vector Product in MPI

The chapter on linear algebra (Chap. 5) will concentrate on distributed algorithms on the oriented ring and torus topologies.

> WWW source code: `MPIMatrixVectorMultiplication.cpp`

```cpp
// filename: MPIMatrixVectorMultiplication.cpp
#include <mpi.h>

int main(int argc, char *argv[]) {
  int A[4][4], b[4], c[4], line[4], temp[4],
      local_value, myid;
  MPI_Init(&argc, &argv);
  MPI_Comm_rank(MPI_COMM_WORLD, &myid);

  if (myid == 0) {/* initialization */
    for (int i=0; i<4; i++) {
      b[i] = 4 ? i;
      for (int j=0; j<4; j++)
        A[i][j] = i + j;
    }
    line[0]=A[0][0];
    line[1]=A[0][1];
    line[2]=A[0][2];
    line[3]=A[0][3];
  }

  if (myid == 0) {
    for (int i=1; i<4; i++) {// slaves perform
        multiplications
      temp[0]=A[i][0];
      temp[1] = A[i][1];
      temp[2] = A[i][2];
      temp[3] = A[i][3];
      MPI_Send( temp, 4, MPI_INT, i, i,
          MPI_COMM_WORLD);
      MPI_Send( b, 4, MPI_INT, i, i, MPI_COMM_WORLD)
          ;
    }
  } else {
    MPI_Recv( line, 4, MPI_INT, 0, myid,
        MPI_COMM_WORLD, MPI_STATUS_IGNORE);
    MPI_Recv( b, 4, MPI_INT, 0, myid, MPI_COMM_WORLD
        , MPI_STATUS_IGNORE);
  }
  {// master node
    c[myid] = line[0] * b[0] + line[1] * b[1] + line
        [2] * b[2] + line[3] * b[3];
    if (myid != 0) {
```

```
      MPI_Send(&c[myid], 1, MPI_INT, 0, myid,
          MPI_COMM_WORLD);
   } else {
      for (int i=1; i<4; i++) {
         MPI_Recv( &c[i], 1, MPI_INT, i, i,
             MPI_COMM_WORLD, MPI_STATUS_IGNORE);
      }
   }
   MPI_Finalize();
   return 0;
}
```

2.9.2   Example of MPI Reduce Operations: Computing the Factorial and Minimum Value of an Array

The following code illustrates how to perform a global calculation in MPI using a collective reduce operation:

> WWW source code: `MPIFactorialReduce.cpp`

```
// filename: MPIFactorialReduce.cpp
#include <stdio.h>
#include "mpi.h"

int main(int argc, char *argv[]) {
  int i,me, nprocs;
  int number, globalFact=-1, localFact;

  MPI_Init(&argc,&argv);

  MPI_Comm_size(MPI_COMM_WORLD,&nprocs);
  MPI_Comm_rank(MPI_COMM_WORLD,&me);

    number=me+1;
    MPI_Reduce(&number,&globalFact,1,MPI_INT,
       MPI_PROD,0,MPI_COMM_WORLD);
    if (me==0) printf("Computing the factorial in
       MPI: %d processus = %d\n",nprocs,globalFact);

    localFact=1; for(i=0;i<nprocs;i++) {localFact*=
       (i+1);}
    if (me==0) printf("Versus local factorial: %d\n"
       ,localFact);

  MPI_Finalize();
}
```

We now turn to a more elaborate example: computing the global minimum value of a set of arrays stored in the local memories of processes:

WWW source code: `MPIMinimumReduce.cpp`

```cpp
// filename: MPIMinimumReduce.cpp
#include <mpi.h>
#include <stdio.h>

#define N    1000

int main(int argc, char** argv) {
  int rank, nprocs, n, i;
  const int root=0;

  MPI_Init(&argc, &argv);
  MPI_Comm_size(MPI_COMM_WORLD, &nprocs);
  MPI_Comm_rank(MPI_COMM_WORLD, &rank);

  float val[N];
  int myrank, minrank, minindex;
  float minval;

  // fill the array with random values (assume UNIX here)
  srand(2312+rank);
  for (i=0; i<N; i++) {val[i]=drand48();}

  // Declare a C structure
  struct { float value; int index; } in, out;

  // First, find the minimum value locally
  in.value = val[0]; in.index = 0;
  for (i=1; i <N; i++)
    if (in.value > val[i]) {
      in.value = val[i]; in.index = i;
    }

  // and get the global rand index
  in.index = rank*N + in.index;

  // now the compute the global minimum
    // the keyword in MPI for the binary commutative operator
      is MPI_MINLOC
  MPI_Reduce( (void*) &in, (void*) &out, 1,
    MPI_FLOAT_INT, MPI_MINLOC, root, MPI_COMM_WORLD
      );
```

```
if (rank == root) {
  minval = out.value; minrank = out.index / N;
      minindex = out.index % N;
  printf("minimal value %f on proc. %d   at
      location %d\n", minval, minrank, minindex);
}

MPI_Finalize();
}
```

2.9.3   Approximating π with Monte-Carlo Stochastic Integration

We describe the Monte-Carlo sampling approach to approximate a complex integral calculation by a discrete sum. Loosely speaking, Monte-Carlo sampling is bypassing the continuous integral $\int$ calculation by approximating it with a discrete sum: $\int \approx \sum$. To approximate π (an irrational number), we draw randomly n points uniformly inside the unit square. We then compute the ratio of the number of points n_c falling inside the unit disk positive orthant over the total number of drawn points. Therefore we can deduce that:

$$\frac{\pi}{4} \approx \frac{n_c}{n}, \pi_n = \frac{4n_c}{n}$$

The approximated value of π converges very slowly in practice, but this estimator is proven to be statistically consistent since we have the following theoretical result:

$$\lim_{n \to \infty} \pi_n = \pi.$$

Fig. 2.7 Monte-Carlo rejection sampling to approximate π: we draw at random n points uniformly in the unit square, and we count the number of points that fall within the unit radius circle centered at the origin (n_c). We approximate $\frac{\pi}{4}$ as the ratio $\frac{n_c}{n}$

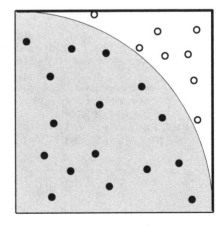

Moreover, this approach is pretty easy to parallelize, and the speed-up is linear, as expected. Figure 2.7 illustrates this Monte-Carlo stochastic estimation of π by the method called *rejection sampling*.

WWW source code: `MPIMonteCarloPi.cpp`

```cpp
// filename: MPIMonteCarloPi.cpp
int main(int argc, char *argv[]) {
  MPI_Init(&argc, &argv);
#define INT_MAX_ 1000000000
    int myid, size, inside=0, outside=0, points
      =10000;
  double x, y, Pi_comp, Pi_real
    =3.14159265358979323846264643;

  MPI_Comm_rank(MPI_COMM_WORLD, &myid);
  MPI_Comm_size(MPI_COMM_WORLD, &size);

  if (myid == 0) {
    for (int i=1; i<size; i++) /* send to slaves
      */
      MPI_Send(&points, 1, MPI_INT, i, i,
        MPI_COMM_WORLD);
  } else
    MPI_Recv(&points, 1, MPI_INT, 0, i,
      MPI_COMM_WORLD, MPI_STATUS_IGNORE);
  rands=new double[2*points];

  for (int i=0; i<2*points; i++ ) {
    rands[i]=random();
    if (rands[i]<=INT_MAX_)
      i++
  }

  for (int i=0; i<points; i++ ) {
    x=rands[2*i]/INT_MAX_;
    y
      =rands[2*i+1]/INT_MAX_;
    if ((x*x+y*y)<1) inside++ /* point inside
      unit circle*/
  }

  delete[] rands;

  if (myid == 0) {
    for (int i=1; i<size; i++) {
      int temp;
      MPI_Recv(&temp, 1, MPI_INT, i, i,
        MPI_COMM_WORLD, MPI_STATUS_IGNORE);
      inside+=temp;
    } /* master sums all */
  } else
```

```
    MPI_Send(&inside, 1, MPI_INT, 0, i,
        MPI_COMM_WORLD); /* send inside to master */
  if (myid == 0) {
    Pi_comp = 4 * (double) inside / (double)(size*
        points);
    cout << "Value obtained: " << Pi_comp << endl <<
        "Pi:" << Pi_real << endl;
  }

  MPI_Finalize();

  return 0;
}
```

2.9.4 Monte-Carlo Stochastic Integration for Approximating the Volume of a Molecule

A molecule M is modeled by a set of n 3D spheres where each sphere represents an atom (with given location and radius). We would like to compute the volume $v(M)$ of the molecule M (that is, the volume of the union of spheres). We shall approximate this volume by performing a stochastic approximation: first, we compute an enclosing bounding box BB, and then we perform rejection sampling inside this bounding box. We draw a set of e uniform variates inside BB and count the number of variates e' falling inside the union of spheres. Then we approximate $v(M)$: $v(M) \simeq \frac{e'}{e} v(\mathrm{BB})$.

Figure 2.8 illustrates the Monte-Carlo rejection sampling for computing the union of a set of 2D balls. The sequential code is given below:

WWW source code: `SequentialVolumeUnionSpheres.cpp`

```
// filename: SequentialVolumeUnionSpheres.cpp
// Sequential implementation of the approximation of the
    volume of a set of spheres
#include <limits>
#include <math.h>
#include <iostream>
#include <stdlib.h>
#include <time.h>

#define n 8*2
#define d 3
#define e 8*1000

double get_rand(double min, double max) {
    double x = rand() / (double)RAND_MAX;
    return x * (max - min) + min;
}
```

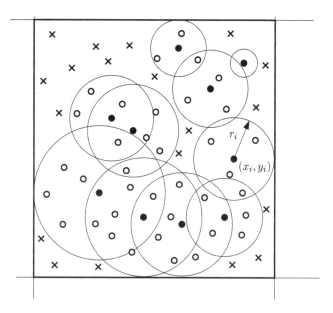

Fig. 2.8 Monte-Carlo rejection sampling to approximate the volume of the union of balls M: first, we compute the bounding box (BB) of the balls. Then we draw uniformly inside BB e samples and approximate the volume of the union of balls by $v(M) \simeq \frac{e'}{e} v(BB)$

```
double distance2(double p0[d], double p1[d]) {
    double x = 0;
    for (int i = 0; i < d; i++) {
        double diff = p0[i] - p1[i];
        x += diff * diff;
    }
    return x;
}

int main(int argc, char** argv) {
    srand(0);
    double radius[n];
    double C[n][d];
    // Generate data
    for (int i = 0; i < n; i++) {

        radius[i] = get_rand(1, 5);
        for (int j = 0; j < d; j++) C[i][j] =
            get_rand(-20, 20);

    }
    // Compute bounding box
    double bb[d][2];
    for (int i = 0; i < d; i++) {
```

```
        bb[i][0] = std::numeric_limits<double>::
            infinity();
        bb[i][1] = -std::numeric_limits<double>::
            infinity();
    }
    for (int i = 0; i < n; i++) {
        for (int j = 0; j < d; j++) {
            bb[j][0] = fmin(bb[j][0], C[i][j] -
                radius[i]);
            bb[j][1] = fmax(bb[j][1], C[i][j] +
                radius[i]);
        }
    }
    // Compute the volume of the bounding box
    double volBB = 1;
    for (int i = 0; i < d; i++) volBB *= bb[i][1] -
        bb[i][0];

    // Draw samples and perform rejection sampling
    int ePrime = 0;

    for (int i = 0; i < e; i++) {
        double pos[d];
        for (int j = 0; j < d; j++) pos[j] =
            get_rand(bb[j][0], bb[j][1]);
        for (int j = 0; j < n; j++) {

            if (distance2(pos, C[j]) < radius[j] *
                radius[j]) {
                ePrime++;
            }
        }
    }
    // Compute the volume
    double vol = volBB * (double)ePrime / double(e);
    std::cout << vol << std::endl;
    std::cout << ePrime << std::endl;
    return 0;
}
```

Let us implement this sequential code on a cluster of machine. Initially, we assume that the collection of spheres is stored on the root process (say, of rank 0), and we shall distribute those data using a scattering operation. Then we compute in parallel the bounding box by taking the bounding box of local bounding boxes using reduce operations (with the binary operators MPI_MIN and MPI_MAX). Then the random variates are sampled by the root process and dispatched to all processes using another scattering operation. Then each process tests whether the variates fall inside the union of its local set of spheres, and finally we aggregate the accepted variates using another reduce operation with the logical OR as the binary operator: MPI_LOR.

The MPI implementation is given below:

> WWW source code: `MPIVolumeUnionSpheres.cpp`

```cpp
// filename: MPIVolumeUnionSpheres.cpp
// Parallel implementation of the approximation of the volume
   of a set of spheres
#include <limits>
#include <math.h>
#include <iostream>
#include <stdlib.h>
#include <time.h>
#include "mpi.h"

#define n 8*2
#define d 3
#define e 8*1000

double get_rand(double min, double max) {
    double x = rand() / (double)RAND_MAX;

}

double distance2(double p0[d], double p1[d]) {
    double x = 0;
    for (int i = 0; i < d; i++) {
        double diff = p0[i] - p1[i];
        x += diff * diff;
    }
    return x;
}

int main(int argc, char** argv) {
    srand(0);
    MPI_Init(&argc, &argv);

    int n_proc, rank;
    MPI_Comm_rank(MPI_COMM_WORLD, &rank);
    MPI_Comm_size(MPI_COMM_WORLD, &n_proc);


    double radius0[n];
    double C0[n][d];
    // Generate data
    if (rank == 0) {
        for (int i = 0; i < n; i++) {
            radius0[i] = get_rand(1, 5);
            for (int j = 0; j < d; j++) C0[i][j] =
                get_rand(-20, 20);
        }

    }
```

```
// Send data to processes
double radius[n];
double C[n][d];
int begin = n / n_proc*rank;
int loc_n = n / n_proc;
MPI_Scatter(radius0, loc_n, MPI_DOUBLE, &(radius
    [begin]), loc_n, MPI_DOUBLE, 0,
    MPI_COMM_WORLD);
MPI_Scatter(C0, 3 * loc_n, MPI_DOUBLE, &(C[begin
    ][0]), 3 * loc_n, MPI_DOUBLE, 0,
    MPI_COMM_WORLD);
double bb[d][2];

// Compute the bounding box
for (int i = 0; i < d; i++) {
    bb[i][0] = std::numeric_limits<double>::
        infinity();
    bb[i][1] = -std::numeric_limits<double>::
        infinity();

    for (int j = begin; j < begin + loc_n; j++)
        {
        bb[i][0] = fmin(bb[i][0], C[j][i] -
            radius[j]);
        bb[i][1] = fmax(bb[i][1], C[j][i] +
            radius[j]);
    }

    MPI_Reduce(rank ? &(bb[i][0]) : MPI_IN_PLACE
        , &(bb[i][0]), 1, MPI_DOUBLE, MPI_MIN, 0,
        MPI_COMM_WORLD);
    MPI_Reduce(rank ? &(bb[i][1]) : MPI_IN_PLACE
        , &(bb[i][1]), 1, MPI_DOUBLE, MPI_MAX, 0,
        MPI_COMM_WORLD);
}

// Compute the volume of the bounding box

double volBB = 1;
for (int i = 0; i < d; i++) volBB *= bb[i][1] -
    bb[i][0];
// Draw variates and perform rejection sampling
double samples[e][3];
if (rank == 0) {

    for (int i = 0; i < e; i++) {
        for (int j = 0; j < d; j++) samples[i][j
            ] = get_rand(bb[j][0], bb[j][1]);
    }
}
MPI_Bcast(samples, 3 * e, MPI_DOUBLE, 0,
    MPI_COMM_WORLD);
```

```
// Testing variates

bool hit[e];
for (int i = 0; i < e; i++) hit[i] = false;
for (int i = 0; i < e; i++) {
    for (int j = begin; j < begin + loc_n; j++)
        {
            if (distance2(samples[i], C[j]) < radius
                [j] * radius[j]) hit[i] = true;
        }
}

// Gather results and count the accepted variates

bool hit0[e];
for (int i = 0; i < e; i++) hit0[i] = false;

MPI_Reduce(hit, hit0, e, MPI_C_BOOL, MPI_LOR, 0,
    MPI_COMM_WORLD);

if (rank == 0) {
    int ePrime = 0;
    for (int i = 0; i < e; i++) {
        if (hit0[i]) ePrime++;
    }
    double vol = volBB * (double)ePrime / double
        (e);
    std::cout << vol << std::endl;
    std::cout << ePrime << std::endl;
}

MPI_Finalize();
return 0;
}
```

2.10 References and Notes

A precursor of the MPI standard was the software library *PVM*[18] that stands for *Parallel Virtual Machine*. That PVM library already had both the synchronous and asynchronous communication primitives. The MPI standard is well-covered in many textbooks dealing with *parallel computing*, see [3, 4] for example. In this chapter, we have only covered the main concepts and primitives of the MPI library. We recommend the interested reader these following books [5, 6] that fully cover all functionalities of the first and second standard versions (called MPI-I and MPI-II). There are many interesting mechanisms in the MPI standard that have been designed to facilitate parallel programming: for example, one can define derived types using

---

[18]http://www.csm.ornl.gov/pvm/.

MPI_type_struct, and so on. The last standard version is *MPI-3* and its usages
are described in the recent book [7]. Parallel prefix operations (or scan) in MPI are
well-studied, highly optimized and benchmarked in the research paper [8].

2.11   Summary

MPI is a standardized *Application Programming Interface* (*API*) that allows one to
provide unambiguously the interface (that is, the declaration of functions, procedures,
data-types, constants, etc.) with the precise semantic of communication protocols and
global calculation routines, among others. Thus a parallel program using distributed
memory can be implemented using *various* implementations of the MPI interface
provided by several vendors (like the prominent OpenMPI, MPICH2,[19] etc.) Communications can either be *synchronous* or *asynchronous*, *bufferized* or not *bufferized*,
and one can define *synchronization barriers* where all processes have to wait for
each other before further carrying computations. There is a dozen MPI implementations available, and those implementations can further be called in many different
languages (usually C, C++ and Python) using an appropriate *language binding* (a
wrapper library to the underlying MPI implementation of the MPI standard). The
last installment of the MPI standard is MPI-3 that it offers beyond the usual basic
communication routines (broadcast, scatter, gather, all-to-all) over 200 functions that
also allow one to also manage the Input/Output (I/O) in a distributed fashion as well.

2.12   Exercises

Exercise 1   Consider the mathematical identity $\pi = \int_0^\infty \frac{4}{1+x^2} \mathrm{d}x$ to approximate π
by a Monte-Carlo stochastic integration. Fill the missing parts of the MPI program
below (using the C++ binding):

> WWW source code: `MPIPiApproximationHole.cpp`

```
// filename: MPIPiApproximationHole.cpp
#include <math.h>
#include "mpi.h"
#include <iostream>
using namespace std;

int main(int argc, char *argv[]){
    int n, rank, size, i;
    double PI = 3.141592653589793238462643;
    double mypi, pi, h, sum, x;
```

---

[19]http://www.mpich.org/.

```
MPI::Init(argc, argv);
size = MPI::COMM_WORLD.Get_size();
rank = MPI::COMM_WORLD.Get_rank();

while (1) {
    if (rank == 0) {
        cout << "Enter n (or an integer < 1 to
            exit) :" << endl;
        cin >> n;
    }

    MPI::COMM_WORLD.Bcast(...);
    if (n<1) {
        break;
    } else {
        h = 1.0 / (double) n;
        sum = 0.0;
        for (i = rank + 1; i <= n; i += size) {
            x = h * ((double)i - 0.5);
            sum += (4.0 / (1.0 + x*x));
        }
        mypi = h * sum;

        MPI::COMM_WORLD.Reduce(...);
        if (rank == 0){
            cout << "pi is approximated by " <<
                pi
                    << ", the error is " << fabs(pi
                        - PI) << endl;
        }
    }
}
MPI::Finalize();
return 0;
}
```

Exercise 2 (*Monte-Carlo rejection sampling in MPI*) In statistics, to sample independently and identically variates following a probability density function $f(x)$ defined over a finite support $[m, M]$ with maximal mode f_M (the largest value of $f(x)$), we can proceed as follows: sample a uniform variate u_1 from the uniform distribution $u_1 \sim U(m, M)$, and then sample a uniform variate u_2 from the uniform distribution $[0, F]$. Accept u_1 if $u_2 \leq f(u_1)$ and reject it otherwise. Intuitively speaking, to explain that this procedure produces independently and identically variates following density $f(x)$, consider throwing darts on a blackboard rectangle $[m, M] \times [0, F]$ and keep only the x-coordinate of darts falling below the density curve. The rejection sampling technique works for non-normalized densities $q(x)$ so that $f(x) = q(x)/Z$ where $Z = \int_x q(x)dx$ is the implicit normalization factor (a constant). Implement a MPI procedure on P processes that draws n random variates of the truncated standard normal distribution defined on the support $[-1, 1]$, with unnormalized density

$q(x) = \exp(-\frac{x^2}{2})$. Observe that this is a generalization of the Monte-Carlo approximation method of π.

Exercise 3 (*Computing the volume of the intersection of balls in MPI*) In Sect. 2.9.4, we provided some sequential and parallel implementations for approximating the volume of the union of balls by a Monte-Carlo stochastic approximation scheme. Show how to adapt the distributed MPI code for approximating the volume of the intersection of a set of balls.

References

1. Kernighan, B.W., Ritchie, D.M.: The C Programming Language, 2nd edn. Prentice Hall Professional Technical Reference, Englewood Cliffs (1988)
2. Stroustrup, Bjarne: The C++ Programming Language, 3rd edn. Addison-Wesley Longman Publishing Co. Inc, Boston (2000)
3. Kumar, V., Grama, A., Gupta, A., Karypis, G.: Introduction to Parallel Computing: Design and Analysis of Algorithms. Benjamin-Cummings Publishing Co. Inc, Redwood City (1994)
4. Casanova, H., Legrand, A., Robert, Y.: Parallel Algorithms. Chapman and Hall/CRC numerical analysis and scientific computing. CRC Press (2009)
5. Snir, M., Otto, S., Huss-Lederman, S., Walker, D., Dongarra, J.: MPI-The Complete Reference, Volume 1: The MPI Core, 2nd edn. MIT Press, Cambridge (1998). (revised)
6. Gropp, W.D., Huss-Lederman, S., Lumsdaine, A., Inc netLibrary: MPI: The Complete Reference. Vol. 2, The MPI-2 Extensions. Scientific and engineering computation series. MIT Press, Cambridge (1998)
7. Gropp, W., Hoefler, T., Thakur, R., Lusk, E.: Using Advanced MPI: Modern Features of the Message-Passing Interface. MIT Press (2014)
8. Sanders, P., Larsson Träff, J.: Parallel prefix (scan) algorithms for MPI. In: Recent Advances in Parallel Virtual Machine and Message Passing Interface, pp. 49–57. Springer (2006)

Chapter 3
Topology of Interconnection Networks

3.1 Two Important Concepts: Static Versus Dynamic Networks, and Logic Versus Physical Networks

In this chapter, a parallel computer is a computer cluster architecture with distributed memory: that is, a set of computers interconnected by a network. We shall consider two types of network:

- *static networks* that are once for all fixed, and cannot be anymore changed on the fly, and
- *dynamic networks* that can always be adapted to suit the traffic conditions of the network or the demand of applications using a connection manager.

When implementing a parallel algorithm (meaning programming it!), we also need to distinguish between the *physical network* and the *logical network*. On one hand, the physical network is the real-world hardware network where each node is a computer (machine, processor or *Processing Element*, PE), and each link between two processors is a direct communication channel between the two corresponding machines. On the other hand, the logical network is an *abstraction* of a communication network that is independent of the hardware architecture: It is a *virtual network* used by your algorithm/program to support communication primitives.

Considering logical networks instead of physical networks frees the parallel algorithm designer from the nitty-gritty details to know about the actual network hardware, and thus makes this programming design flexible to various hardware environments: At run time, we simply need to map the logical network to the physical network by a mechanism that is called an *embedding* or a *network transposition*. Of course, we obtain in practice an ideal performance when the physical network coincides with the logical network. When it is not the case, we seek for a transposition or an embedding of the logical network onto the physical network that minimizes the loss of efficiency of communication primitives.

© Springer International Publishing Switzerland 2016
F. Nielsen, *Introduction to HPC with MPI for Data Science*, Undergraduate Topics in Computer Science, DOI 10.1007/978-3-319-21903-5_3

3.2   Interconnection Network: Graph Modeling

Let P processors communicate between them (each one with its own independent local memory attached to). We have many ways to design the communication architecture! At the two opposite extremes, we can either consider (i) an architecture linking all processors using a shared *communication bus* but that has to deal with potential messages colliding when messages are simultaneously sent, or (ii) a *point-to-point network* linking all pairs of processors using a dedicated link to transmit messages. Although this last solution seems to be the best scenario, it unfortunately does not scale since this communication design requires a quadratic number $\binom{P}{2} = \frac{P(P-1)}{2} = O(P^2)$ of links (think of the physical constraints for all the cables!). *Topology*[1] of a network is described by a *graph* $G = (V, E)$ with:

- V: the set of *vertices* representing processes (or machines or processors, *PEs*),
- E: the set of *edges* representing communication links between processes (mapped onto processors).

Note that communication edges can either be oriented or not. In the former case, we rather use the term *communication arcs* instead of (bidirectional) edges.

Thus in order to build a good topology, we seek to set a trade-off between two opposing criteria:

- minimize the number of links in order to decrease the material cost, and
- maximize the number of direct communication links (arcs/edges) in order to decrease the communication cost of parallel algorithms.

The communication links can either be considered unidirectional or bidirectional. In the latter case, this simply amounts conceptually to double the edges with opposite arc directions. The *half-duplex model* is a model for bidirectional links with the bandwidth shared by transmitted messages using opposite directions. When the bandwidth is kept for both directional, we have the so-called *full-duplex model*.

When we have multiple concurrent communications, we can benefit from overlapping factors: Indeed, we shall assume that processes can both send and receive messages (non-blocking) and perform local computation at the same time. On a logical node of degree l, we can also define the maximum number of concurrent physical communications: When sending/receiving on all links are permitted, we have the *multi-port model*. Otherwise, we say we have a *k-port model* when at most k message sending and receiving operations can be processed simultaneously in parallel. The *1-port model* is a particular case often considered in practice.

In the remainder, we assume that routing messages in the network is done without message loss: That is, no message is rejected (due to a buffer overflow) and we do not take into account considerations about potential contentions. In practice, this requires

---

[1]Etymologically speaking, the word 'topology' stems from the field of geometry and defines the global property of objects and spaces. That is, for example the number of connected components or the number of holes/handles in objects. Geometric topology characterizes the genus of geometric objects, etc.

to implement a message flow controller on the links/nodes using a communication manager that needs to apply some policy for transmitting, storing, and dropping messages. Communication with contention means that processors attached to the network can send and receive messages whenever they need it, and this can make *collision exception* when a communication link is already in use. Thus communication by contention fosters competition to access network resources.

We shall now characterize in greater details the properties of interconnection network by studying the topology (that is, the general features) of their induced graphs.

3.3 Some Attributes Characterizing Topologies

A *path* in a graph $G = (V, E)$ is a sequence of nodes $V_1, \ldots, V_C$ so that edges $(V_i, V_{i+1}) \in E$ for all $1 \le i \le C - 1$. The length of a path in a graph is its number of edges: $L = C - 1$. The *distance* between two nodes in a graph is the length of the *shortest path* between these two nodes.

3.3.1 Degree and Diameter

We define the main structural attributes of a *network communication graph* $G = (V, E)$ as follows:

- *dimension*: the number of nodes in graph G (with $p = |V|$),
- *number of links* (edges), $l = |E|$,
- *degree* of a node: number of incoming links and outcoming links of a node, d. For oriented graphs, for a vertex s, we have $d(s) = d^{\text{incoming}}(s) + d^{\text{outcoming}}(s)$. When all nodes have the same degree, the graph G is said to be *regular*, and we denote by $d(G)$ the degree of the regular graph.
- *diameter* D: the maximum distance between any two nodes of the graph.

3.3.2 Connectivity and Bisection

In practice, it is very interesting to increase the number of nodes of a cluster of computers according to the data-set sizes of the problem to solve. That requires to be able to build *generic topologies* that scales up: that is, extendable topologies. One can characterize recursively topologies from sub-topologies by defining the following notions:

- *network connectivity*: Defined as the minimum number of links (edges) to remove in order to obtain two connected networks.

- *bisection width*, *b*: minimum number of links required to link two half sub-topologies. The *bisection bandwidth* is the bandwidth between the two equal segmented parts: It is an important criterion for measuring the performance of the network.

3.3.3 Criteria for a Good Network Topology

What are good topologies for an interconnection network? Here, we emphasize that a topology is a family of graphs satisfying a set of properties. We consider the following wish list:

- minimize the degree of a regular network in order to get a cheap hardware cost,
- minimize the network diameter in order to get short paths used by the communication network.
- maximize the network dimension: that is, increase P (the number of nodes/processors) for handling larger volumes of data (scalability).

We can also list those properties in order to compare topologies:

- positive aspects of a topology:

    - being uniform or symmetric,
    - property to scale up or scale down the topology while keeping the properties of the topology,
    - property to scale up in order to increase the performance of a parallel system,
    - property of a topology to simulate other virtual topologies easily,
    - ease of message routing on the topology.

- negative aspects of a topology:

    - high cost or high complexity for routing messages (large degree),
    - not robust to hardware failure (low degree or weak connectivity),
    - not efficient for communication primitives (low degree and large diameter),
    - not efficient for high performance computing (topology only available for small dimensions, that is small values of P).

We shall now quickly review the main usual topologies met in practice.

3.4 Common Topologies: Simple Static Networks

3.4.1 Complete Graphs: The Cliques

The complete network of P nodes is represented by the *complete graph* (also technically called a *clique*). This network is illustrated in Fig. 3.1. On one hand, it is the ideal

Fig. 3.1 The complete
network (here, represented
by the complete graph or
clique with 10 vertices,
denoted by K_{10}) minimizes
the communication costs but
has a high hardware cost or
is limited by physical
restrictions to be able to
scale up in practice

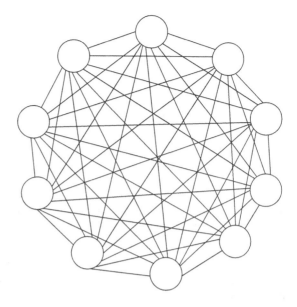

network for communications between processors since they are all at a unit distance
between each other (that is, diameter $D = 1$). On the other hand, the degree of nodes
is $d = p - 1$ (large), and the number of communication links (edges) is quadratic:
$\binom{P}{2} = \frac{P(P-1)}{2} = O(P^2)$. Of course, the complete graph network of P nodes allows
one to simulate easily *any* other topology of P nodes as a sub-graph but unfortunately
has a prohibitive high cost and nevertheless faces physical restrictions.[2] Thus this
clique topology can be use in practice only for small values of P.

3.4.2 Star-Shaped Graph

The *star graph* is depicted in Fig. 3.2a. Although it is efficient for communications
(low diameter $D = 2$), the topology of the star is weak to failure when the central
node becomes unavailable.

3.4.3 Rings and Chordal Rings

The *ring graph* and its topology are illustrated in Fig. 3.2. The ring topology allows
one to implement pipeline algorithms (using cascading operations) like the matrix-
vector product, etc. The ring links can either be unidirectional (represented by an

---

[2]Indeed, it is difficult to have too many cables getting out of a computer in practice.

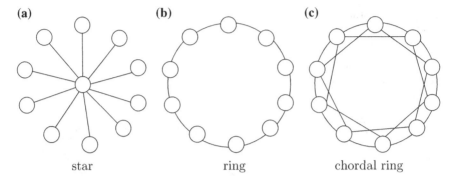

(a)   **(b)**   **(c)**

star   ring   chordal ring

Fig. 3.2 The star topology (**a**) with $P = 11$ nodes guarantees a diameter of 2 for communications but can be easily disrupted when a failure occurs on the central node. Ring topology (**b**) and chordal ring topology (**c**): Adding chordal communication links allows one to decrease the diameter of the ring

oriented graph) or bidirectional (non-oriented graph). One of the major drawback of the ring topology is the time it takes to communicate between two extreme nodes: The communication time (in steps) is $D = P - 1$, the diameter of the oriented ring, or $D = \lfloor \frac{P}{2} \rfloor$ for the non-oriented ring topology. Here, the *floor function* $\lfloor x \rfloor$ returns the largest integer that is smaller of equal to x.

In order to minimize the impact of large communication cost in rings, we can add several chords on the ring, and obtain the so-called *chordal ring*: Communications are now faster because the diameter D becomes smaller. The diameter decreases according to the number of added chords. To get a regular topology (node symmetry, meaning that all nodes play the same role in the network) for the chordal ring, we need to choose the step of chords to be a common divisor of the total number of nodes P. For example, for $P = 10$ nodes, we can choose a step of either 2 or 5 (see Fig. 3.2).

3.4.4 Meshes (Grids) and Torii (Plural of Torus)

The topology of the *grid* or *near-neighbor mesh* is very well-suited to problems dealing with image domains (say, 2D for pixels, or 3D grid topology for voxels[3] used in medical imaging), and on parallel algorithms implemented on matrices. One of the main drawback of the grid topology is that it is not a regular topology since nodes located on the border of the grids have not the same degree as the internal nodes. That means, that one has to take special care when implementing algorithms to consider these two cases: inner nodes and border nodes. The *torus* topology allows to remedy this drawback by being regular and therefore ease the parallel programming task. Figure 3.3 illustrates the difference between the irregular grid topology and the

---

[3] Voxel stands for volume element.

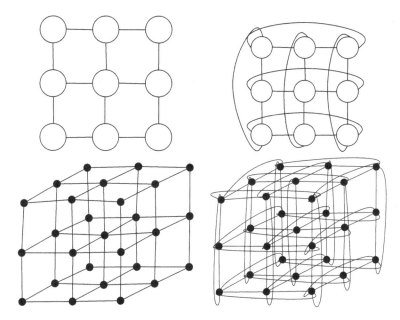

Fig. 3.3 Irregular topology of the grid and regular topology of the torus (illustrated in 2D and in 3D)

regular torus topology. Note that the ring topology can be interpreted as a 1D torus topology. Topology of grids and *torii* (plural of torus) can be extended to any arbitrary dimension. This is all the more important for modern processing applications based on the framework of tensor computing.

3.4.5 The 3D Cube and the Cycle Connected Cube (CCC)

The topology of the *cube* is regular and has diameter $D = 3$. We can increase the number of nodes by replacing each cube vertex with a ring: We thus obtain the so-called topology of *Cycle Connected Cube (CCC)*[4]. These topologies are often used in practice because they can be easily generalized in high dimensions. Figure 3.4 illustrates the cube and the topology of the Cycle Connected Cube.

3.4.6 Trees and Fat Trees

Many parallel algorithms use as inner data-structures trees for making queries. Trees also allow to easily implement *depth-first search* exploration or *breadth-first search*

---

[4]The advantage of the CCC topology is that the degree becomes 3 instead of d in dimension s. The number of nodes is $P = 2^s s$, the diameter $D = 2s - 2 + \lfloor \frac{s}{2} \rfloor$ for $s \gg 4$ and $D = 6$ when $s = 3$.

(a)   **(b)**

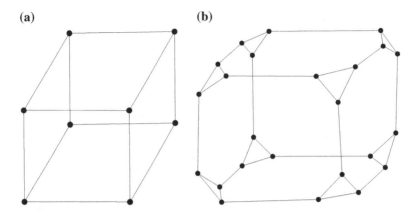

Fig. 3.4 Topology of the cube (**a**), and of **b** the Cycle Connected Cube, or CCC for short

(a)   **(b)**   **(c)**

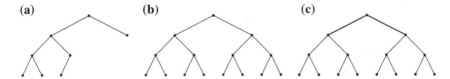

Fig. 3.5 Tree topologies: **a** tree, complete tree (**b**) and fat tree (**c**). For fat trees, the bandwidth of the communication links increase with respect to the distance of nodes to the tree root

exploration. It is thus important to choose the topology of the physical network to suit the topology of those algorithms (also called logical topology, or sometimes virtual topology). We observe that the closer to the tree root, the higher the bandwidth we wish as we need to communicate more messages (often aggregating information from the sub-trees, or leaves). Thus, in order to take into account this bandwidth requirement that decreases with the heights of the nodes in the tree, we build yet another topology: The fat trees (Fig. 3.5).

Let us summarize in Table 3.1 the main characteristics of the usual topologies we have introduced here.

Next, we introduce a key topology ubiquitously met in parallel computing: The hypercube.

Table 3.1 Principal characteristics of the common simple topologies, with P denoting the number of nodes, and b the bisection width

Topology	Processors P	Degree k	Diameter D	#links l	b
Compl. graph	P	$P-1$	1	$\frac{P(P-1)}{2}$	$\frac{P^2}{4}$
Ring	P	2	$\lfloor \frac{P}{2} \rfloor$	P	2
2D grid	$\sqrt{P}\sqrt{P}$	2, 4	$2(\sqrt{P}-1)$	$2P - 2\sqrt{P}$	$\sqrt{P}$
2D torus	$\sqrt{P}\sqrt{P}$	4	$2\lfloor \frac{\sqrt{P}}{2} \rfloor$	$2P$	$2\sqrt{P}$
Hypercube	$P = 2^d$	$d = \log_2 P$	d	$\frac{1}{2}P\log_2 P$	$P/2$

3.5 Topology of Hypercubes and Node Labeling Using the Gray Code

3.5.1 Recursive Construction of the Hypercube

The *hypercube* in dimension d, also called d-cube, is a generalization of the 2D square and 3D cube. We build recursively a hypercube of dimension d from two hypercubes of dimension $d - 1$ by linking the matched vertices together. Figure 3.6 illustrates the construction process of hypercubes. Therefore, we can deduce from this recursive construction that in d-dimension, the hypercube has 2^d vertices and each vertex has exactly degree d (or d edges). The hypercube provides a regular topology of degree d, for $d \in \mathbb{N}$.

How one should label the nodes of the hypercube in order to get efficient routing/communication algorithms for sending/receiving messages? A first strategy one could think of, is to label arbitrarily the nodes. However, in that case we need to have a *routing table* to know for each node the labels of its d neighbors. This method does not scale up and moreover requires extra memory storage. We rather search for a labeling representation so that the neighboring nodes of the hypercube, say node P and node Q, differ by at most one bit in their binary representation of their node labels. That would then be easy to check for example that $P = (0010)_2$ and $Q = (1010)_2$ are neighbors since P XOR $Q = 1000$. We recall the truth table of the logical XOR or exclusive OR:

XOR	0	1
0	0	1
1	1	0

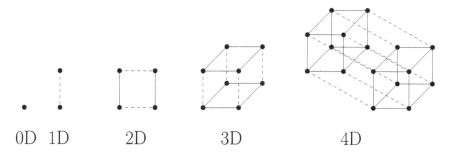

0D 1D   2D   3D   4D

Fig. 3.6 Recursive construction of the hypercube: Hypercubes in dimension 0, 1, 2, 3 and 4. A d-dimensional hypercube H_d is built recursively from two hypercubes of dimension $d - 1$ by linking the corresponding vertices

Moreover, we wish that the d bits of the labels encoding the 2^d different nodes correspond to the d axes of the hypercube: Thus, if P and Q differ by a single bit on the dth bit, we could deduce that they can communicate from/to P to/from Q by using this dth link. This special labeling of nodes of the hypercube is called the Gray code.

3.5.2 Numbering Hypercube Nodes Using the Gray Code

The *Gray code* $G(i, x)$ is a *reflected binary code* that has the particularity of asserting that two neighbor nodes of the hypercube have their binary labeling different by exactly one bit. Historically, the Gray code has been patented in the US in 1953 by Frank Gray (Bell Labs). The mathematical definition of the Gray code can be written recursively as follows:

$$G_d = \{0G_{d-1}, 1G_{d-1}^{\text{mirrored}}\}, \quad G_{-1} = \emptyset.$$

Let i denote the rank and x be number of bits of the Gray code. Then we have:

$$G(0, 1) = 0,$$
$$G(1, 1) = 1,$$
$$G(i, x + 1) = G(i, x), i < 2^x,$$
$$G(i, x + 1) = 2^x + G(2^{x+1} - 1 - i, x), i \geq 2^x.$$

For example, we get those following Gray codes using 2, 3 and 4 bits, respectively:

- $G(2) = (0G(1), 1G^r(1)) = (00, 01, 11, 10)$
- $G(3) = (0G(2), 1G^r(2)) = (000, 001, 011, 010, 110, 111, 101, 100)$
- $G(4) = (0G(3), 1G^r(3)),$ $(0000, 0001, 0011, 0010, 0110, 0111, 0101, 0100,$
  $1100, 1101, 1111, 1110, 1010, 1011, 1001, 1000)$
- etc.

Figure 3.7 illustrates the fact that the Gray code is called a reflected code.

The Gray code has many interesting properties beyond the fact that adjacent nodes have labels different by one bit: For example, the Gray code is a cyclic code, and a decreasing sequence amounts to an increasing sequence when we flip the front bit $(0 \leftrightarrow 1)$.

Fig. 3.7 Gray code construction as a reflected code

	$G(1)$	mirror	$G(2)$ prefix	mirror	$G(3)$ prefix
			00	00	000
	0	0			
	1	1	01	01	001
		1	11	11	011
		0	10	10	010
				10	110
				11	111
				01	101
				00	100

Decimal code	Binary code	Gray code (reflected binary)
0	000	000
1	001	001
2	010	011
3	011	010
4	100	110
5	101	111
6	110	101
7	111	100

The *Hamming distance* on the hypercube allows one to compute the distance (as the edge length of a shortest path) between any two arbitrary nodes. Let $P = (P_{d-1} \ldots P_0)_2$ and $Q = (Q_{d-1} \ldots Q_0)_2$ be two vertices of the hypercube in dimension d. The distance between P and Q is the length of the shortest path and amounts to the Hamming distance on their binary representation:

$$\text{Hamming}(P, Q) = \sum_{i=0}^{d-1} 1_{P_i \neq Q_i}$$

For example, we have $\text{Hamming}(1011, 1101) = 2$ We compute the Hamming distance between P and Q simply by counting the number of 1-bits in a XOR of P and Q.

3.5.3 Generating Gray Codes in C++

First, we start by giving a simple implementation of the reflected code using strings in C++:

WWW source code: `GrayString.cpp`

```cpp
// filename: GrayString.cpp
// Naive recursive implementation of the Gray code using strings
#include <iostream>
#include <string.h>
using namespace std;

string * Mirror(string * s, int nb)
{ string * res;
  res=new string[nb];
  int i;
  for (i=0; i<nb; i++)
    { res[i]=s[nb-1-i]; // copie
    }
  return res;
}

string * GrayCode(int dim)
{ string * res;
  int i, card=1<<(dim-1);

  if (dim==1)
  { res=new string[2]; res[0]="0";  res[1]="1";
  } else
  {
    string *GC=GrayCode(dim-1);
    string * GCreflected=Mirror(GC, card);
    res=new string[2*card];

    // prefixe
    for (i=0; i<card; i++)
    { res[i]="0"+GC[i];
      res[i+card]="1"+GCreflected[i];
    }
  }
  return res;
}

void printCode(string * code, int nb)
{
  int i;
  for (i=0; i<nb; i++)
  {
    cout<<code[i]<<endl;
  }
}

int main()
{
  int i, dim=4;
  string * GC=GrayCode(dim);
  printCode(GC, 1<<dim);
}
```

Now, we give below a better C++ source code using the STL to generate a Gray code in any arbitrary dimension n:

```cpp
// filename: GraySTL.cpp
// C++ code using the STL class vector
class Gray {
public:
    vector<int> code(int n) {
        vector<int> v;
        v.push_back(0);

        for(int i = 0; i < n; i++) {
            int h = 1 << i;
            int len = v.size();
            for(int j = len - 1; j >= 0; j--) {
                v.push_back(h + v[j]);
```

```
                }
            }
        return v;
        }
};
```

We can then use this class as follows:

```
#include <iostream>
#include <vector>
#include <bitset>

using namespace std;

int main() {
    Gray g;
        vector<int> a = g.code(4);

    for(int i = 0; i < a.size(); i++)
            {cout << a[i] << "\t";}
        cout << endl;

        for(int i = 0; i < a.size(); i++)
            {cout << (bitset<8>) a[i] << "\t";}
    cout << endl;

        return 0;
}
```

After compiling, running this code yields the following result on the output console:

```
0          1          3          2          6          7          5          4
           12         13
15         14         10         11         9          8
00000000              00000001              00000011              00000010
           00000110
00000111              00000101              00000100              00001100
           00001101
00001111              00001110              00001010              00001011
           00001001
00001000
```

Figure 3.8 illustrates the Gray code on a 4D hypercube.

3.5.4 Converting Gray Codes to and from Binary Codes

Figure 3.9 illustrates schematically the conversion principle between the Gray code and the binary code. For the binary code, we add an extra bit set to 0 as the *Most Significant Bit (MSB)* of the binary code. The ith bit of the Gray code g_i is set to zero if and only if the corresponding neighbor bits of the binary code match. This test can be implemented using a XOR logical gate.

It follows that when converting a binary code to a Gray code, the bits g_i can be simultaneously computed in parallel (say, on the CREW PRAM model). When converting a Gray code to a binary code, we start by computing the *Most Significant Bit*, and then perform a cascading conversion until we reach the *Least Significant Bit* (LSB).

Figures 3.9 and 3.10 illustrate some conversion examples.

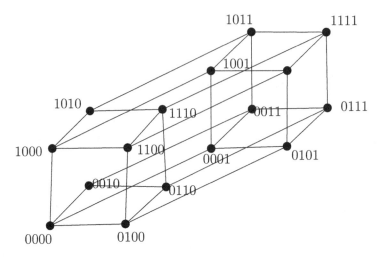

Fig. 3.8 Gray codes labeling the $2^4 = 16$ nodes of a 4D hypercube

$$g_i = 0 \Leftrightarrow b_{i+1} \text{ XOR } b_i = 0$$

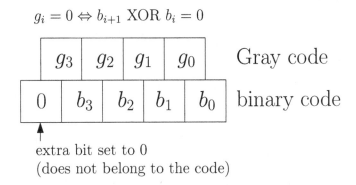

extra bit set to 0
(does not belong to the code)

Fig. 3.9 Procedure to convert a Gray code to an equivalent binary code, and vice versa

3.5.5 Cartesian Product □ of Graphs

The *cartesian graph product* is denoted by the binary operator ⊗. Let $G_1 = (V_1, E_1)$ and $G_2 = (V_2, E_2)$ be two connected graphs. Their cartesian product $G = G_1 \otimes G_2 = (V, E)$ is defined as follows:

- vertex set V: $V = V_1 \times V_2 = \{(u_1, u_2), \ u_1 \in V_1, u_2 \in V_2\}$,
- set E of edges:

$$((u_1, u_2), (v_1, v_2)) \in E \Leftrightarrow \begin{cases} u_1 = v_1 & (u_2, v_2) \in E_2 \\ u_2 = v_2 & (u_1, v_1) \in E_1 \end{cases}$$

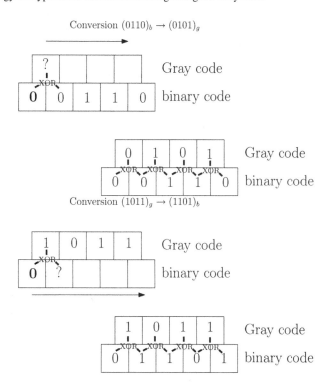

Fig. 3.10 Two examples of Gray ↔ binary code conversion: Converting the binary code $(0110)_b$ to its equivalent $(0101)_g$ code, and converting the Gray code $(1011)_g$ to its equivalent binary code $(1101)_b$

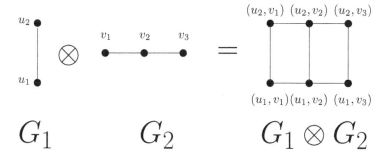

Fig. 3.11 Example of a Cartesian product of graphs

Figure 3.11 shows an example of a cartesian graph product (its inverse operation may be interpreted as a factorization of graphs).

The product of two edges is a 4-vertex cycle: $K_2 \otimes K_2 = C_4$, where K_2 denotes the clique with two nodes: an edge! The product of K_2 with a path is called a *ladder graph*. The product of two (linear) paths gives a grid, etc.

Now, the hypercube in dimension d can be obtained as d Cartesian graph products of 1D edges:

$$\underbrace{K_2 \otimes \cdots \otimes K_2}_{d \text{ times}} = \text{Hypercube}_d$$

We can thus deduce the following closure property of hypercubes using the graph cartesian product:

$$\text{Hypercube}_{d_1} \otimes \text{Hypercube}_{d_2} = \text{Hypercube}_{d_1+d_2}.$$

3.6 Some Communication Algorithms on Topologies

Let us consider the ring topology with P nodes: $P_0, \ldots, P_{P-1}$. We assume unidirectional links so that the ring is oriented (say, in the clockwise order, CW). We recall the two usual MPI functions: `Comm_size()` that returns the value of P, the number of nodes, and `Comm_rank()` that gives the rank, indexed from 0 to $P-1$.

Let us assume the *SPDM* (*Single Program Multiple Data*) mode of computation on the ring: All processors execute the same code, and all computations are carried out on the local memory space of their process. We give the two elementary primitives of communication: `send` and `receive` that allow to process P_i to communicate as follows:

- `send(address, length)`: send a message stored in the local memory space at address `address` to $\boxed{P_{(i+1) \bmod P}}$ (of length `length` in bytes)
- `receive (address, length)`: receive a message from $\boxed{P_{(i-1) \bmod P}}$ and store it into the local memory space of P_i at address `address`

Compare to the MPI interface,[5] we do not consider the *tag* attributes here in messages, and all nodes belong to the same communication group (same "communicator").

The communication primitives `send` and `receive` are synchronous and blocking, and we can thus potentially reach undesirable deadlocks. We could alternatively also consider non-blocking `Isend()` with blocking `receive()`, or the scenario that deals with both non-blocking `Isend()` and `Ireceive()`.

In order to measure the communication cost, let us denote by l the length of a message. The cost of a send or receive operation is modeled in the so-called $\alpha - \tau$ *model* as a linear function $\alpha + \tau l$ with:

---

[5]The MPI syntax provides far more options. See http://www.mcs.anl.gov/research/projects/mpi/sendmode.html.

- α: the initialization cost for communication that cannot be shrunk and yields latency, and
- τ: the rate of transmission.

Thus sending or receiving a message of length l at distance $d \leq P - 1$ from a calling process naively cost $d(\alpha + \tau l)$.

The four basic communication operations on the (oriented) ring are:

- *broadcast*,
- personalized broadcast called *scatter*,
- *gather*,
- gossip (*all-to-all, total exchange*)

This list of primitives is not exhaustive since in the MPI standard, there exist far many more communication modes like the personalized total exchange, and so on.

3.6.1 Communication Primitives on the Oriented Ring

Without loss of generality, we assume that it is process P_0 (the root process) that sends a message of length l to all other processes $P_1, \ldots, P_{P-1}$ of the oriented ring, step by step, as it is shown in Fig. 3.12.

This broadcasting operation requires $P - 1$ stages, with messages being sent iteratively to $P_1, \ldots, P_{P-1}$. Indeed, for a message to be transmitted from P_a to P_b, we need $b - a + 1$ stages. The cost of broadcasting in the (α, τ)-model is therefore $(P - 1)(\alpha + \tau l)$. We can observe the relative weights of parameters α and τ with respect to the message length.

An implementation based on blocking communications is given below in pseudo-code:

```
// Pseudo-code for the broadcast operation on the ring:
// - initial calling process P_k
// - length of message l
// - message is stored at memory address 'address'
broadcast(k, address, l)
{
        r = Comm_rank();
        p = Comm_size();

        if (r == k) {
           // I am P_k the calling process = I send the initial
              message
                send(address,l); }
        else
                if (r == k-1 mod p) {
                   // I am the last process = I receive
                        receive(address,l);
                        }
```

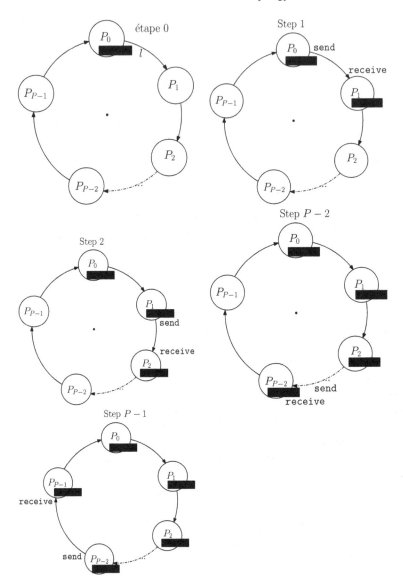

Fig. 3.12 Broadcasting on the oriented ring

```
else {
// I am a process in between, therefore I
    receive and send
receive(address,1);
send(address,1);}
}
```

We used the *round robin* technique for circulating messages on the ring.
A full MPI implementation is given below:

WWW source code: `MPIBroadcastRing.cpp`

```cpp
// filename: MPIBroadcastRing.cpp
// Broadcasting on the oriented ring
# include <mpi.h>
# include <cstdio>
# include <cstdlib>
using namespace std;

int next()
{
  int rank,size;
  MPI_Comm_rank ( MPI_COMM_WORLD , &rank );
  MPI_Comm_size ( MPI_COMM_WORLD , &size ) ;
  return ((rank + 1) % size);
}

int previous()
{
int rank,size;
  MPI_Comm_rank ( MPI_COMM_WORLD , &rank );
  MPI_Comm_size ( MPI_COMM_WORLD , &size ) ;
  return ((size + rank - 1) % size);
}

int main ( int argc , char * argv []) {
  int rank , value , size ;
  if (argc == 2)
    value = atoi(argv[1]);
  else
    value = rand % 1001;
  MPI_Status status ;
  MPI_Init (& argc , & argv ) ;
  MPI_Comm_rank ( MPI_COMM_WORLD , &rank ) ;
  MPI_Comm_size ( MPI_COMM_WORLD , &size ) ;
  if ( rank == 0) {
  /* Master Node sends out the value */
    MPI_Send ( &value , 1 , MPI_INT , next() , 0 ,
       MPI_COMM_WORLD) ;
  }
  else {
    /* Slave Nodes block on receive then send on the value
       */
    MPI_Recv ( &value , 1 , MPI_INT , previous() , 0 ,
       MPI_COMM_WORLD , &status ) ;
    if ( rank < size - 1) {
      MPI_Send ( &value , 1 , MPI_INT , next() , 0 ,
         MPI_COMM_WORLD ) ;
    }
    printf ( "process %d received %d \n" , rank , value ) ;
  }
  MPI_Finalize();
  return 0;
}
```

3.6.1.1 Scattering: Personalized Broadcasting

Scattering is a personalized broadcasting operation that consists in sending a personalized message to each process of the ring. Let us assume that P_0 is the calling process, and that P_0 wishes to send message M_i to process P_i. All messages are stored on the local memory of P_0. Let address be an array of message pointers, and address[i] denotes the pointer of M_i. We shall use non-blocking communication primitive Isend() and the blocking primitive receive(). We chose blocking receive() in order to ensure that messages are received in the proper ordering. We shall present an efficient technique using overlapping between the different communications! Figure 3.13 illustrates the scattering operation.

Fig. 3.13 Illustration of the scattering operation on the ring (from *top* to *bottom*, and from *left* to *right*)

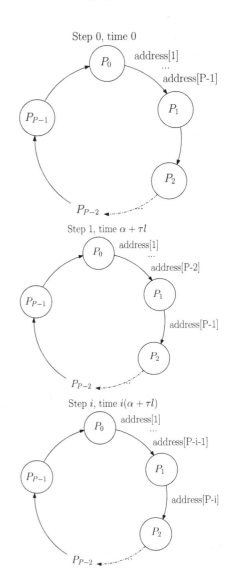

An implementation of the ring scattering communication primitive is reported in pseudo-code below:

```
// Scattering operation on the ring (personalized messages) :
// - initial calling process P_k
// - length of message l
// - individual messages are stored in an array 'address'
scatter(k, address, l)
{
        q = Comm_rank();
        p = Comm_size();

        if (q == k)
            {
            // I am the calling process P_k
            // I send using a non-blocking operation

                        for (i=1;i<p;i=i+1)
                                {Isend(address[k-i mod
                                        p],i);}
            }
        else
        {
        receive(address,l);

        for (i=1;i<k-q mod p;i = i+1)
                {Isend(address,l);
                receive(temp,l);
                address = temp; }
        }
}
```

Thus we can evaluate the complexity of a ring scattering operation as $(P-1)(\alpha + \tau l)$. The communication complexity is therefore identical to the cost of a broadcasting operation thanks to the overlapping strategy.

> WWW source code: `MPIScatteringRing.cpp`

```
// filename: MPIScatteringRing.cpp
// Scattering on the oriented ring
# include <mpi.h>
# include <cstdio>
# include <cstdlib>
using namespace std;

int main ( int argc , char * argv []) {
  int rank , size ;
  MPI_Status status ;
  MPI_Init (& argc , & argv ) ;
  MPI_Comm_rank ( MPI_COMM_WORLD , &rank ) ;
  MPI_Comm_size ( MPI_COMM_WORLD , &size ) ;
  MPI_Request request;

  if (rank == 0){
    int values[size-1];
    for(int i=0;i<size;i++){
      values[i]=i*i;
    }
```

```
for (int i =1; i < size; i++){
   printf("process 0 is sending value %d to process %d
      intended for process %d\n",values[size-1-i],1,
      size-i);
   MPI_Isend(&values[size-1-i],1,MPI_INT,1,0,
      MPI_COMM_WORLD,&request);
   }
}
else{
   int my_received_val;
   int val_to_transfer;
   for (int i = rank; i < size-1; i++){
      MPI_Recv(&val_to_transfer,1,MPI_INT,rank-1,0,
         MPI_COMM_WORLD,&status);
      printf("process %d received value %d for process %d
         which it now transfers to process %d\n",rank,
         val_to_transfer,size-1-i+rank,rank+1);
      MPI_Isend(&val_to_transfer,1,MPI_INT,rank+1,0,
         MPI_COMM_WORLD, &request);
   }
   MPI_Recv(&my_received_val,1,MPI_INT,rank-1,0,
      MPI_COMM_WORLD,&status);
   printf("process %d received value %d from process %d\n",
      rank,my_received_val,rank-1);
}
MPI_Finalize();
return  0;
}
```

3.6.1.2 Total Exchange (Gossiping or All-to-All Communication)

Total exchange also called gossip is a communication procedure that consists for all processes to send a personalized message to all other processes. Initially, each P_i has all its proper message $M_{i,j}$ (for $1 \leq j \leq P$) stored locally in an array myAddress. At the end of the gossip call, all processes have an array address [] such that address[j] contains the message send by process P_j.

An implementation of the all-to-all primitive on the ring is given in pseudo-code below:

```
// Total exchange collective communication
all-to-all(myAddress,adr,l)
{
    q = Comm_rank();
    p = Comm_size();

    address[q] = myAddress;

    for (i=1;i<p;i++) {
        send(address[q-i+1 mod p],l);
        Ireceive(address[q-i mod p],l);
    }
}
```

The cost of an all-to-all total exchange on the ring is thus $(P - 1)(\alpha + \tau l)$. That costs is the same if we consider a personalized total exchange.

3.6.1.3 Pipeline Broadcasting for Shrinking Communication Times

Since the simple broadcasting algorithm has the same cost (that is, $(P-1)(\alpha + \tau l)$) as the scattering algorithm (that used pipeline operations), we can improve the complexity of the broadcasting primitive as follows:

- We partition message M into r portions (let us assume that $l \bmod r = 0$, that is l can be divided by r),
- The calling process successively sends the p pieces of the message in order to pipeline operations.

Let address[0], ... address[r-1] denote the addresses of the r pieces of the message. An implementation of the *pipeline broadcasting primitive* on the oriented ring is given is the following algorithm written in pseudo-code style:

```
broadcast(k, address, 1)
{
  q = Comm_rank();
  p = Comm_size();

  if (q == k)
  {
    for (i=0; i<r; i++) send(address[i], 1/r);
  } else
    if (q == k-1 mod p)
  {
    for (i=0; i<r; i++) Ireceive(address[i], 1/r);
  } else {
    Ireceive(address[0], 1/r);

    for (i=0; i<r-1; i++) {
      send(address[i], 1/r);
      receive(address[i+1], 1/r);
    }
  }
}
```

Now, let us consider the communication complexity of this pipeline broadcasting: The first piece of message, M_0, is received by the last process P_{P-1} in time $(P-1)\left(\alpha + \tau \frac{l}{r}\right)$, then the $r-1$ remaining pieces arrive one by one. Thus we add $(r-1)\left(\alpha + \tau \frac{l}{r}\right)$ time. Overall, the global cost is:

$$f(r) = (P-2+r)\left(\alpha + \tau \frac{l}{r}\right).$$

In order to obtain the best complexity, we need to choose the best size r of pieces. Simple calculations yield:

$$r^* = \sqrt{\frac{l(P-2)\tau}{\alpha}}.$$

It follows that the cost of the pipeline broadcast is:

$$\left(\sqrt{(P-2)\alpha} + \sqrt{\tau l}\right)^2 .$$

Let us observe that when the length l of the messages become large enough (or asymptotically when $l \to \infty$), the cost of the pipeline broadcast becomes τl. It is therefore independent of P because the terms in P can be neglected for a fixed value of P.

In this chapter, we have described the fundamental communication algorithms on the ring. It is also very interesting to consider other topologies, and understand how the topology affects these communication algorithms. For example, how different are the communication primitives on the star topology compared to the ring topology? On the star graph, the maximal distance is 2 but we need to consider buffer operations (and take care of potential buffer overflows). Similarly, what happens when we consider the chordal ring with bidirectional links instead of the ring? We shall now concisely review a broadcast algorithm on the hypercube that demonstrates tree-like communications on that topology.

3.6.2 Broadcasting on the Hypercube: Tree-Like Communications

Between two arbitrary nodes P and Q of the hypercube, we have exactly Hamming (P, Q)! (! for the factorial notation) distinct paths. For example, we have Hamming $(00, 11) = 2! = 2$, and there exist two distinct paths: $00 \to 10 \to 11$ et $00 \to 01 \to 11$.

$$
\begin{array}{ccc}
00 & \leftrightarrow & 01 \\
\updownarrow & & \updownarrow \\
10 & \leftrightarrow & 11
\end{array}
$$

Let us consider the broadcasting primitive: A message is sent from a root process to all other processes. One could first send from the root node to all neighbors (at distance 1) using the communication links, and then all processes at distance 1, could send to their direct neighbors (that is, at distance 2 from the root process), and so one! However this yields inefficient algorithm because we will have redundancy of messages communicated over the links!

A far better routing algorithm consists in starting from the least significant bits[6] (LSB), and send the message by transforming the binary representation of node P to node Q by flipping bits at the locations where P XOR Q has the bits set at one. For example, to communicate from $P = 1011$ to $Q = 1101$, we first compute

---

[6]We can alternatively, consider the Most Significant Bit (MSB) too.

P XOR $Q = 0110$. We deduce that P sends a message to $P' = 1001$ on the axis link 1, and then P' sends a message to $P'' = 1101 = P$ on the link 2, etc.

We are now ready to consider the broadcast algorithm on the hypercube. Starting from the calling node process $P_0 = (0\ldots0)_2$ that we rename as $(10\ldots0)_2$ by adding an extra bit, we proceed as follows: Processes receive the message on the link corresponding to their first bit at 1, and send the message on the links of the axis where this 1 position occurred. Thus it requires $d = \log_2 P$ stages, where P denotes the number of processes.

Figure 3.14 illustrates those different communication stages. There exist better broadcast algorithms on the hypercube that we voluntarily omitted in this textbook for sake of conciseness.

The *broadcast tree* obtained from the broadcast algorithm is called a *binomial covering tree* of the hypercube. Figure 3.15 illustrates such a binomial tree.

We give the complete MPI implementation below:

> WWW source code: `MPIBroadcastHypercube.cpp`

```cpp
// filename: MPIBroadcastHypercube.cpp
// Broadcasting on the hypercube
#include <mpi.h>
#include <iostream>
#include <vector>
#include <bitset>
#include <cstdio>
#include <cstdlib>
using namespace std;


class Gray{
public:
  vector <int> code(int n){
    vector <int> v;
    v.push_back(0);
    for(int i=0; i < n; i++){
      int h = 1 << i; // 100000 with i zeros
      int len = v.size();
      for(int j = len-1;j>=0;j--){
    v.push_back(h+v[j]);
      }
    }
    return v;
  }
};

int lowest_non_zero_bit(int order, int code){
// we take the convention from the course, that the lowest nonzero bit
    of 0 is 1 << i where i == "order of the gray code"

  if(code == 0)
    return order;
  else{
    int temp = code;
    int i=0;
    while(temp % 2 == 0){
      i++;
      temp = temp / 2;
    }
    return i;
  }
}

vector<int> neighbours(int order, int code){
```

Fig. 3.14 Broadcasting on the hypercube: Visualization of the different communication stages

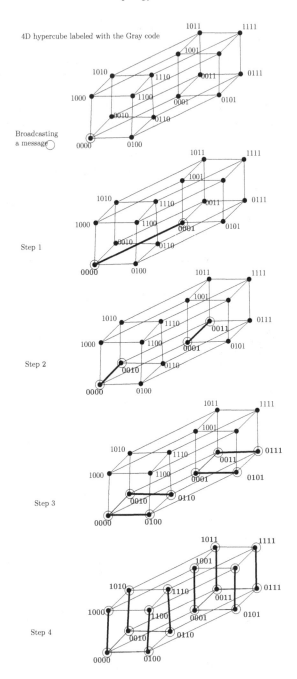

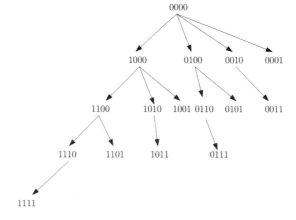

Fig. 3.15 Binomial tree covering the hypercube (here, of dimension 4 with 16 nodes). Observe that at a given level, the number of bits set to 1 is constant

```
    vector<int> res;
    int lnz = lowest_non_zero_bit(order,code);
    if (lnz==0)
      return res;
    else{
      for(int i=0;i<lnz;i++){
        res.push_back(code + (1 << (lnz-1-i)));
      }
      return res;
    }
}

vector<int> reverse_lookup(vector<int> * graycode){
  int n = graycode->size();
  vector<int> res(n);
  for(int i=0;i<n;i++){
    res[(*graycode)[i]]=i;
  }
  return res;
}

int main(int argc, char * argv[]){
  int rank,size,order;
  MPI_Status status ;
  MPI_Init (& argc , & argv ) ;
  MPI_Comm_rank ( MPI_COMM_WORLD , &rank ) ;
  MPI_Comm_size ( MPI_COMM_WORLD , &size ) ;

  order=0;
  while((1 << order) < size){
    order++;
  }
  Gray g;
  vector<int> toGray = g.code(order);
  vector<int> fromGray = reverse_lookup(&toGray);
  // we build a reverse lookup table from the Gray codes of all nodes
  //    so as to be able to retrieve their actual rank in constant time

  if (rank==0){
    int value = rand() % 1001;
    printf("I am process 0 and am now sending out the value
        %d\n",value);
    vector<int> rootNeighbors = neighbours(order,0);
    for(int i=0;i< rootNeighbors.size();i++){
      int neighbRank = fromGray[rootNeighbors[i]];
```

```
        // we retrieve the actual rank of the current neighbour from
           its Gray code
        if (neighbRank<size){
        // remember we "rounded up" to the smallest hypercube
           containing all nodes, so we need to check this is an actual
           neighbor
     printf("process %d: my current neighbor is %d\n",rank,
        neighbRank);
     MPI_Send(&value,1,MPI_INT,neighbRank,0,MPI_COMM_WORLD);
        }
    }
  }
  else{
    int grayRank = toGray[rank];
    int lnb = lowest_non_zero_bit(order,grayRank);
    int grayPredecessor = (grayRank - (1 << lnb));
    int predecessor = fromGray[grayPredecessor];
    cout << "I am process " << rank << " of gray code " <<
        (bitset<8>) grayRank << " and I am waiting for a
        message from my predecessor in the binomial tree "
        << predecessor << endl;
    int received_value;
    MPI_Recv(&received_value,1,MPI_INT,predecessor,0,
        MPI_COMM_WORLD,&status);
    vector<int> rootNeighbors = neighbours(order,grayRank);
    if (rootNeighbors.size() == 0){
      cout <<  "I am process " <<  rank << " of gray code "
          << (bitset<8>) grayRank <<  " and I have no
          descendants, so I will stop here!" << endl;
    }
    else{

      cout << "I am process " <<  rank << " of gray code "
          << (bitset<8>) grayRank <<   " and am now sending
          out the value " << received_value << " to my
          neighbors "<<  endl;
      for(int i=0;i< rootNeighbors.size();i++){
    int neighbRank = fromGray[rootNeighbors[i]]; // we
        retrieve the actual rank of the current neighbour from its
        Gray code
    if (neighbRank<size){
    // remember we "rounded up" to the smallest hypercube
        containing all nodes, so we need to check this is an actual
        neighbor
        MPI_Send(&received_value,1,MPI_INT,neighbRank,0,
           MPI_COMM_WORLD);
    }
        }
    }
  }
  MPI_Finalize();
  return 0;
}
```

The hypercube is a renown topology because it is a regular topology that can be scaled up, and that allows to simulate the ring and torus topologies in practice. Indeed, the ring topology of size $2^r \times 2^s$ can be embedded in a $(d = r + s)$-hypercube by labeling the nodes with the Gray code (Gray$_r$, Gray$_s$). We shall further discuss those *topology embeddings* in the next section.

3.7 Embedding (Logical) Topologies in Other (Physical) Topologies

In the beginning of this chapter, we have explained the difference between the physical network that relies on hardware characteristics and the logical network (also called the virtual network) that is the network considered by designers for implementing parallel algorithms. When both these physical and logical networks coincide, we obtain an optimal performance, otherwise we need to simulate the logical network onto the physical network by an embedding that specifies the correspondences between the physical nodes and the logical nodes. There are basically two parameters to optimize when embedding a topology into another: First, the *dilatation* that is defined as the maximal distance in the physical network between two arbitrary neighbor nodes of the logical network. Second, the *expansion* that is defined as the following ratio:

$$\text{expansion} = \frac{\#\text{nodes in physical network}}{\#\text{nodes in logical network}}.$$

A good embedding seeks to have a dilatation of 1 with an expansion of 1 in order to avoid loosing some communication performance (that necessarily occurs when the dilatation is greater than 1). It is quite easy to embed the ring of $P = 2^d$ nodes onto the hypercube $H_d = \{0, 1\}^d$: This is schematically illustrated in Fig. 3.16. However, this first strategy is not optimal because it yields a high dilatation when linking two neighbor nodes of the ring: Indeed, the dilatation obtained by this scheme matches the dimension of the hypercube (here, 3).

Fortunately, we can obtain an optimal embedding with both the dilatation and expansion factors of 1 by mapping the node A_i of the ring to the node $H_{G(i,d)}$ of the hypercube, where $G(i, d)$ is the ith code word of Gray with d bits. We thus realize the ring cycle on the hypercube by using the cyclic property of the Gray code. Figure 3.17 illustrates this optimal network transposition.

We can also embed optimally the 2D grid (with node degrees either 2 for border nodes or 4 for inner nodes), and binary trees on the hypercube.

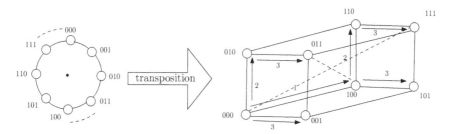

Fig. 3.16 Example of an embedding of the ring with 8 nodes onto a hypercube of dimension 3 (optimal expansion). The logical edges of the ring that require three (the dimension of the hypercube) physical links on the hypercube are shown in *dashed style*. Therefore the dilatation is 3

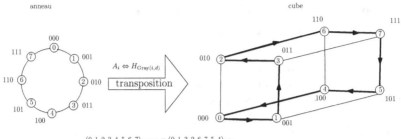

$(0, 1, 2, 3, 4, 5, 6, 7)_{\text{anneau}} = (0, 1, 3, 2, 6, 7, 5, 4)_{\text{cube}}$

Fig. 3.17 Optimal embedding of the logical ring network onto the physical hypercube network: To each node A_i of the ring corresponds a node $H_{G(i,d)}$ of the hypercube, where $G(i, d)$ is the ith codeword of Gray with d bits

3.8   Complex Regular Topologies

Recall that by definition a regular topology is a topology where each node plays the same role: Therefore nodes have all the same degree. Let $N(d, D) = P$ denote the *maximum number* of nodes in a regular graph of degree d and diameter D. We have $N(d, D) = P$ in the following cases:

- the ring with $d = 2$ and $D = \lfloor \frac{P}{2} \rfloor$,
- the complete graph with $d = P - 1$ and $D = 1$,
- the hypercube with $d = \log_2 p$ and $D = \log_2 p$.

Figure 3.18 displays a regular topology that is more complex: The *Petersen graph* with $d = 3$ and $D = 2$. We can also obtain complex regular topologies by using the graph Cartesian product of regular graphs: For example, $K_3 \otimes C_5$ (C_5 denotes the ring, that is the cycle with 5 nodes), etc.

Generally speaking, we define *Moore inequalities* that provide upper bounds on the maximal number of nodes P a regular topology can have if it is constrained to have (regular) degree d and bounded diameter D:

Fig. 3.18 Example of a complex regular topology: The Petersen graph (with $d = 3$, $D = 2$ and $P = 10$)

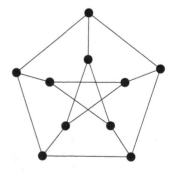

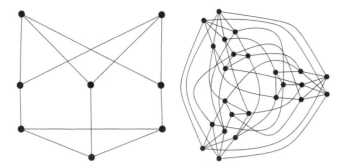

Fig. 3.19 Regular topology of $K3 \otimes X8$ ($X8$ is drawn on the *left*): $P = 24$ vertices of degree $d = 5$. The diameter is $D = 2$

- $N(2, D) \leq 2D + 1$
- $N(d, D) \leq \frac{d(d-1)^D - 2}{d-2}, d > 2$
- $N(16, 10) = 12, 951, 451, 931$

For the Petersen graph, we check that Moore's upper bound $N(3, 2)$ yields $\frac{3 \times 2^2 - 2}{1} = 10$. It is therefore optimal since the Petersen's graph has 10 nodes. In general, Moore upper bounds are not tight. For example, the Cartesian graph product of $X8$ with the clique K_3 yields a regular topology with $P = 24$ nodes, $d = 5$ and $D = 2$ (Fig. 3.19). But Moore's upper bound is equal to 26. Finding better bounds is still an open research problem. We refer the reader to [1] for a state-of-the-art survey on Moore's bounds.

3.9 Interconnection Network on a Chip

Modern processors are multi-core: Often, quad-cores or octo-cores, but even sometimes processors massively multi-cores on dedicated architectures. For example, the Intel Xeon® Phi[7] is a $x86$ processor that gives 3 TFLOPS of performance using 72 cores. It is an example of *Many Integrated Core* (MIC) architecture. Chips are manufactured using lithography processes (for the Xeon processor, using 14 nanometers), and super-computers are built from these chips by gathering them into rack modules. Nowadays, we aim at building super-computer with TeraFLOPS (TFLOPS) performance.

In order to minimize the latency of calculations that need memory access to load and store variables, we deal in practice with a hierarchy of memory types (and caches): Registers, caches, dynamic RAM, etc. Using dynamic random access memory (DRAM) costs approximately $\times 100$ clock cycles to access the values of those variables! We also need an interconnection network for the cores to communicate

---

[7]http://en.wikipedia.org/wiki/Xeon_Phi.

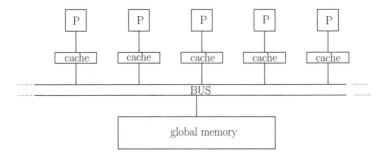

Fig. 3.20 Communications on a shared bus and contention: When two processors (or cores) try to communicate at the same time on the bus, we have a collision. Contention are solved by using a single software token that is required to have for sending messages

between them. That is, we need *on-chip interconnection networks*. With the advances of processor technologies, we shifted the design of CPUs from function-centric chips to communication-centric chips.

Figure 3.20 illustrates the communication using a shared bus: A single node at a time can send a message on a bus that can be listened by all other processors (concurrent read, CR for short). When two processors try to access the bus at the same time, we have a collision! Thus broadcasting is very efficient on a bus but not a gathering primitive! To avoid contentions, one can use a communication protocol using a token. We ensure that there is no collision when sending a message by requiring to have a special token that is guaranteed to be unique.

A *communication switch* requires a starting time when it is created but once created guarantees by construction to have no collisions (and therefore we do not need any arbitrage to take care of). Several message transfers are possible when we use mutually exclusive switches.

Routing can be done by *circuit switching* or by *packet switching*:

Circuit switching.   First, links are booked for a connection between the source and the destination. Then messages are sent. For example, the phone network is an example of network using circuit switching.

Packet switching.   Each packet is routed separately. Links are only used when data are transferred. For example, the Internet protocol is such an example of packet switching.

A *crossbar network*, illustrated in Fig. 3.21, allows to each pair of processors to communicate with small delays. The drawback of crossbars is its high hardware complexity: Indeed, it requires a quadratic number of switches, $O(P^2)$ (Fig. 3.22).

In order to scale up, one can use an *omega network*. An omega network has $\frac{P}{2} \log P$ switches that are 2×2 crossbars, organized into $\log P$ levels. Omega networks require less complexity per link compared to a crossbar network, but the delay is now in $O(\log P)$. Figure 3.23 illustrates an *omega network*, and show a routing example when sending a message between processor 000 and processor 110. The routing algorithm is simple but the network is blocking because we cannot send several messages at the same time without message collisions.

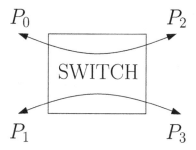

Fig. 3.21 A 4 × 4 crossbar initialized for communications between processors P_1 and P_3, and P_2 and P_4

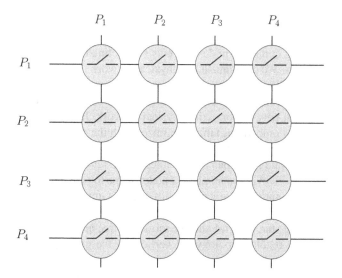

Fig. 3.22 A crossbar network

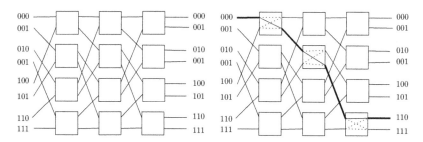

Fig. 3.23 Dynamic multi-stage omega network: Illustrating the communication between processor 000 and processor 110. Messages commute between 2 × 2 switches

3.10   Notes and References

Classical textbooks dealing with parallel algorithms [2, 3] describe the various topologies and their use in parallel algorithms. The book of Hennessy and Patterson [4] focuses on the performance evaluation of various computer architectures (the nodes of the topologies). To upper bound the maximal number of nodes in a regular topology of given degree d and diameter D is still nowadays an open research problem: See [1] for recent progress in that direction.

3.11   Summary

An interconnection network of computers is modeled mathematically as a graph with vertices representing computer nodes and edges depicting the communication links between those nodes. We distinguish the physical network from the logical network that is used by a parallel algorithm to operate its communications. When a logical network is different from the underlying physical network, one needs to transpose or embed the logical network onto the physical network. In that case, we seek the best transposition (or embedding) that minimizes both the dilatation (defined as the maximal distance between nodes on the physical network for neighbor nodes on the logical network) and the expansion (defined as the ratio of the number of nodes in the physical network over the number of nodes in the logical network). The topology of network is the study of characteristics of generic families of graphs that depend on the number of nodes. Common topologies met in practice are the ring (oriented or non-oriented), the star, the grid and the torus, the tree and the hypercube, just to mention a few. In a regular topology, all vertices of the graph play the same role (that is, vertices cannot be distinguished by their incoming/outcoming set of edges, meaning there is a vertex symmetry) and this makes life easier when implementing parallel algorithms since we do not need to take into account the type of nodes: They are all the same in a regular topology. The hypercube has a regular topology of degree d for $P = 2^d$ nodes and is often used in applications since it allows one to easily implement the various basic communication primitives like broadcasting by using an effective Gray code to label its nodes. The hypercube also allows one to simulate other common topologies like rings, trees and grids. But there are many other families of graphs used in parallel computing like the *De Bruijn graphs* also known as the *shuffle-exchange graphs*, etc.

References

1. Miller, M., Siran, J.: Moore graphs and beyond: a survey of the degree/diameter problem. Electron. J. Comb. **61**(DS14), 1–61 (2005)
2. Hwang, K.: Advanced Computer Architecture: Parallelism, Scalability, Programmability, 1st edn. McGraw-Hill Higher Education, New York (1992)
3. Casanova, H., Legrand, A., Robert, Y.: Parallel Algorithms. Chapman & Hall/CRC Numerical Analysis and Scientific Computing. CRC Press, Boca Raton (2009)
4. Hennessy, J.L., Patterson, D.A.: Computer Architecture: A Quantitative Approach, 5th edn. Morgan Kaufmann Publishers Inc., San Francisco (2011)

Chapter 4
Parallel Sorting

4.1 Quick Review of Sequential Sorting

Let $X = \{x_1, \ldots, x_n\}$ be a set of n real values stored in an array at locations $X[0], \ldots, X[n-1]$. Note that the index i is shifted by one: $X[i] = x_{i+1}$, starting from 0 to $n-1$. We ask to sort in increasing order, that is to report the sorted sequence $(x_{(1)}, \ldots, x_{(n)})$ with $x_{(1)} \leq \cdots \leq x_{(n)}$. Sorting amounts to find a permutation σ on the indices $(1, \ldots, n)$ such that $x_{\sigma(1)} \leq \cdots \leq x_{\sigma(n)}$ (often in order statistics, we write for short $\sigma(i) = (i)$). Since there exist $n!$ (factorial n) such distinct permutations, we can also unsort (shuffle) in $n!$ different ways a sorted sequence, say $(1, \ldots, n)$.

We assume when sorting on a memory-distributed parallel architecture with P processes that all data are already allocated to the processes into P arrays denoted by $X_0, \ldots X_{P-1}$. At the end of a parallel sorting procedure, all elements of X_i are sorted in increasing order, and less or equal to all elements of X_{i+1} for $0 \leq i \leq P - 2$.

Let us concisely review a few common sequential sorting algorithms.

4.1.1 Main Sequential Sorting Algorithms

BubbleSort. This *bubble sorting* procedure is incremental and use a propagation mechanism: It consists in letting the largest element of the input array to move up until it finds its place, and repeat this procedure for the second largest until the it reaches the smallest element. This sorting procedure bears its name from the analogy of an air bubble underwater that goes up to the surface. Figure 4.1 illustrates an example of bubble sorting. This algorithm is quite naive but very easy to program. Its worst-case complexity for sorting n elements is quadratic, in $O(n^2)$.

QuickSort. *QuickSort* is a randomized recursive algorithm that chooses an element, called the *pivot*, and cost $\tilde{O}(n \log n)$ in amortized time. We first apply a random permutation on the input array in linear time before calling the QuickSort sorting

© Springer International Publishing Switzerland 2016
F. Nielsen, *Introduction to HPC with MPI for Data Science*, Undergraduate
Topics in Computer Science, DOI 10.1007/978-3-319-21903-5_4

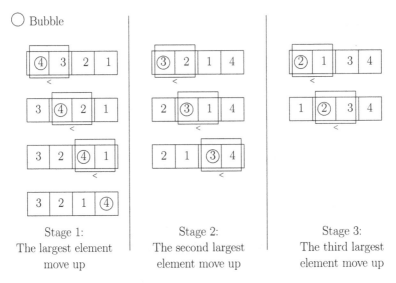

Stage 1:
The largest element
move up

Stage 2:
The second largest
element move up

Stage 3:
The third largest
element move up

Fig. 4.1 Example of BubbleSort sorting that requires quadratic time to sort: we compare pairs of consecutive elements. After the first stage is completed, the largest element reached the last position of the array. Then we iteratively proceed for the second largest to move up, and so on

procedure. Then Quicksort chooses the first element $X[0]$ as the pivot element, and partitions X into three sub-arrays: an array $X_<$ of elements strictly less than the pivot value, an array $X_>$ of elements strictly great than the pivot, and an array $X_=$ of elements equal to the pivot value (always of size 1 when all elements are distinct). QuickSort finally calls recursively itself on smaller-size arrays $X_<$ and $X_>$, and return the sorted list by concatenating the sorted sub-arrays:

$$\text{QuickSort}(X) = (\text{QuickSort}(X_<), X_=, \text{QuickSort}(X_>)).$$

Beware that if you do not choose the pivot randomly, then you need first to apply a random permutation to guarantee an amortized time of $\tilde{O}(n \log n)$. Otherwise, Quicksort may take quadratic time if you sort a sorted array! A more careful analysis proves that Quicksort requires $\tilde{O}(n + n \log p)$ time where p is the number of distinct elements. Thus when all elements are identical, we have the sorted sequence in linear time, as expected.

MergeSort.   The *MergeSort* sorting algorithm proceeds recursively as follows: first, we split data into two lists and perform this splitting recursion until getting elementary lists of single elements (henceforth sorted by definition!, this is the terminal case of recursion). Then we merge those sorted lists two by two until we get the overall sorted list of all elements. Figure 4.2 illustrates the MergeSort. The main primitive consists in merging two sorted lists into a sorted list: this can be done easily in linear time, and therefore MergeSort costs overall $O(n \log n)$ time.

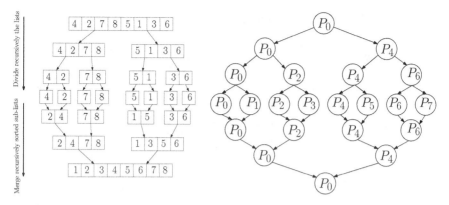

Fig. 4.2 Illustrating the parallel merge sort algorithm (fine grained parallelism)

RadixSort.   The *RadixSort* sorting algorithm relies on the binary representation of numbers into b bits: $x_i = \sum_{j=0}^{b-1} x_i^{(j)} 2^j$. First, we sort elements into two groups according the value of their bit value (1 or 0), starting from the *Least Significant Bit* (LSB) to the *Most Significant Bit* (MSB). The time complexity of RadixSort is $O(bn)$. Note that if we use integers represented using b bits, we can have at most $n = 2^b$ distinct numbers. That is, we need to have $b \geq \log_2 n$ to guarantee that all elements can be distinct, and in that case, the complexity of radix sort is $O(n \log n)$, matching the time complexity of the MERGESORT algorithm.

4.1.2   Complexity of Sorting: A Lower Bound

To get a *lower bound* of the complexity of sorting n distinct elements by comparisons $<$, let us observe that a single comparison $<$ splits the permutation space into two parts. Thus to find the right permutation that sorts all elements, we start from the identity permutation and by making comparison operations we split the permutation space until we get a singleton permutation set: the permutation solution for sorting. That is, we ask for the depth of a *decision tree* on the permutation set. For a binary tree with n nodes, the depth of the tree is at least $\lfloor \log_2 n \rfloor$ (with $\lfloor \cdot \rfloor$ denoting the floor function), and since we have $n!$ potential permutations, we can deduce that the minimal depth of a decision tree is $\lfloor \log_2 n! \rfloor$. Using *Stirling formula* for approximating the factorial $n!$: $n! \sim \sqrt{2\pi n}(\frac{n}{e})^n$, we deduce that $\log_2 n! = O(n \log n)$. This proves that sorting sequentially requires $\Omega(n \log n)$ elementary comparison operations. Let us emphasize that a lower bound holds only on the considered computation model. We usually assume the *real-RAM model* where elementary arithmetic operations can be computed on the reals in constant time and without any numerical precision issues. On other computation models, we can sort deterministically in $O(n \log \log n)$ time using linear memory space [1] by a technique called integer sorting. There exists also *adaptive algorithms* that sort provably quicker already partially sorted sequences [2].

4.2 Parallel Sorting by Merging Lists

Figure 4.2 shows how to parallelize the merge sort algorithm, by a fine-grained parallelism. We use $P = n$ processes to divide data and merge recursively the sorted sub-lists. Let us study the sequential time of this algorithm with this complexity analysis:

$$t_{\text{seq}} = O\left(\sum_{i=1}^{\log n} 2^i \frac{n}{2^i}\right) = O(n \log n).$$

To contrast with, the complexity of a parallel implementation of merge sort is:

$$t_{\text{par}} = O\left(2 \sum_{i=0}^{\log n} \frac{n}{2^i}\right) = O(n),$$

since $\sum_{k=0}^{n} q^k = \frac{1-q^{n+1}}{1-q}$.

This method is thus inefficient since the obtained speed-up is $\frac{t_{\text{seq}}}{t_{\text{par}}} = O(\log n)$. Ideally, we aim at an optimal linear speed-up factor of $O(P) = O(n)$. As depicted in Fig. 4.2, when we merge sub-lists, some processes happen to have no workload.

4.3 Parallel Sorting Using Ranks

An important question is whether we can sort in parallel in $O(\log n)$ time? We shall see that this is possible indeed with a trivial parallel algorithm based on computing the ranks of elements. However this RankSort algorithm does not yield an optimal speed-up.

For each data element $X[i]$, let us compute its *rank* in the array defined by:

$$R[i] = |\{X[j] \in X \mid X[j] < X[i]\}|.$$

That is, the rank $R[i]$ of $X[i]$ is the number of array elements strictly less than itself. The smallest element has rank 0 and the largest element has rank $n - 1$. Then we put the elements into a new auxiliary array, Y, that will be sorted as follows: $Y[R[i]] = X[i] \forall i$. Here, we have assumed that all elements were distinct to avoid degenerate rank definition (and get a total order on the elements).

Computing the rank of an element can also be parallelized easily on $P = n$ nodes as follows: For a given element $X[i]$, we evaluate the predicate $X[j] < X[i], \forall j \in \{1, \ldots, n\}$, and we aggregate all predicate evaluations by counting 0 when the predicate is false, and 1 when the predicate is true. That is, we have:

$$R[i] = \sum_{j=0}^{n-1} \underbrace{1_{[X[j]<X[i]]}}_{\text{Boolean predicate value converted to 0 (false) or 1 (true)}}$$

The sequential RankSort is described by the following code using a double loop:

```
for  (i  =  0;  i  <  n;  i++)
      {  // for each element
      rang  =  0;
      for  (j  =  0;  j  <  n;  j++)
            {// we count the number of elements smaller than
                  itself
            if  (a[i]  >  a[j])
                                    {rang++;}
      }
      // then we copy the element at its right position
            into new array b[]
      b[rang]  =  a[i];
}
```

Sequential rank sorting costs quadratic time, $t_{\text{seq}} = O(n^2)$, since it costs linear time to compute the rank of a single element. But its parallel implementation using $P = n$ processors is linear, $t_{\text{par}} = O(P) = O(n)$.

Now, let us consider parallel RankSort with $P = n^2$ processes. This can be done in practice for small values of n by using the *Graphical Processing Units* (GPUs) that are made of thousands of graphics cores.

To compute the rank of an element, we now use n processes for evaluating the predicate and performs a reduce operation (a prefix sum, `MPI_Reduce/MPI_Sum` in MPI). Therefore we use $P^2 = n^2$ for computing all ranks. Process $P_{i,j}$ evaluates boolean predicate $1_{[X[j]<X[i]]}$, and we compute the rank of $X[i]$ by aggregating all predicate values of processes $P_{i,*}$. Here, the $P_{i,*}$ denotes the group of processes $P_{i,j}$ pour $1 \le j \le P$ (Fig. 4.3).

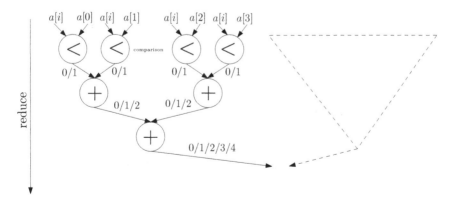

Fig. 4.3 Computing the rank in RankSort by aggregating the result of the boolean predicates $1_{[X[j]<X[i]]}$, counting one each time it is true: This is a collaborative reduce operation

Overall, the parallel time of rank sort with a quadratic number of processes is the time required by a collaborative reduce operation. This reduce operation depends on the topology of the interconnection network. It can be done in logarithmic time for an hypercube topology of dimension $\log n$, but takes linear time for the ring topology. Thus, by using $P = n^2$ processors on the hypercube topology, we get:

$$t_{\text{par}} = O(\log n).$$

When we choose the complete interconnection graph for the topology (the clique), then the reduce operation can be calculated in constant time (assuming that we can receive at the same time the $P - 1$ data from its neighbors), and the RankSort algorithm with $P = n^2$ processes requires constant time, $O(1)$.

4.4 Parallel Quicksort

We recall that for a pivot value x, we partition data into two arrays: $X_<$ and $X_>$. Here, for the sake of conciseness, we merged the $X_<$ array with the $X_=$ array. Then we recursively sort the sub-arrays $X_{\leq x} \leftarrow \text{QuickSort}(X_{\leq x})$ and $X_{>x} \leftarrow \text{QuickSort}(X_{>x})$, and finally we get the sorted array by concatenation as:

$$\text{QuickSort}(X) = (\text{QuickSort}(X_{\leq x}), \text{QuickSort}(X_{>x})).$$

When we choose randomly $x \in X$, we get a randomized algorithm with expected-time complexity $\tilde{O}(n \log n)$. Otherwise, when the pivot is chosen deterministically, we may compute the *median element* (an order statistics operation in linear time) to balance fairly the two sub-arrays, and we obtain a deterministic algorithm, in $O(n \log n)$ time.

The QuickSort algorithm in C++ using the Standard Template Library (STL) is given below:

WWW source code: `SequentialQuickSort.cpp`

```cpp
// filename: SequentialQuickSort.cpp
# include <vector.h>
# include <iostream.h>
# include <multiset.h>
# include <algo.h>

// pivot
template <class T>
void quickSort(vector<T>&v, unsigned int low,
    unsigned int high)
{
  if (low >= high) return;
  // select median element for the pivot
  unsigned int pivotIndex = (low + high) / 2;
```

```
    // partition
    pivotIndex = pivot (v, low, high, pivotIndex);
    // sort recursively
    if (low < pivotIndex) quickSort(v, low, pivotIndex
      );
    if (pivotIndex < high)  quickSort(v, pivotIndex +
      1, high);
}

template <class T> void quickSort(vector<T> & v)
{
  unsigned int numberElements = v.size ();
  if (numberElements > 1)
    quickSort(v, 0, numberElements - 1);
}

template <class T>
unsigned int pivot (vector<T> & v, unsigned int
    start,
unsigned int stop, unsigned int position)
{ //swap pivot with initial position
  swap (v[start], v[position]);
  // partition values
  unsigned int low = start + 1;
  unsigned int high = stop;
  while (low < high)
    if (v[low] < v[start])
      low++;
    else if (v[--high] < v[start])
      swap (v[low], v[high]);
  // swap again pivot with initial element
  swap (v[start], v[--low]);
  return low;
}

void main() {
  vector<int> v(100);
  for (int i = 0; i < 100; i++)
    v[i] = rand();
  quickSort(v);
  vector<int>::iterator itr = v.begin();
  while (itr != v.end ()) {
    cout << *itr << " ";
    itr++;
  }
  cout << "\n";
}
```

The median element for $n = 2m + 1$ elements is the middle element of the sorted array, located at position $m = \frac{n-1}{2}$. For even number of elements, we choose the median element to be at position $\lfloor \frac{n}{2} \rfloor$. Algorithm 1 recalls the classic recursive linear-time algorithm to compute the median (or any other ranked element by a divide and conquer technique with pruning). These selection algorithms are called order statistics.

Data: S a set of $n = |S|$ number, $k \in \mathbb{N}$
Result: Return the k-th element of S
if $n \leq 5$ **then**
   | // Terminal case of recursion
   | Sort S and return the k-th element of S;
else
   | Partition S in $\lceil \frac{n}{5} \rceil$ groups;
   | // The last group has 5 (complete) or n mod 5
   | elements (incomplete)
   | Compute recursively the group medians $M = \{m_1, ..., m_{\lceil \frac{n}{5} \rceil}\}$;
   | // Calculate the pivot x as the median
   | $x \leftarrow \text{SELECT}(M, \lceil \frac{n}{5} \rceil, \lfloor \frac{\lceil \frac{n}{5} \rceil + 1}{2} \rfloor)$;
   | Partition S into two sub-sets $L = \{y \in S : y \leq x\}$ and
   | $R = \{y \in S : y > x\}$;
   | **if** $k \leq |L|$ **then**
   | | **return** $\text{SELECT}(L, |L|, k)$;
   | **else**
   | | **return** $\text{SELECT}(R, n - |L|, k - |L|)$;
   | **end**
end

Algorithm 1: Computing the k-th element (median when $k = \lfloor \frac{n}{2} \rfloor$) using a recursive procedure SELECT (deterministic) in linear time.

Now, let us parallelize Quicksort: Let P computers (each taking charge of a process). We seek to sort data already distributed on the local memory of the machines $P_0, \ldots, P_{P-1}$ into P sub-sets $X_0, \ldots, X_{P-1}$ of size $\frac{n}{P}$. Without loss of generality, we assume that n can be divided by P: $n \mod P = 0$.

We shall write $X_i \leq X_j$ if and only if $\forall x_i \in X_i, \forall x_j \in X_j, \ x_i \leq x_j$. Initially, all groups $X_0, \ldots, X_{P-1}$ are unordered. The key idea of this first parallelization of Quicksort is to partition data on processes by exchanging messages so that at the end of the partition, we have $X_0 \leq \cdots \leq X_{P-1}$. A straightforward implementation consists in randomly choosing the pivot x, and to broadcast this pivot value to all the other processes. Then each process P_p partitions its array into two sub-arrays $X_{\leq}^{p}$ and $X_{>}^{p}$ using the pivot. Furthermore, each process of the upper process group $p \geq P/2$ sends its lower list $X_{\leq}^{p}$ to a corresponding process $p' = p - P/2 \leq P/2$, and receives an upper list $X_{>}^{p'}$, and vice-versa. Processes then split into two groups, and we recursively apply the parallel quicksort algorithm. Figure 4.4 illustrates this algorithm denoted by Quicksort //, a short cut for Parallel QuickSort.

Notice that the sequential Quicksort algorithm with $\log P$ recursive levels yields a tree of calling functions that we can visualize on the function stack. It partitions data: $X_0 \leq X_1 \leq \cdots \leq X_{P-1}$ in expected time $\tilde{O}(n \log P)$ (randomized algorithm) such that the group data X_i are not yet sorted but that we have $X_i \leq X_j$ for all $i \leq j$.

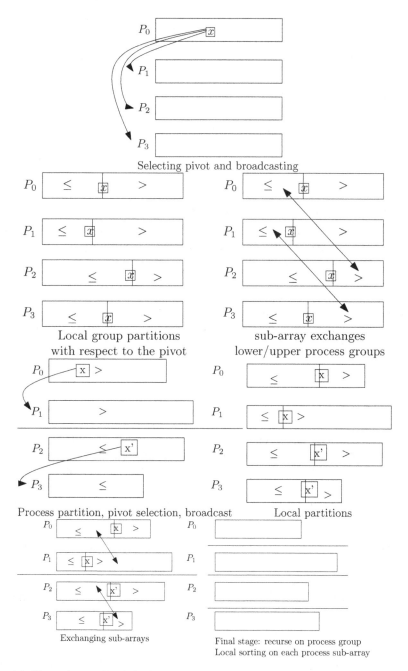

Fig. 4.4 Illustrating parallel QuickSort: selecting the pivot, broadcasting the pivot, partitioning locally data with the pivot, exchanging sub-arrays between corresponding processes, and performing recursion. Notice that depending on the pivot choices the sub-arrays can be quite unbalanced

It then remains to sort locally data inside each process using a dedicated sequential sorting algorithm, like the sequential QuickSort or the sequential mergesort.

Let us summarize our first parallelization of the Quicksort algorithm as follows:

- the upper processes (with rank greater than $P/2$) have data values above the pivot, and the lower processes (with rank less than $P/2$) have data values less than the pivot,
- after $\log P$ recursive calls, each process has a list of values disjoint from all the others, and
- the largest element of process P_i is less or equal than the smallest element of P_{i+1} for all i, and
- in the terminal case of the recursion, each process sorts its own group of data using a sequential sorting algorithm like QuickSort.

One of the major drawback of Quicksort // is that processes have potentially very different workload (size of their sub-lists). Indeed, the size of the process sub-lists depends of the chosen pivots that are broadcasted when splitting the process groups. This load-unbalancing phenomenon is illustrated in Fig. 4.4 where it is graphically indicated that the size of sub-lists can be quite different from one stage to another stage. We shall now study two algorithms that consider the load-balancing issue at the heart of their parallelization: The HyperQuickSort algorithm and the Parallel Sorting by Regular Sampling (or PSRS for short) algorithm.

4.5 HyperQuickSort

In the *HyperQuickSort* algorithm, the P processes first start by calling a sequential sorting procedure on their $\frac{n}{P}$ local data elements, in $O(\frac{n}{P} \log \frac{n}{P})$ time. Then the process that has in charge to choose the pivot, choose the median from its sorted list (hence, at index $\frac{n}{2P}$). This "pivot process" broadcasts the pivot to all other processes of its group. Processes then partition their data into two sub-lists $X_\le$ and $X_>$ according to the pivot value. Then we proceed similarly as for QuickSort //: Processes exchange upper and lower sub-lists with partner process, and on each process, we merge the two sorted sub-lists into a sorted list (in linear time). Finally, we recursively call HyperQuickSort on the processes of its group. Figure 4.5 illustrates this recursive HyperQuickSort algorithm.

Let us analyze the amortized mean complexity of HyperQuickSort by making the following hypotheses: Lists are assumed to be more or less balanced, and communication times are dominated by transmission time (that is, latency times are ignored). The initial sequential Quicksort call costs $\tilde{O}(\frac{n}{P} \log \frac{n}{P})$, the comparisons for the $\log P$ merging stages cost $\tilde{O}(\frac{n}{P} \log P)$, and the cost of communications for the $\log P$ sub-list exchange is $\tilde{O}(\frac{n}{P} \log P)$. Thus the overall parallel global time is in $\tilde{O}(\frac{n}{P} \log(P + n))$. Therefore, we obtain an optimal speed-up factor in $\tilde{O}(P)$ (under our mild no latency and well-balanced sub-list assumptions).

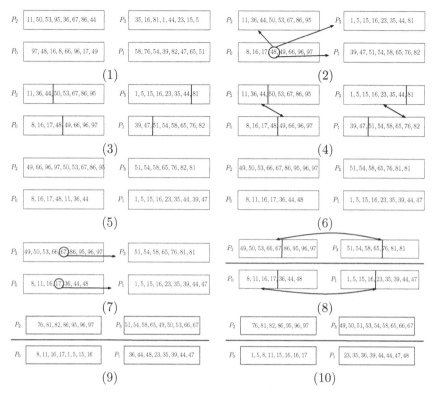

Fig. 4.5 Illustration of the HyperQuickSort algorithm: (1) Initialization, (2) chosen pivot 48, (3) data partitioning with respect to 48, (4) sub-list exchange between pairs of processes, (5) lists have been exchanged, (6) merging lists, (7) recursive calls → Pivot 67||17, (8) partition and exchange, (9) lists exchanged, (10) merging sorted sub-lists

In practice, the process lists that we have assumed more or less balanced are not well balanced in real-world applications! Thus we shall present our last alternative choice for parallel sorting. This last algorithm chooses better pivots that make partitions further well balanced in practice. This method goes by the name Parallel Sort Regular Sampling (PSRS).

4.6 Parallel Sort Regular Sampling (PSRS)

The *Parallel Sort Regular Sampling algorithm* (or *PSRS* method for short) proceeds in four stages. Here, we do not assume anymore that the number of processes is a power of 2, and P can be an arbitrary natural number. Let us describe the algorithm PSRS as follows:

1. Each process P_i sorts its own local data using a sequential algorithm (say, QuickSort), and choose P elements sampled at the following *regular* positions:

$$0, \frac{n}{P^2}, \frac{2n}{P^2}, \ldots, \frac{(P-1)n}{P^2}$$

We thus obtain a regular sampling of the sorted data.

2. A process gathers and sorts all these regular samples, and then selects $P - 1$ pivots among these $P \times P$ samples. This process broadcasts these $P - 1$ pivots, and all processes partition their local data into P pieces.

3. Each process P_i keeps its ith partition, and sends its jth partition to process $P_i, \forall j \neq i$. This is a total exchange (or all-to-all) collaborative communication primitive.

4. Each process merges its P partitioned arrays into a final sorted list.

Figure 4.6 schematically illustrates the work flow of the PSRS algorithm on a given toy data-set.

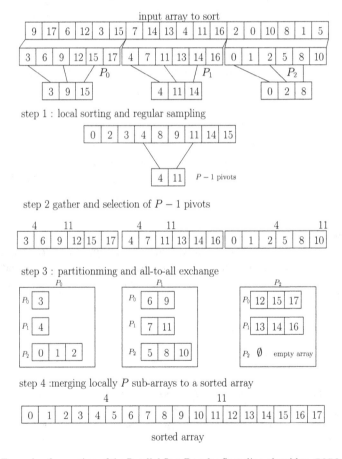

Fig. 4.6 Example of execution of the Parallel Sort Regular Sampling algorithm, PSRS

We analyze the complexity of this sorting algorithm as follows: Each process merges about $\frac{n}{P}$ elements, and this is the time experimentally observed empirically in practice! We assume that the interconnection network of the processes allows to have P simultaneous communications. Let us summarize the costs of these different stages of PSRS as follows:

- Local computation cost:

    - QuickSort in time $\tilde{O}(\frac{n}{P} \log \frac{n}{P})$,
    - Sorting regular samples : $O(P^2 \log P)$,
    - Merging sub-lists : $O(\frac{n}{P} \log P)$.

- Communication cost:

    - Gathering samples, broadcasting pivots,
    - Total exchange: $O(\frac{n}{P})$.

4.7 Sorting on Grids: ShearSort

Here, we demonstrate a simple parallel sorting algorithm well suited to the grid topology: the ShearSort parallel algorithm. At the final stage, the sorted sequence can either be ordered line by line on the grid, or ordered following a snake pattern as depicted in Fig. 4.7. Let $P = \sqrt{P}\sqrt{P} = n$ be the number of grid processors.

To sort on the process grid, we alternatively sort on rows and sort on columns until we get the sorted sequence after $\log n$ stages. For the snake pattern, we only need to alternate the sorting directions (meaning in increasing order or in decreasing order) on lines.

Let us analyze the complexity of this ShearSort sorting on a 2D grid of dimension $P = \sqrt{n} \times \sqrt{n} = n$. By sorting in parallel $\sqrt{n}$ numbers in $O(\sqrt{n})$ time, the

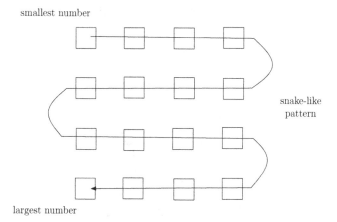

smallest number

snake-like
pattern

largest number

Fig. 4.7 Here, after completion of the ShearSort parallel sorting, the sorted elements are stored in the snake pattern

parallel time we get is $t_{par} = O((\log n) \times \sqrt{n}) = O(\sqrt{n} \log n)$. The cost of the sequential algorithm is $t_{seq} = O(n \log n)$. Thus we obtain a speed-up in $\frac{T_{seq}}{T_{par}} = O(\sqrt{n}) = O(\sqrt{P})$, that is not optimal!

Figure 4.8 illustrates the various sorting stages of the ShearSort algorithm for a given input sequence.

Fig. 4.8 The various stages of the ShearSort: $\log n$ steps are required to produce a final totally ordered sequence

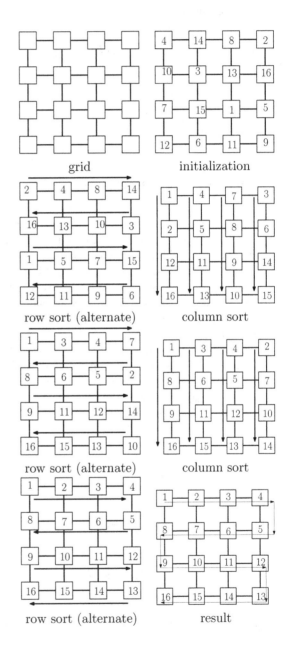

4.8   Sorting Using Comparison Network: Odd–Even Sorting

Let us now consider sorting by comparing pairs of elements. We introduce a sorting network, called *odd–even transposition* (or *odd–even sorting*). The main principle relies on the bubble sort idea. Here, sorting requires two stages per cycle, namely:

- Odd stage: we compare and exchange (swap) the odd pairs of elements:

$$(X[0], X[1]), (X[2], X[3]), \ldots.$$

- Even stage: we compare and exchange (swap) the even pairs of elements:

$$(X[1], X[2]), (X[3], X[4]), \ldots.$$

To sort an array of n elements, this algorithm requires n cycles of odd–even stages. Figure 4.9 depicts a running example for this comparison network sorting algorithm.

In the C/C++ programming language, this algorithm can be concisely implemented as follows:

> WWW source code: OddEvenSort.cpp

```
// filename: OddEvenSort.cpp
void OddEvenSort(int a[], int n)
{
  int phase, i;
  for (phase = 0; phase < n; phase++)
    if (phase % 2 == 0)
        {// even stage
      for (i = 1; i < n; i += 2)
        {if (a[i-1] > a[i])
           swap(&a[i], &a[i-1]);}
           }
    else
     {// odd stage
            for (i = 1; i < n-1; i += 2)
         {if (a[i] > a[i+1])
           swap(&a[i], &a[i+1]);}
         }
}
```

We can generalize this odd–even sorting algorithm by considering pairs of *groups of elements* instead of pairs of singleton elements. We sort the n/P local elements inside each group of the process (say, using your favorite sequential algorithm like the sequential QuickSort), and then we send and receive the corresponding elements from the pairs of adjacent processes. When the rank of the process is less than the rank of the process of its matching pair, we keep half of the smaller values, otherwise we keep half of the larger values. We repeat P times this group odd–even cycle. Thus we

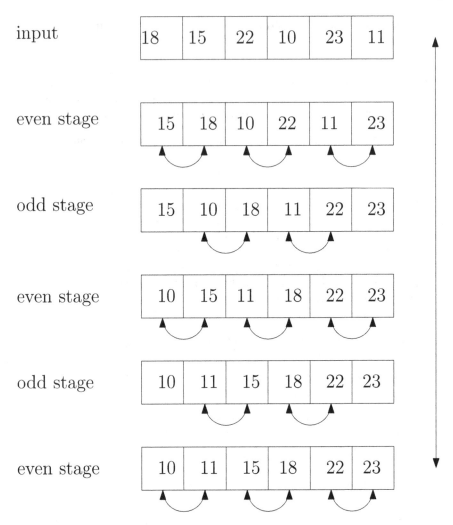

Fig. 4.9 Sorting by odd–even transposition: it requires n odd–even cycles to produce a sorted sequence

can tune up the *granularity* of the parallelism by considering P ranging from $P = n$ (fine grained parallelism) to $P = 2$ (coarsest-grained parallelism). Notice that this algorithm can be fairly easily implemented. Figure 4.10 illustrates the different steps of this algorithm.

Let us now analyze the complexity of this group odd/even sorting algorithm: the initial sequential sorting requires $O(\frac{n}{P} \log \frac{n}{P})$ for sorting groups of size $\frac{n}{P}$. Then we repeat P cycles by sorting the smallest values from the largest values in time $O(\frac{n}{P})$ (by merging lists and by keeping the right half for each process), and we communicate

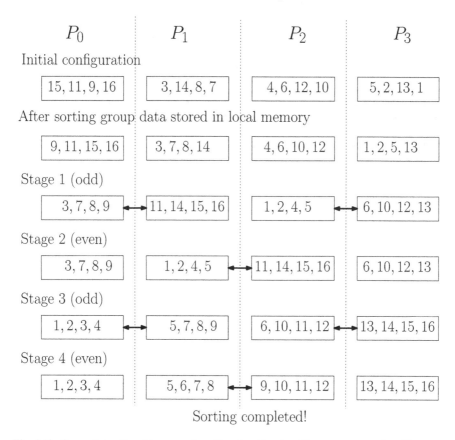

Fig. 4.10 Generalizing the odd–even pair sorting algorithm to odd–even group sorting. The granularity of the parallelism depends on the group size of data stored in the local memory of processes

to each process $O(\frac{n}{p})$ elements. Neglecting the latency times of communications, we thus obtain an overall complexity in time $O(\frac{n}{p} \log \frac{n}{p} + n)$. This algorithm is very interesting on a communication network that uses the *bidirectional ring topology*.

4.9 Merging Sorted Lists Using a Comparison Network

From a comparison-swap block, we can build a tailored circuit that implements algorithms sorting numbers. Figure 4.11 illustrates the basic element of these circuits: the comparison-swap box. We can sort two sorted sub-lists by using a *comparison network* implemented in hardware as shows in Fig. 4.12. Thus we can build a physical comparison network *recursively* as it is depicted in Fig. 4.12.

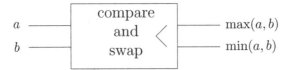

Fig. 4.11 The comparison-swap elementary hardware box that takes as input two numbers and returns in output the minimum and the maximum of the input elements.

Fig. 4.12 Comparison network for merging two sorted sub-lists (*top*) built generically recursively (*bottom*) from basic comparison-swap blocks

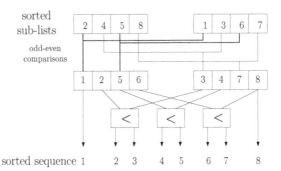

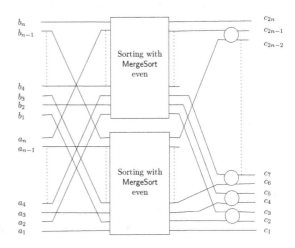

4.10   The Bitonic Merge Sort

Finally, to conclude this chapter on parallel sorting, let us describe the *bitonic merge sort* algorithm that was first proposed by Ken Batcher.[1] A sequence is said bitonic if it is a unimodal sequence (that is, with a unique extremum point, let it be minimum or maximum) by considering the cyclic sequence. Now, we can search efficiently

---

[1] http://en.wikipedia.org/wiki/Ken_Batcher.

for an element in a bitonic sequence in logarithmic time by using a bisection search algorithm. To obtain a bitonic partition, we proceed as follows:

- We associate to each element of the first half of the list, an element of the second half of the list: $x_i \leftrightarrow x_{i+\frac{n}{2}}$.
- We compare these pairs of elements and sort them, so they are ordered following the (min, max) ordering.
- Thus each element of the first half is guaranteed to be smaller than all elements of the second half by construction.
- The two half lists are bitonic sequences of length $\frac{n}{2}$.
- Observe that this comparison sequence does not depend semantically of the data. This property is important and is different with respect to the MergeSort algorithm whose behavior depends on the semantic of the data.

Therefore we get a binary splitting, and obtain as output two bitonic sequences B_1 and B_2 such that the elements of B_1 are all smaller than the elements of B_2. The terminal case of the recursion is when we have a sequence with a single element: in that case, it is trivially a sorted bitonic list! Figure 4.13 shows the workflow of this algorithm. An example of sorting with bitonic sort is reported in Fig. 4.14.

Let us analyze the complexity of the BitonicMergeSort: (1) Each bitonic partition costs $\frac{n}{2}$ comparisons, (2) We have $\log n$ recursion levels of bitonic sequence splitting, and (3) $\log n$ levels of merging of bitonic sequences. Thus the overall number of

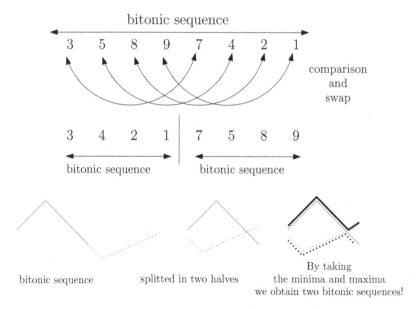

Fig. 4.13 *Top* Splitting a bitonic sequence into two bitonic sequences using comparison-swap blocks between elements x_i and $x_{i+\frac{n}{2}}$. *Bottom* An intuitive visual proof that by taking the minimum and the maximum on these two sub-sequences, we indeed obtain two bitonic sequences

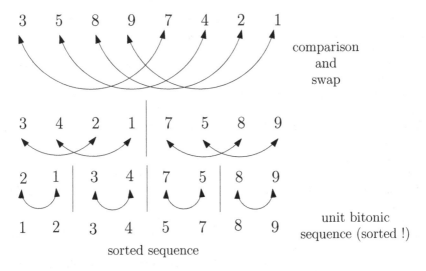

Fig. 4.14 Recursive calls for splitting bitonic sequences into bitonic sub-sequences

comparison-swap elementary operations is in $O(n \log^2 n)$. Figure 4.15 shows the bitonic sorting algorithm implemented using a comparison network.

4.11 Notes and References

The celebrated parallel sorting algorithms are covered in the following textbook [3]. Sorting in $O(\log n (\log \log n)^2)$ on the hypercube has been investigated in [4]. Even if sorting has a well-known lower bound of $\Omega(n \log n)$ on the real-RAM model of computation, we observe that in practice that it can be more or less easy to sort already partially sorted sequences: thus, we rather seek for *adaptive algorithms* [2] for sorting that take into account other input parameters in order to be more competitive in practice, and in the worst-case to yield the unadaptive complexity of $O(n \log n)$ time.

The fundamental primitive in sorting is the comparison operation that given a pair of elements produce a sorted pair as output:

$$(a, b) \xrightarrow{\text{comparison}<} (\min(a, b), \max(a, b))$$

One can choose the granularity of parallelism by considering A and B as group of elements, and not as single elements anymore. Then the operation $A < B$ means to sort $A \cup B$ and to return the pair (A', B') with A' the first half of sorted elements, and B' the second half of sorted elements. Thus we can build sorting network for parallel algorithms that control the granularity of the parallelism by adjusting the size of the groups for the basic sorting comparison-swap primitive.

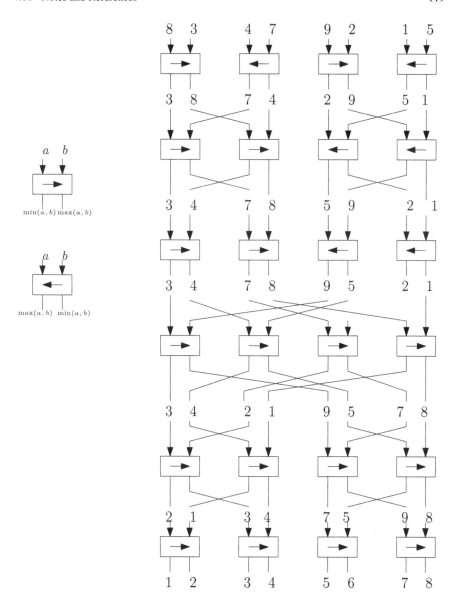

Fig. 4.15 Comparison network for bitonic sorting: the network is static and does not depend on the input data. We get the same running time whether we sort an already sorted sequence or an inversely sorted sequence

4.12 Summary

There exist plenty sequential algorithms to sort n numbers that achieve the optimal time complexity of $\Theta(n \log n)$. We can sort on parallel architectures with distributed memory by considering the granularity of local sorting. The QuickSort algorithm chooses randomly its pivot element and can be parallelized straightforwardly, but yields unfair workload on the processes (that is, not a good balancing property). To overcome this drawback, the HyperQuickSort algorithm first starts by sorting locally data before choosing the pivot element. The Parallel Sort Regular Sampling (PSRS) algorithm is even better, and proceeds into two stages to choose simultaneously several pivots in order to get a fair workload among all the processes. Sorting can also be performed in hardware using comparator networks, that we can simulate on parallel computers by taking group of data instead of single data element when evaluating comparisons. This allows us to tune the granularity of the parallelism.

4.13 Exercises

Exercise 1 (ShearSort *on groups*) Generalized the ShearSort algorithm on the grid by considering groups of $\frac{n}{P}$ elements for each node. What is the complexity of this algorithm, and its speed-up? Provide a MPI implementation of your algorithm.

Exercise 2 (*Programming* HyperQuickSort *in MPI*) Writes in pseudo-code the Hyper-QuickSort algorithm. What happens when we assume that there are only k distinct elements among the n elements, with $l \ll n$?

References

1. Han, Y.: Deterministic sorting in $O(n \log \log n)$ time and linear space. J. Algorithms **50**(1), 96–105 (2004)
2. Barbay, J., Navarro, G.: On compressing permutations and adaptive sorting. Theor. Comput. Sci. **513**, 109–123 (2013)
3. Casanova, H., Legrand, A., Robert, Y.: Parallel Algorithms. Chapman & Hall/CRC Numerical Analysis and Scientific Computing. CRC Press, Boca Raton (2009)
4. Cypher, R., Greg Plaxton, C.: Deterministic sorting in nearly logarithmic time on the hypercube and related computers. J. Comput. Syst. Sci. **47**(3), 501–548 (1993)

Chapter 5
Parallel Linear Algebra

5.1 Distributed Linear Algebra

5.1.1 Linear Algebra for Data Science

The field of algorithms covering *linear algebra* implementations is very rich and versatile. In computer science, we ubiquitously use computational linear algebra in algorithms, often by using a dedicated software library that hides the tedious nitty-gritty details of the optimized implementations of the fundamental algorithms (mainly matrix arithmetic operations and factorization primitives). Those matrix software libraries contain common product operations, various factorization techniques (like the Singular Value Decomposition, etc.), and matrix factorization routines like the LU factorization or the Cholesky $L^\top L$ factorization, etc. We find those core linear algebra techniques in most scientific domains. *Data Science* (DS) is no exception and also heavily relies on efficient implementation of linear algebra primitives in these three main categories:

Clustering. We seek for homogeneous group of data in data-sets: It is a class discovery procedure in data exploratory, also called *unsupervised classification*.

Classification. Given a training set of data labeled with their class, we seek to label new unlabeled data by means of a *classifier*. That is, we predict a discrete class variable.

Regression. Given a data-set and a function on this data-set, we ask for the best model of the function that explains the data. This allows one to interpolate or extrapolate values of this function for new data. In general, *regression* is a mechanism that allows to study the relationship of a variable with another.

Those three fundamental problems are visually depicted in Fig. 5.1.

Let us concisely review the mathematics underpinning the principle of the *linear regression* modeling of data-sets: we are asked to predict the value $\hat{y} = f(x)$ of a function at a query position x with $f(x) = \hat{\beta}_0 + \sum_{i=1}^{d} \hat{\beta}_i x_i$, a linear (affine)

© Springer International Publishing Switzerland 2016

F. Nielsen, *Introduction to HPC with MPI for Data Science*, Undergraduate
Topics in Computer Science, DOI 10.1007/978-3-319-21903-5_5

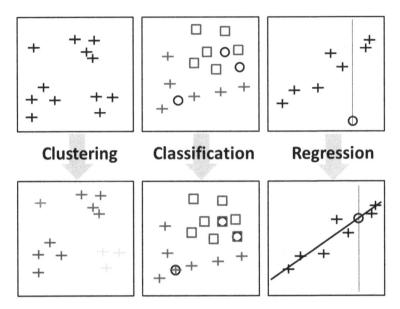

Fig. 5.1 The three pillars of learning in data science: clustering (flat or hierarchical), classification and regression

function (geometrically, represented by a hyperplane). First, we can augment the dimensionality of data by adding an extra coordinate $x_0 = 1$ to unify the function evaluation as a *dot product*: indeed, consider $x \leftarrow (x, 1)$ and $f(x) = \sum_{i=0}^{d} \hat{\beta}_i x_i = x_i^{\top} \beta$ ($d + 1$ parameters to evaluate). We are given a collection of observations $\{(x_1, y_1), \ldots, (x_n, y_n)\} \in \mathbb{R}^d$ and we want to fit the best model function by minimizing the *Residual Sum of Squares* (RSS)

$$\hat{\beta} = \min_{\beta} \sum_{i=1}^{n} (y_i - x_i^{\top} \beta)^2$$

The ordinary linear regression considers a data matrix X of dimension $n \times (d + 1)$ with a column vector y of dimension n and the hyperplane parameter vector β to estimate of dimension $d + 1$ (Fig. 5.2). We write the residual sum of squares as follows:

$$\text{RSS}(\beta) = \sum_{i=1}^{n} (y_i - x_i^{\top} \beta)^2 = (y - X\beta)^{\top} (y - X\beta)$$

By taking the gradient $\nabla_{\beta} \text{RSS}(\beta)$ (vector of partial derivatives), we get the so-called *normal equation*:

$$\boxed{X^{\top}(y - X\beta) = 0}$$

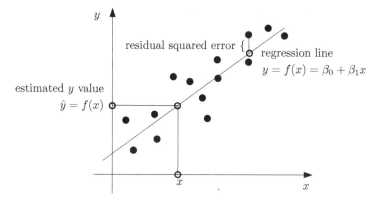

Fig. 5.2 Linear regression fits a linear model, that is an affine equation representing a hyperplane (in 2D, *a line*), to a data-set by minimizing the sum of the residual squared errors

When $X^\top X$ is not singular, we get estimate $\hat{\beta}$ minimizing the least squares by computing the *Penrose–Moore pseudo-inverse matrix*:

$$\hat{\beta} = (X^\top X)^{-1} X^\top y = X^\dagger y$$

with $X^\dagger = (X^\top X)^{-1} X^\top$.

Using the *SciLab*[1] open source software for numerical computation, we can easily demonstrate the linear regression fitting of noisy observations:

WWW source code: `ExampleLinearRegression.scilab`

```
// filename: ExampleLinearRegression.scilab
rand('seed',getdate('s'))
x = -30:30;  a=0.8; b=5; y=a*x+b;
// add a uniform noise
mynoise=rand(1,61,'uniform')-0.5;
y = y+10*mynoise;
// call the linear regression in scilab
[aa, bb] = reglin(x, y);
// plot the result
plot(x, y,'r+' );
plot(x, a*x+b,'bo-')
```

Figure 5.3 displays the output produced by this SciLab snippet code.

How to measure the error of the data to the model? Here, in the ordinary least squares fitting, we have considered vertical projection errors, and we saw that the minimization yielded a direct *closed-form formula* involving matrix operations

---

[1] Freely available online at http://www.scilab.org/.

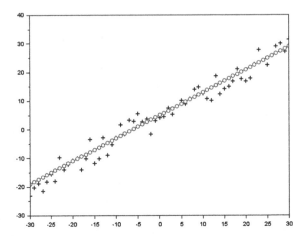

Fig. 5.3 Example of an ordinary linear regression computed from noisy observations

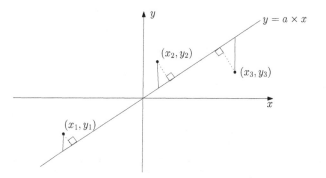

Fig. 5.4 Illustrating the difference between an ordinary regression and a total regression: total regression (total least squares) seeks to minimize the squared orthogonal projection lengths of data to the model hyperplane while ordinary regression (ordinary least squares) asks to minimizes the squared vertical projection lengths of data to the model hyperplane

$(X^\top X)^{-1}X^\top$ and a matrix–vector product $X^\dagger y$. A different approach would be to measure the error as the squared *orthogonal projection* lengths of data to the predicted values: this is called the *total regression* or *total least squares method*. Figure 5.4 illustrates the difference between the vertical projection and the orthogonal projection for the linear regression fitting. Total least squares is more complicated to calculate as there is no simple closed-form solution for solving it directly.

Regression can also be used for classification, but this is beyond the scope of this textbook.

5.1.2 Classic Linear Algebra

Traditionally, linear algebra has considered column vectors (and not row vectors, that are transposed vectors):

$$v = \begin{bmatrix} v_1 \\ \vdots \\ v_l \end{bmatrix} \text{ and matrices } M = \begin{bmatrix} m_{1,1} & \cdots & m_{1,c} \\ \vdots & \ddots & \vdots \\ m_{l,1} & \cdots & m_{l,c} \end{bmatrix}, \text{ with } l \text{ rows and } c \text{ columns,}$$

squared matrices or not.

There exist many types of matrices like *dense matrices* of dimension $l \times c$ that require $O(lc)$ memory space to store all their coefficients, diagonal matrices that require $O(l)$ memory space, tri-diagonal matrices, symmetric matrices, symmetric positive definite[2] matrices that are often met in statistics as covariance or precision[3] matrices, triangular matrices (upper or lower), Toeplitz[4] matrices, *sparse matrices* that require $o(lc)$ memory to store a new number of non-zero coefficients, etc. Vectors and matrices (and scalars) are particular cases of tensors (that extend linear algebra to multi-linear algebra). The most basic linear algebra operations are the addition and the multiplication. Let us consider $l = c = d$ for the dimensions of the square matrices and column vectors. The *scalar product* between two vectors is defined by:

$$\langle u, v \rangle = \sum_{i=1}^{d} u^{(i)} v^{(i)} = u^{\top} \times v,$$

and can be computed in linear time, $O(d)$.

The matrix–vector product $y = Ax$ requires quadratic time, $O(d^2)$.

The matrix–matrix product (or matrix product for short) $M = M_1 \times M_2$ can be straightforwardly computed in cubic time, $O(d^3)$.

Let us observe in passing, that the optimal complexity of matrix multiplication is not yet known! It is one of the oldest and hardest unsolved problem in theoretical computer science. For example, one of the very first algorithm to beat the cubic time naive algorithm is Strassen algorithm that requires $O(d^{\log_2 7}) = O(n^{2.8073549221})$ multiplications. This algorithm relies on a matrix block decomposition and minimizes the number of multiplications (compared to additions that can be performed much faster in practice). The so far best matrix multiplication algorithm is the so-called Coppersmith and Winograd [1] algorithm that has a complexity in $O(n^{2.3728639})$ [2].

Many matrix factorization algorithms including the LU (Lower Upper) decomposition are implemented in the most famous library for linear algebra: The *BLAS*[5] that stands for *Basic Linear Algebra Subroutines*. This library is organized into

---

[2]A matrix is said symmetric positive definite if and only if: $\forall x \neq 0, x^{\top} M x > 0$. Positive definite matrices have all positive eigenvalues.

[3]By terminology, the precision matrix is the inverse of the covariance matrix.

[4]A matrix is Toeplitz if all its diagonals are constant.

[5]http://www.netlib.org/blas/.

several hierarchical layers of primitives depending on the complexity of the routines. In C++, we can use the `boost ublas`[6] library to process efficiently matrices.

We shall now describe several classic algorithms for the multiplication primitive implemented either on the ring topology or on the torus topology.

5.1.3   The Matrix–Vector Product: $y = Ax$

The *matrix–vector* product computes $y = A \times x$ for a square matrix A of dimension $d \times d$ and x a d-dimensional column vector. The coefficients of the column vector y can be computed as follows:

$$y_i = \sum_{k=1}^{d} a_{i,k} x_k.$$

Each element y_i is independent of the others y_j, and only depend on the x vector and a single row of A. Thus all y_i coefficients can be *simultaneously computed independently*. This is crucial observation that yields a rich field of parallelization approaches for the matrix product that can be interpreted as independent scalar products:

$$y_i = \langle a_{i,}, x \rangle,$$

where $a_{i,}$ denotes by convention the ith row of matrix A.

To parallelize the vector-matrix product on P processes using distributed memory, we allocate initially to each process, $\frac{n}{P}$ rows of matrix A. Thus, we partition the problem (using a scatter MPI primitive), and we locally compute the $\frac{n}{P}$ scalar products on processes (that all contain the data for vector x), and finally we combine these results (using a MPI reduce operation) to obtain the y vector. We shall see soon another technique on the ring where it is partitioned data of x that circulates by blocks on the oriented ring.

The vector–matrix product is very well suited to Graphics Processor Units (GPUs) architectures (using the *General Purpose GPU programming*, or GPGPU for short). GPUs can be used for high performance computing but then one has to take care whether the *IEEE 754 floating point operations* are implemented or not, for numerical reproducibility of computations across various machines. Indeed, we would like the GPU code to run faster but deliver the same numerical results as a slower CPU implementation.

Before introducing the various matrix products on several topologies, let us first describe the main ways to partition matrix data onto the local memory of processors.

---

[6]http://www.boost.org/doc/libs/1_57_0/libs/numeric/ublas/doc/.

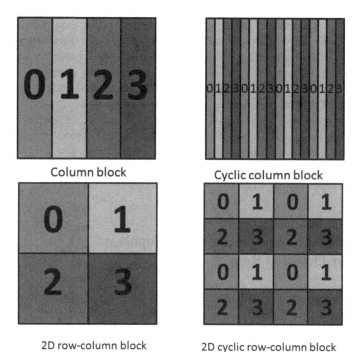

Column block Cyclic column block

2D row-column block 2D cyclic row-column block

Fig. 5.5 Several data partitioning patterns for assigning data to the local memory of processors. Patterns can be adapted to the underlying topology: the 1D column block is well suited to the ring topology, and the 2D checkerboard pattern to the 2D grid/torus topology

5.1.4 Data Patterns for Parallelism

One of the main advantages of HPC is to be able to handle larger volumes of data by partitioning them into local memories of machines. We then are interested in algorithms that can compute locally with the local data stored at the node, and to minimize the communication cost when exchanging data between processors. We can distinguish several patterns for partitioning and distributing local data to processors.

For example, we have the *block-column pattern*, or the *cyclic block-column pattern*, where b denotes the block width, often chosen to be $\frac{n}{P}$. This data pattern is illustrated in Fig. 5.5, and is often used in linear algebra computations on the ring topology. Similarly, we have the *row-block pattern* and *cyclic row-block pattern* that are just the former block-column pattern, or the cyclic block-column pattern when one considers the matrix transpose.

On the 2D grid or torus topology, we prefer *checkerboard patterns*: We have the *2D block pattern* or the *cyclic 2D clock pattern*, as depicted in Fig. 5.5.

Let us revisit the matrix–vector product for dense matrices using the 1D column-block pattern. In BLAS, a basic operation is the matrix–vector product *with accumulation*:

$$y \leftarrow y + Ax.$$

Let $A(i)$ denote the row block matrix of size $\frac{n}{p} \times n$ that is initially stored on processor P_i. To perform a product operation $y = Ax$, we first use a personalized broadcasting of x (a scattering MPI operation), so that each processor receives its own sub-vector $x(i)$, and is then able to perform locally its computation: $y(i) = A(i) \times x(i)$. Finally, a collaborative gather communication is called to receive and agglomerate all the sub-vectors of y into the full vector y.

Parallel algorithms computing the matrix product may differ depending on the chosen pattern, the underlying topology of the interconnection network, and the types of collaborative communications used.

Let us start by considering the vector–matrix product on the ring before introducing several classic matrix–matrix product on the torus.

5.2   Matrix–Vector Product on the Topology of the Oriented Ring

Let A be a matrix of dimension (n, n) and x a column vector with n coefficients (indexed from 0 to $n - 1$):

$$x = \begin{bmatrix} x_0 \\ \vdots \\ x_{n-1} \end{bmatrix}.$$

We would like to compute the matrix–vector product $y = A \times x$ on the ring topology with P processors, with $\frac{n}{P} = r \in \mathbb{N}$. As we mentioned earlier, this matrix–vector product can be interpreted as n scalar products. Thus we can compute the matrix–vector product in quadratic time using two nested loops:

```
for (i=0; i<n; i++) {
  for (j=0; j<n; j++) {
    y[i] = y[i]+a[i][j]*x[j];
    // we can also write as
    // y[i] += a[i][j]*x[j]
  }
}
```

We obtain a quadratic algorithm, in $O(n^2)$ time. We can perform this operation in parallel using the single instruction multiple data (SIMD) paradigm of vector computers:

$$y = a[i,]^\top x.$$

This basic operation is very well optimized on modern processors (for example, by using the Intel SSE® instruction set). We can distribute the computation of Ax by splitting the n scalar products onto the P processes: Each process P_i has in memory $r = n/P$ rows of A. Processor P_i contains the rows indexed from ir to $(i + 1)r − 1$, and similarly the portions of the vectors x and y. Thus all input data and the result are fairly distributed among the local memory of the ring nodes. We used data partitioning using the row block pattern of matrix A. Let us now illustrate the principle of computation by taking the simple ring with $P = 2$ nodes: By choosing $r = 1$, we perform local computations on matrices/vectors of dimension $n = rP = 2$. The matrix vector product $y = Ax$ can therefore be explicitly carried out in the following way:

$$\begin{bmatrix} y_1 \\ y_2 \end{bmatrix} = \begin{bmatrix} a_{1,1} & a_{1,2} \\ a_{2,1} & a_{2,2} \end{bmatrix} \times \begin{bmatrix} x_1 \\ x_2 \end{bmatrix},$$

$$\begin{bmatrix} y_1 \\ y_2 \end{bmatrix} = \begin{bmatrix} a_{1,1}x_1 + a_{1,2}x_2 \\ a_{2,1}x_1 + a_{2,2}x_2 \end{bmatrix}.$$

In that case, we imagine how we can make data turn around the ring (say, in clockwise order, CW) in order to compute locally as follows:

- Step 1: x_i is on P_i and we compute:

$$\begin{bmatrix} y_1 \\ y_2 \end{bmatrix} = \begin{bmatrix} \boxed{a_{1,1}x_1} + a_{1,2}x_2 \\ a_{2,1}x_1 + \boxed{a_{2,2}x_2} \end{bmatrix}$$

- Step 2: x_i is on $P_{(i+1) \bmod P}$ and we compute:

$$\begin{bmatrix} y_1 \\ y_2 \end{bmatrix} = \begin{bmatrix} a_{1,1}x_1 + \boxed{a_{1,2}x_2} \\ \boxed{a_{2,1}x_1} + a_{2,2}x_2 \end{bmatrix}$$

In the general case, we let a sub-vector of x of size $\frac{n}{P} = r$ be transmitted on the ring, and we compute the local products by accumulating the results on the y vector. The product is decomposed in blocks (of size $\frac{n}{P} = r$) as follows:

$$\begin{bmatrix} y_1 \\ \vdots \\ y_P \end{bmatrix} = \begin{bmatrix} A_1 \\ \vdots \\ A_P \end{bmatrix} \times \begin{bmatrix} x_1 \\ \vdots \\ x_P \end{bmatrix}.$$

We denote by X the block vector : $X = \begin{bmatrix} x_1 \\ \vdots \\ x_P \end{bmatrix}$.

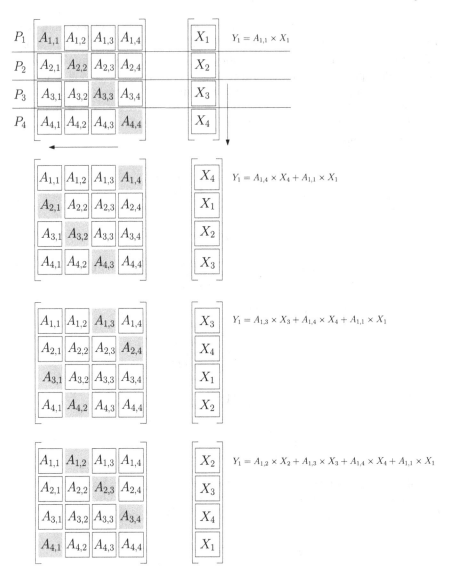

Fig. 5.6 Illustrating the matrix–vector product $Y = A \times X$ by blocks on the topology of the oriented ring

At step 0, we begin by initializing $y \leftarrow 0$, then we repeat P times the product of a sub-matrix of size $r \times r$ with the sub-vector of x, and we accumulate results on the corresponding sub-vector of y. Figure 5.6 illustrates this process. To illustrate this algorithm, let us take the following case $n = 8$, $P = 4$, and $r = \frac{n}{P} = 2$.

We start by initializing y to the zero vector, and the data of matrix A and vector x are allocated to the processes as follows:

$$
\begin{array}{c}
P_0 \\
P_1 \\
P_2 \\
P_3
\end{array}
\left[
\begin{array}{cccccccc}
a_{0,0} & a_{0,1} & a_{0,2} & a_{0,3} & a_{0,4} & a_{0,5} & a_{0,6} & a_{0,7} \\
a_{1,0} & a_{1,1} & a_{1,2} & a_{1,3} & a_{1,4} & a_{1,5} & a_{1,6} & a_{1,7} \\ \hline
a_{2,0} & a_{2,1} & a_{2,2} & a_{2,3} & a_{2,4} & a_{2,5} & a_{2,6} & a_{2,7} \\
a_{3,0} & a_{3,1} & a_{3,2} & a_{3,3} & a_{3,4} & a_{3,5} & a_{3,6} & a_{3,7} \\ \hline
a_{4,0} & a_{4,1} & a_{4,2} & a_{4,3} & a_{4,4} & a_{4,5} & a_{4,6} & a_{4,7} \\
a_{5,0} & a_{5,1} & a_{5,2} & a_{5,3} & a_{5,4} & a_{5,5} & a_{5,6} & a_{5,7} \\ \hline
a_{6,0} & a_{6,1} & a_{6,2} & a_{6,3} & a_{6,4} & a_{6,5} & a_{6,6} & a_{6,7} \\
a_{7,0} & a_{7,1} & a_{7,2} & a_{7,3} & a_{7,4} & a_{7,5} & a_{7,6} & a_{7,7}
\end{array}
\right]
\left[
\begin{array}{c}
x_0 \\ x_1 \\ x_2 \\ x_3 \\ x_4 \\ x_5 \\ x_6 \\ x_7
\end{array}
\right]
$$

At the beginning of each stage, we let a subvector of x turns on the ring, and the processes compute their local block matrix–vector product, and add this result to the corresponding y sub-sector:

- Step 1: Compute local matrix × block vector:

$$
\begin{array}{c}
P_0 \\
P_1 \\
P_2 \\
P_3
\end{array}
\left[
\begin{array}{cccccccc}
\mathbf{a}_{0,0} & \mathbf{a}_{0,1} & a_{0,2} & a_{0,3} & a_{0,4} & a_{0,5} & a_{0,6} & a_{0,7} \\
\mathbf{a}_{1,0} & \mathbf{a}_{1,1} & a_{1,2} & a_{1,3} & a_{1,4} & a_{1,5} & a_{1,6} & a_{1,7} \\ \hline
a_{2,0} & a_{2,1} & \mathbf{a}_{2,2} & \mathbf{a}_{2,3} & a_{2,4} & a_{2,5} & a_{2,6} & a_{2,7} \\
a_{3,0} & a_{3,1} & \mathbf{a}_{3,2} & \mathbf{a}_{3,3} & a_{3,4} & a_{3,5} & a_{3,6} & a_{3,7} \\ \hline
a_{4,0} & a_{4,1} & a_{4,2} & a_{4,3} & \mathbf{a}_{4,4} & \mathbf{a}_{4,5} & a_{4,6} & a_{4,7} \\
a_{5,0} & a_{5,1} & a_{5,2} & a_{5,3} & \mathbf{a}_{5,4} & \mathbf{a}_{5,5} & a_{5,6} & a_{5,7} \\ \hline
a_{6,0} & a_{6,1} & a_{6,2} & a_{6,3} & a_{6,4} & a_{6,5} & \mathbf{a}_{6,6} & \mathbf{a}_{6,7} \\
a_{7,0} & a_{7,1} & a_{7,2} & a_{7,3} & a_{7,4} & a_{7,5} & \mathbf{a}_{7,6} & \mathbf{a}_{7,7}
\end{array}
\right]
\left[
\begin{array}{c}
x_0 \\ x_1 \\ x_2 \\ x_3 \\ x_4 \\ x_5 \\ x_6 \\ x_7
\end{array}
\right]
$$

- Step 1': We let the sub-vector of x turn on the ring in the direction $\downarrow$:

$$
\begin{array}{c}
P_0 \\
P_1 \\
P_2 \\
P_3
\end{array}
\left[
\begin{array}{cccccccc}
a_{0,0} & a_{0,1} & a_{0,2} & a_{0,2} & a_{0,4} & a_{0,5} & a_{0,6} & a_{0,7} \\
a_{1,0} & a_{1,1} & a_{1,2} & a_{1,3} & a_{1,4} & a_{1,5} & a_{1,6} & a_{1,7} \\ \hline
a_{2,0} & a_{2,1} & a_{2,2} & a_{2,3} & a_{2,4} & a_{2,5} & a_{2,6} & a_{2,7} \\
a_{3,0} & a_{3,1} & a_{3,2} & a_{3,3} & a_{3,4} & a_{3,5} & a_{3,6} & a_{3,7} \\ \hline
a_{4,0} & a_{4,1} & a_{4,2} & a_{4,3} & a_{4,4} & a_{4,5} & a_{4,6} & a_{4,7} \\
a_{5,0} & a_{5,1} & a_{5,2} & a_{5,3} & a_{5,4} & a_{5,5} & a_{5,6} & a_{5,7} \\ \hline
a_{6,0} & a_{6,1} & a_{6,2} & a_{6,3} & a_{6,4} & a_{6,5} & a_{6,6} & a_{6,7} \\
a_{7,0} & a_{7,1} & a_{7,2} & a_{7,3} & a_{7,4} & a_{7,5} & a_{7,6} & a_{7,7}
\end{array}
\right]
\left[
\begin{array}{c}
x_6 \\ x_7 \\ x_0 \\ x_1 \\ x_2 \\ x_3 \\ x_4 \\ x_5
\end{array}
\right]
$$

- Step 2: Local product computation:

$$P_0 \begin{bmatrix} a_{0,0} & a_{0,1} & a_{0,2} & a_{0,3} & a_{0,4} & a_{0,5} & \mathbf{\underline{a}}_{0,6} & \mathbf{\underline{a}}_{0,7} \\ a_{1,0} & a_{1,1} & a_{1,2} & a_{1,3} & a_{1,4} & a_{1,5} & \mathbf{\underline{a}}_{1,6} & \mathbf{\underline{a}}_{1,7} \end{bmatrix} \begin{bmatrix} x_6 \\ x_7 \end{bmatrix}$$

$$P_1 \begin{bmatrix} \mathbf{\underline{a}}_{2,0} & \mathbf{\underline{a}}_{2,1} & a_{2,2} & a_{2,3} & a_{2,4} & a_{2,5} & a_{2,6} & a_{2,7} \\ \mathbf{\underline{a}}_{3,0} & \mathbf{\underline{a}}_{3,1} & a_{3,2} & a_{3,3} & a_{3,4} & a_{3,5} & a_{3,6} & a_{3,7} \end{bmatrix} \begin{bmatrix} x_0 \\ x_1 \end{bmatrix}$$

$$P_2 \begin{bmatrix} a_{4,0} & a_{4,1} & \mathbf{\underline{a}}_{4,2} & \mathbf{\underline{a}}_{4,3} & a_{4,4} & a_{4,5} & a_{4,6} & a_{4,7} \\ a_{5,0} & a_{5,1} & \mathbf{\underline{a}}_{5,2} & \mathbf{\underline{a}}_{5,3} & a_{5,4} & a_{5,5} & a_{5,6} & a_{5,7} \end{bmatrix} \begin{bmatrix} x_2 \\ x_3 \end{bmatrix}$$

$$P_3 \begin{bmatrix} a_{6,0} & a_{6,1} & a_{6,2} & a_{6,3} & \mathbf{\underline{a}}_{6,4} & \mathbf{\underline{a}}_{6,5} & a_{6,6} & a_{6,7} \\ a_{7,0} & a_{7,1} & a_{7,2} & a_{7,3} & \mathbf{\underline{a}}_{7,4} & \mathbf{\underline{a}}_{7,5} & a_{7,6} & a_{7,7} \end{bmatrix} \begin{bmatrix} x_4 \\ x_5 \end{bmatrix}$$

- Step 2': We let the x-subvector turn clockwise on the ring:

$$P_0 \begin{bmatrix} a_{0,0} & a_{0,1} & a_{0,2} & a_{0,3} & a_{0,4} & a_{0,5} & a_{0,6} & a_{0,7} \\ a_{1,0} & a_{1,1} & a_{1,2} & a_{1,3} & a_{1,4} & a_{1,5} & a_{1,6} & a_{1,7} \end{bmatrix} \begin{bmatrix} x_4 \\ x_5 \end{bmatrix}$$

$$P_1 \begin{bmatrix} a_{2,0} & a_{2,1} & a_{2,2} & a_{2,3} & a_{2,4} & a_{2,5} & a_{2,6} & a_{2,7} \\ a_{3,0} & a_{3,1} & a_{3,2} & a_{3,3} & a_{3,4} & a_{3,5} & a_{3,6} & a_{3,7} \end{bmatrix} \begin{bmatrix} x_6 \\ x_7 \end{bmatrix}$$

$$P_2 \begin{bmatrix} a_{4,0} & a_{4,1} & a_{4,2} & a_{4,3} & a_{4,4} & a_{4,5} & a_{4,6} & a_{4,7} \\ a_{5,0} & a_{5,1} & a_{5,2} & a_{5,3} & a_{5,4} & a_{5,5} & a_{5,6} & a_{5,7} \end{bmatrix} \begin{bmatrix} x_0 \\ x_1 \end{bmatrix}$$

$$P_3 \begin{bmatrix} a_{6,0} & a_{6,1} & a_{6,2} & a_{6,3} & a_{6,4} & a_{6,5} & a_{6,6} & a_{6,7} \\ a_{7,0} & a_{7,1} & a_{7,2} & a_{7,3} & a_{7,4} & a_{7,5} & a_{7,6} & a_{7,7} \end{bmatrix} \begin{bmatrix} x_2 \\ x_3 \end{bmatrix}$$

- Step 3: Local computation matrix $\times$ vector :

$$P_0 \begin{bmatrix} a_{0,0} & a_{0,1} & a_{0,2} & a_{0,3} & \mathbf{\underline{a}}_{0,4} & \mathbf{\underline{a}}_{0,5} & a_{0,6} & a_{0,7} \\ a_{1,0} & a_{1,1} & a_{1,2} & a_{1,2} & \mathbf{\underline{a}}_{1,4} & \mathbf{\underline{a}}_{1,5} & a_{1,6} & a_{1,7} \end{bmatrix} \begin{bmatrix} x_4 \\ x_5 \end{bmatrix}$$

$$P_1 \begin{bmatrix} a_{2,0} & a_{2,1} & a_{2,2} & a_{2,3} & a_{2,4} & a_{2,5} & \mathbf{\underline{a}}_{2,6} & \mathbf{\underline{a}}_{2,7} \\ a_{3,0} & a_{3,1} & a_{3,2} & a_{3,3} & a_{3,4} & a_{3,5} & \mathbf{\underline{a}}_{3,6} & \mathbf{\underline{a}}_{3,7} \end{bmatrix} \begin{bmatrix} x_6 \\ x_7 \end{bmatrix}$$

$$P_2 \begin{bmatrix} \mathbf{\underline{a}}_{4,0} & \mathbf{\underline{a}}_{4,1} & a_{4,2} & a_{4,3} & a_{4,4} & a_{4,5} & a_{4,6} & a_{4,7} \\ \mathbf{\underline{a}}_{5,0} & \mathbf{\underline{a}}_{5,1} & a_{5,2} & a_{5,3} & a_{5,4} & a_{5,5} & a_{5,6} & a_{5,7} \end{bmatrix} \begin{bmatrix} x_0 \\ x_1 \end{bmatrix}$$

$$P_3 \begin{bmatrix} a_{6,0} & a_{6,1} & \mathbf{\underline{a}}_{6,2} & \mathbf{\underline{a}}_{6,3} & a_{6,4} & a_{6,5} & a_{6,6} & a_{6,7} \\ a_{7,0} & a_{7,1} & \mathbf{\underline{a}}_{7,2} & \mathbf{\underline{a}}_{7,3} & a_{7,4} & a_{7,5} & a_{7,6} & a_{7,7} \end{bmatrix} \begin{bmatrix} x_2 \\ x_3 \end{bmatrix}$$

- Step 3': We let the x sub-vector turns on the ring:

$$P_0 \begin{bmatrix} a_{0,0} & a_{0,1} & a_{0,2} & a_{0,3} & a_{0,4} & a_{0,5} & a_{0,6} & a_{0,7} \\ a_{1,0} & a_{1,1} & a_{1,2} & a_{1,3} & a_{1,4} & a_{1,5} & a_{1,6} & a_{1,7} \end{bmatrix} \begin{bmatrix} x_2 \\ x_3 \end{bmatrix}$$

$$P_1 \begin{bmatrix} a_{2,0} & a_{2,1} & a_{2,2} & a_{2,3} & a_{2,4} & a_{2,5} & a_{2,6} & a_{2,7} \\ a_{3,0} & a_{3,1} & a_{3,2} & a_{3,3} & a_{3,4} & a_{3,5} & a_{3,6} & a_{3,7} \end{bmatrix} \begin{bmatrix} x_4 \\ x_5 \end{bmatrix}$$

$$P_2 \begin{bmatrix} a_{4,0} & a_{4,1} & a_{4,2} & a_{4,3} & a_{4,4} & a_{4,5} & a_{4,6} & a_{4,7} \\ a_{5,0} & a_{5,1} & a_{5,2} & a_{5,3} & a_{5,4} & a_{5,5} & a_{5,6} & a_{5,7} \end{bmatrix} \begin{bmatrix} x_6 \\ x_7 \end{bmatrix}$$

$$P_3 \begin{bmatrix} a_{6,0} & a_{6,1} & a_{6,2} & a_{6,3} & a_{6,4} & a_{6,5} & a_{6,6} & a_{6,7} \\ a_{7,0} & a_{7,1} & a_{7,2} & a_{7,3} & a_{7,4} & a_{7,5} & a_{7,6} & a_{7,7} \end{bmatrix} \begin{bmatrix} x_0 \\ x_1 \end{bmatrix}$$

- Step 4: We compute locally the matrix × vector:

$$
\begin{array}{c}
P_0 \\[20pt]
P_1 \\[20pt]
P_2 \\[20pt]
P_3
\end{array}
\begin{bmatrix}
a_{0,0}\ a_{0,1}\ \mathbf{a}_{0,2}\ \mathbf{a}_{0,3}\ a_{0,4}\ a_{0,5}\ a_{0,6}\ a_{0,7} \\
a_{1,0}\ a_{1,1}\ \mathbf{a}_{1,2}\ \mathbf{a}_{1,3}\ a_{1,4}\ a_{1,5}\ a_{1,6}\ a_{1,7} \\ \hline
a_{2,0}\ a_{2,1}\ a_{2,2}\ a_{2,3}\ \mathbf{a}_{2,4}\ \mathbf{a}_{2,5}\ a_{2,6}\ a_{2,7} \\
a_{3,0}\ a_{3,1}\ a_{3,2}\ a_{3,3}\ \mathbf{a}_{3,4}\ \mathbf{a}_{3,5}\ a_{3,6}\ a_{3,7} \\ \hline
a_{4,0}\ a_{4,1}\ a_{4,2}\ a_{4,3}\ a_{4,4}\ a_{4,5}\ \mathbf{a}_{4,6}\ \mathbf{a}_{4,7} \\
a_{5,0}\ a_{5,1}\ a_{5,2}\ a_{5,3}\ a_{5,4}\ a_{5,5}\ \mathbf{a}_{5,6}\ \mathbf{a}_{5,7} \\ \hline
\mathbf{a}_{6,0}\ \mathbf{a}_{6,1}\ a_{6,2}\ a_{6,3}\ a_{6,4}\ a_{6,5}\ a_{6,6}\ a_{6,7} \\
\mathbf{a}_{7,0}\ \mathbf{a}_{7,1}\ a_{7,2}\ a_{7,3}\ a_{7,4}\ a_{7,5}\ a_{7,6}\ a_{7,7}
\end{bmatrix}
\begin{bmatrix}
x_2 \\ x_3 \\ x_4 \\ x_5 \\ x_6 \\ x_7 \\ x_0 \\ x_1
\end{bmatrix}
$$

Thus the matrix–vector product algorithm can be written in pseudo-code as follows:

```
matrixVector(A, x, y) {
  q = Comm_rank();
  p = Comm_size();

  for (step=0; step<p; step++) {
    send(x, r);
    // local computations
    for (i=0; i<r; i++) {
      for (j=0; j<r; j++) {
        y[i] = y[i]+a[i, (q-step mod p)r+j]*x[
          j];
      }
    }
    receive(temp, r);
    x = temp;
  }
}
```

Let us now analyze the complexity of this algorithm. Let u denote the elementary computation and τ the transfer rate of the communication links of the ring network. We repeat P times the same identical steps, and each step takes the maximum time of

1. Local matrix–vector product in $r^2 u$ and
2. Send/receive x sub-vector with a communication time using the $\alpha + \tau r$ model: $\max(r^2 u, \alpha + \tau r)$.

For large matrices (n large), we thus have $r^2 u \gg \alpha + \tau r$, and we obtain a global complexity in $\frac{n^2}{P} u$. The efficiency of the parallelization tends to 1 since the speed-up tends to P.

In summary, by using simultaneously the P processors has allowed us to partition matrix A by rows into P pieces: This corroborates the fact that the HPC does not only allow to process data faster, but also allows one to solve larger problems. That is, large volumes of data by fairly distributing the input data on the different local memories of the different machines of a computer cluster. (In the ideal case, one process is allocated to one processor.)

5.3   Matrix Product on the Grid: The Outer Product Algorithm

We describe a simple algorithm to compute $C = A \times B$ on a 2D grid of processors. All matrices are of fixed dimension $n \times n$. Assume that $P = n \times n$, and that the scalar elements $a_{i,j}$, $b_{i,j}$ and $c_{i,j}$, coefficients of the matrices, are already stored in the local memory of processor $P_{i,j}$. The goal is to compute $c_{i,j} = \sum_{k=1}^{n} a_{i,k} \times b_{k,j}$. This calculation of coefficient $c_{i,j}$ starts by initializing it to zero: $c_{i,j} = 0$.

At stage k (with $k \in \{1, \ldots, n\}$), we use both a horizontal broadcast and a vertical broadcast communication primitives as follows:

- Horizontal broadcast: $\forall i \in \{1, \ldots, P\}$, processor $P_{i,k}$ broadcasts horizontally coefficient $a_{i,k}$ on the ith row. That is, to all processors $P_{i,*}$ (all processors $P_{i,j}$ with $j \in \{1, \ldots, n\}$),
- Vertical broadcast: $\forall j \in \{1, \ldots, P\}$, processor $P_{k,j}$ broadcasts vertically $b_{k,j}$ on the kth row. That is, to all processors $P_{*,j}$ (all processors $P_{i,j}$ with $i \in \{1, \ldots, n\}$),
- Local independent multiplications: Each processor $P_{i,j}$ updates its coefficient $c_{i,j}$ as follows: $c_{i,j} \leftarrow c_{i,j} + a_{i,k} \times b_{k,j}$.

Of course, we can perform also locally matrix block products instead of scalar coefficient products. This algorithm is implemented in the *ScaLAPACK*[7] software library under the name: outer product algorithm.

5.4   Matrix Products on the Topology of the 2D Torus

Let us now consider the 2D torus topology, and the matrix product $M = M_1 \times M_2$. We consider $\sqrt{P} \in \mathbb{N}$ to be the side width of the torus so that it has $\sqrt{P} \times \sqrt{P} = P$ processors. Each processor P_i can communicate to its four neighbors (regular topology) as depicted in Fig. 5.7: We refer to the neighbors as North, South, East, West.

When manipulating matrices, it is often useful to introduce the *Hadamard product* and the *Krönecker product* that are defined as follows:

- Hadamard product (or scalar–scalar product):

---

[7]http://www.netlib.org/scalapack/.

Fig. 5.7 The topology of the 2D torus is regular: each processor can communicate with its four neighbors, denoted by North, South, East and West

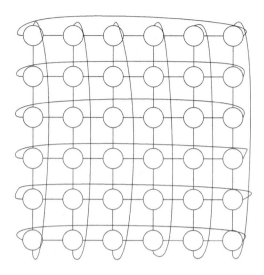

$$A \circ B = [A \circ B]_{i,j} = [a_{i,j} \times b_{i,j}]_{i,j},$$

$$\begin{bmatrix} a_{11} & a_{12} & a_{13} \\ a_{21} & a_{22} & a_{23} \\ a_{31} & a_{32} & a_{33} \end{bmatrix} \circ \begin{bmatrix} b_{11} & b_{12} & b_{13} \\ b_{21} & b_{22} & b_{23} \\ b_{31} & b_{32} & b_{33} \end{bmatrix} = \begin{bmatrix} a_{11} b_{11} & a_{12} b_{12} & a_{13} b_{13} \\ a_{21} b_{21} & a_{22} b_{22} & a_{23} b_{23} \\ a_{31} b_{31} & a_{32} b_{32} & a_{33} b_{33} \end{bmatrix}.$$

- Krönecker product (or scalar-block product):

$$A \otimes B = \begin{bmatrix} a_{11} B & \ldots & a_{1n} B \\ \vdots & \ddots & \vdots \\ a_{m1} B & \ldots & a_{mn} B \end{bmatrix}$$

We shall see three algorithms for computing the matrix product on the torus:

1. *Cannon's algorithm*,
2. *Fox's algorithm*, and
3. *Snyder's algorithm*.

Mathematically, the matrix product $C = A \times B = [c_{i,j}]_{i,j}$ computes C as:

$$c_{i,j} = \sum_{k=1}^{n} a_{i,k} \times b_{k,j} \quad \forall 1 \le i, j \le n.$$

We can rewrite this calculation using scalar product as follows:

$$c_{i,j} = \langle a_{i,\cdot}, b_{\cdot,j} \rangle,$$

with $a_{i,\cdot}$ the ith row of matrix A vector, and $b_{\cdot,j}$ the jth column of matrix B vector.

In order to compute locally on processors, we need to have data $a_{i,k}$ and $b_{k,j}$ already stored locally on $P_{i,j}$ before performing the multiplication. Initially, data of matrices A and B are already partitioned by blocks of size $\sqrt{\frac{n}{P}} \times \sqrt{\frac{n}{P}}$ and distributed among the processors. In these three different algorithms (Cannon/Fox/Snyder), processor $P_{i,j}$ takes charge of computing $C_{i,j} = \sum_{k=1}^{\sqrt{P}} A_{i,k} \times B_{k,j}$. It is the communication strategy and the communication primitives that differ in these three algorithms.

5.4.1 Cannon's Algorithm

In order to illustrate this matrix product algorithm, let us consider the initial configuration on the 2D torus of size 4×4:

$$
\begin{bmatrix} c_{0,0} & c_{0,1} & c_{0,2} & c_{0,3} \\ c_{1,0} & c_{1,1} & c_{1,2} & c_{1,3} \\ c_{2,0} & c_{2,1} & c_{2,2} & c_{2,3} \\ c_{3,0} & c_{3,1} & c_{3,2} & c_{3,3} \end{bmatrix} \leftarrow \begin{bmatrix} a_{0,0} & a_{0,1} & a_{0,2} & a_{0,3} \\ a_{1,0} & a_{1,1} & a_{1,2} & a_{1,3} \\ a_{2,0} & a_{2,1} & a_{2,2} & a_{2,3} \\ a_{3,0} & a_{3,1} & a_{3,2} & a_{3,3} \end{bmatrix} \times \begin{bmatrix} b_{0,0} & b_{0,1} & b_{0,2} & b_{0,3} \\ b_{1,0} & b_{1,1} & b_{1,2} & b_{1,3} \\ b_{2,0} & b_{2,1} & b_{2,2} & b_{2,3} \\ b_{3,0} & b_{3,1} & b_{3,2} & b_{3,3} \end{bmatrix}
$$

Cannon's algorithm require pre-processing and post-processing operations that are *pre-skewing* and *post-skewing* (inverse of pre-skewing) primitives. The algorithm sends matrix block of A and B using horizontal and vertical rotations, respectively. These rotations are simply either row or column shifts (wrapped using the 1D torus topology property).

First, let us pre-process matrices A and B by pre-skewing them horizontally and vertically, respectively:

- Matrix A: We shifts vertically by sliding columns the elements so that the first diagonal becomes the "leftmost" column (*preskew*), $A \overset{skew}{\longleftarrow}$

$$
\begin{bmatrix} a_{0,0} & a_{0,1} & a_{0,2} & a_{0,3} \\ a_{1,1} & a_{1,2} & a_{1,3} & a_{1,0} \\ a_{2,2} & a_{2,3} & a_{2,0} & a_{2,1} \\ a_{3,3} & a_{3,0} & a_{3,1} & a_{3,2} \end{bmatrix}
$$

- Matrix B: We shift horizontally by sliding rows the elements so that the first diagonal becomes to "topmost" row (*preskew*), $B \uparrow$ skew

$$
\begin{bmatrix} b_{0,0} & b_{1,1} & b_{2,2} & b_{3,3} \\ b_{1,0} & b_{2,1} & b_{3,2} & b_{0,3} \\ b_{2,0} & b_{3,1} & b_{0,2} & b_{1,3} \\ b_{3,0} & b_{0,1} & b_{1,2} & b_{2,3} \end{bmatrix}
$$

Thus after preprocessing, the initial configuration on the torus is the following:

$$
\begin{bmatrix}
c_{0,0} & c_{0,1} & c_{0,2} & c_{0,3} \\
c_{1,0} & c_{1,1} & c_{1,2} & c_{1,3} \\
c_{2,0} & c_{2,1} & c_{2,2} & c_{2,3} \\
c_{3,0} & c_{3,1} & c_{3,2} & c_{3,3}
\end{bmatrix}
=
\begin{bmatrix}
a_{0,0} & a_{0,1} & a_{0,2} & a_{0,3} \\
a_{1,1} & a_{1,2} & a_{1,3} & a_{1,0} \\
a_{2,2} & a_{2,3} & a_{2,0} & a_{2,1} \\
a_{3,3} & a_{3,0} & a_{3,1} & a_{3,2}
\end{bmatrix}
\times
\begin{bmatrix}
b_{0,0} & b_{1,1} & b_{2,2} & b_{3,3} \\
b_{1,0} & b_{2,1} & b_{3,2} & b_{0,3} \\
b_{2,0} & b_{3,1} & b_{0,2} & b_{1,3} \\
b_{3,0} & b_{0,1} & b_{1,2} & b_{2,3}
\end{bmatrix}
$$

Therefore, we can compute locally the matrix bloc products and accumulates the result in the corresponding block of matrix C since the indices match: $c_{i,j} \leftarrow c_{i,j} + a_{i,l} \times b_{l,j}$. Then we perform a 1D rotation on A (we let rows shift upward) and a 1D rotation on B(we let columns shift leftward) to obtain this configuration:

$$
\begin{bmatrix}
c_{0,0} & c_{0,1} & c_{0,2} & c_{0,3} \\
c_{1,0} & c_{1,1} & c_{1,2} & c_{1,3} \\
c_{2,0} & c_{2,1} & c_{2,2} & c_{2,3} \\
c_{3,0} & c_{3,1} & c_{3,2} & c_{3,3}
\end{bmatrix}
=
\begin{bmatrix}
a_{0,1} & a_{0,2} & a_{0,3} & a_{0,0} \\
a_{1,2} & a_{1,3} & a_{1,0} & a_{1,1} \\
a_{2,3} & a_{2,0} & a_{2,1} & a_{2,2} \\
a_{3,0} & a_{3,1} & a_{3,2} & a_{3,3}
\end{bmatrix}
\times
\begin{bmatrix}
b_{1,0} & b_{2,1} & b_{3,2} & b_{0,3} \\
b_{2,0} & b_{3,1} & b_{0,2} & b_{1,3} \\
b_{3,0} & b_{0,1} & b_{1,2} & b_{2,3} \\
b_{0,0} & b_{1,1} & b_{2,2} & b_{3,3}
\end{bmatrix}
$$

Again, indices match again for all processes, and we compute the local matrix block product and accumulate the results on the corresponding block of matrix C. Overall, we repeat these rotation-computation steps $\sqrt{P}$ times. After we have completed the matrix product computation, we need to rearrange matrix A and B by post-skewing them. Algorithm 2 describes Cannon's algorithm in pseudo-code:

Data: P processors on the torus: $P = \sqrt{P} \times \sqrt{P}$. Matrix A, B stored locally by block on the processors.
Result: Return the matrix product $C = A \times B$
```
// Pre-processing of matrices A eand B
// Preskew ← : diagonal elements of A aligned vertically on
   the first column
```
HorizontalPreskew(A);
```
// Preskew ↑ : diagonal elements of B aligned horizontall on
   the first column
```
VerticalPreskew(B);
```
// Initialize blocks of C to 0
```
$C = 0$;
for $k = 1$ *to* $\sqrt{P}$ **do**
  $\quad C \leftarrow C +$LocalProduct(A,B);
  ```
  // Horizontal shift ←
  ```
  $\quad$ HorizontalRotation(A);
  ```
  // Vertical shift ↑
  ```
  $\quad$ VerticalRotation(B);
end
```
// Post-processing of matrices A and B : reciprocal inverse
   of pre-processing
// Preskew →
```
HorizontalPostskew(A);
```
// Preskew ↓
```
VerticalPostskew(B);

Algorithm 2: Cannon's algorithm for computing the matrix product $C = A \times B$ on the torus topology.

Figure 5.8 illustrates the different steps of Cannon's algorithm on a 3×3 torus. Note that Cannon's algorithm only requires to have direct *point-to-point communication* between neighbors on the torus. The blocks of matrix C always stay fixed at their position. To optimize the code, observe that local matrix product computations can be overlapped with communication primitives (using a buffer for sending/receiving matrix blocks). To check that Cannon's algorithm is indeed correct, we simply need to verify that all local matrix product computations have been processed:

$$C_{i,j} = \sum_{k=1}^{\sqrt{P}} A_{i,k} \times B_{k,j} \quad \forall 1 \leq i, j \leq \sqrt{P}.$$

5.4.2   Fox's Algorithm: The Broadcast-Multiply-Roll Matrix Product

Fox's algorithm does not require any pre-processing nor post-processing. That is, initially matrix blocks of A and B does not move. The underlying principle of Fox's algorithm is to perform horizontal broadcasting operations of the diagonals of A (shifted stepwise to the right), and vertical upward rotations of B. Figure 5.9 illustrates the three diagonals of a square matrix A of dimension 3×3.

Let us consider 4×4 matrices. The initial configuration is the following:

$$\begin{bmatrix} c_{0,0} & c_{0,1} & c_{0,2} & c_{0,3} \\ c_{1,0} & c_{1,1} & c_{1,2} & c_{1,3} \\ c_{2,0} & c_{2,1} & c_{2,2} & c_{2,3} \\ c_{3,0} & c_{3,1} & c_{3,2} & c_{3,3} \end{bmatrix} \leftarrow \begin{bmatrix} a_{0,0} & a_{0,1} & a_{0,2} & a_{0,3} \\ a_{1,0} & a_{1,1} & a_{1,2} & a_{1,3} \\ a_{2,0} & a_{2,1} & a_{2,2} & a_{2,3} \\ a_{3,0} & a_{3,1} & a_{3,2} & a_{3,3} \end{bmatrix} \times \begin{bmatrix} b_{0,0} & b_{0,1} & b_{0,2} & b_{0,3} \\ b_{1,0} & b_{1,1} & b_{1,2} & b_{1,3} \\ b_{2,0} & b_{2,1} & b_{2,2} & b_{2,3} \\ b_{3,0} & b_{3,1} & b_{3,2} & b_{3,3} \end{bmatrix}$$

We start by broadcasting the first diagonal of A (note that we use a working buffer for A and that the blocks of A are always stored on their initial processor too):

$$\begin{bmatrix} c_{0,0} & c_{0,1} & c_{0,2} & c_{0,3} \\ c_{1,0} & c_{1,1} & c_{1,2} & c_{1,3} \\ c_{2,0} & c_{2,1} & c_{2,2} & c_{2,3} \\ c_{3,0} & c_{3,1} & c_{3,2} & c_{3,3} \end{bmatrix} \leftarrow \begin{bmatrix} a_{0,0} & a_{0,0} & a_{0,0} & a_{0,0} \\ a_{1,1} & a_{1,1} & a_{1,1} & a_{1,1} \\ a_{2,2} & a_{2,2} & a_{2,2} & a_{2,2} \\ a_{3,3} & a_{3,3} & a_{3,3} & a_{3,3} \end{bmatrix} \times \begin{bmatrix} b_{0,0} & b_{0,1} & b_{0,2} & b_{0,3} \\ b_{1,0} & b_{1,1} & b_{1,2} & b_{1,3} \\ b_{2,0} & b_{2,1} & b_{2,2} & b_{2,3} \\ b_{3,0} & b_{3,1} & b_{3,2} & b_{3,3} \end{bmatrix}$$

Since indices match, we can perform local computations: That is, the second index of a corresponds to the first index of b. Then we perform a vertical rotation of B (upward shift), and we broadcast the second diagonal of A to obtain this configuration:

$$\begin{bmatrix} c_{0,0} & c_{0,1} & c_{0,2} & c_{0,3} \\ c_{1,0} & c_{1,1} & c_{1,2} & c_{1,3} \\ c_{2,0} & c_{2,1} & c_{2,2} & c_{2,3} \\ c_{3,0} & c_{3,1} & c_{3,2} & c_{3,3} \end{bmatrix} \overset{+=}{\longleftarrow} \begin{bmatrix} a_{0,1} & a_{0,1} & a_{0,1} & a_{0,1} \\ a_{1,2} & a_{1,2} & a_{1,2} & a_{1,2} \\ a_{2,3} & a_{2,3} & a_{2,3} & a_{2,3} \\ a_{3,0} & a_{3,0} & a_{3,0} & a_{3,0} \end{bmatrix} \times \begin{bmatrix} b_{1,0} & b_{1,1} & b_{1,2} & b_{1,3} \\ b_{2,0} & b_{2,1} & b_{2,2} & b_{2,3} \\ b_{3,0} & b_{3,1} & b_{3,2} & b_{3,3} \\ b_{0,0} & b_{0,1} & b_{0,2} & b_{0,3} \end{bmatrix}$$

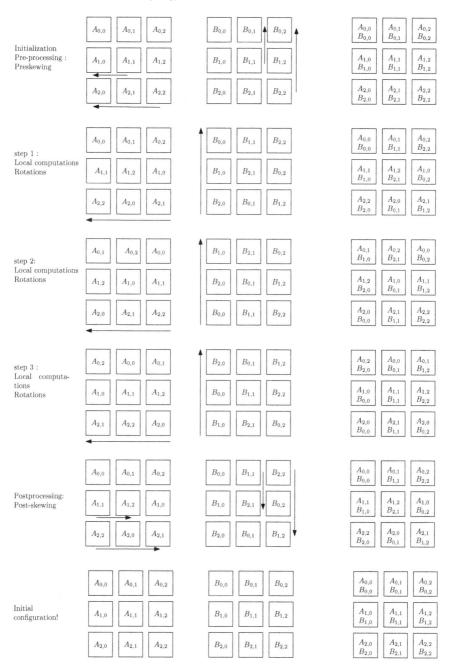

Fig. 5.8 Illustrating Cannon's algorithm: pre-skewing, loop of local matrix product and communication by rotations, and post-skewing

Fig. 5.9 Diagonals of a square matrix (here, of dimension 3 × 3) (Colour figure online)

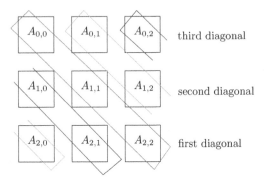

Again, matrix block indices of A and B match, and we can perform local matrix product computations, by accumulating the results in the corresponding local block of matrix C. Overall, we repeat these steps $\sqrt{P}$ times (side size of the torus). Algorithm 3 states Fox's algorithm in pseudo-code.

Data: P processes on the torus: $P = \sqrt{P} \times \sqrt{P}$. Matrix A, B stored locally by block on
        processes.
Result: Compute the matrix product $C = A \times B$
```
// Initialize blocks of C to 0
```
$C = 0$;
for $i = 1$ *to* $\sqrt{P}$ **do**
```
    // Broadcast
```
    Broadcast the i-th diagonal of A on the torus rows;
```
    // Multiply
```
    $C \leftarrow C + \text{LocalProduct}(A,B)$;
```
    // Roll
    // Vertical rotation: vertical shift upward ↑
```
    VerticalRotation(B);
end

Algorithm 3: Fox's algorithm for the matrix product on the torus topology.

Figure 5.10 illustrates Fox's algorithm when performing matrix product on the 3×3 torus. Historically, this algorithm has been designed for the hypercube topology in Caltech (US): but as explained in the topology chapter, we can map the logical torus topology onto the hypercube topology. This algorithm is often referred in the literature as the broadcast-multiply-roll algorithm.

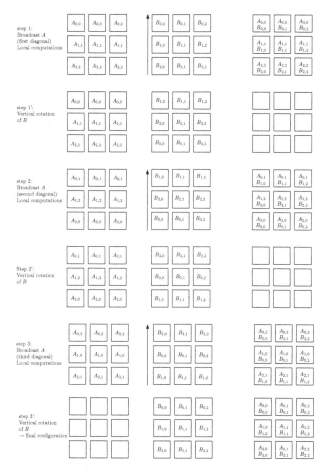

Fig. 5.10 Illustration of the broadcast-multiply-roll matrix product algorithm known as Fox's algorithm: There is no pre-processing nor post-processing operations. At stage i, we broadcast the ith diagonal of matrix A, compute local block matrix products, and perform a vertical rotation on B

5.4.3 Snyder's Algorithm: Accumulating Local Products on the Diagonal

In Snyder's algorithm, we first start by pre-processing matrix B by transposing it: $B \leftarrow B^{\top}$. We then compute the global sum on the processor rows (this amounts to calculate an inner product on matrix blocks of A and B) and accumulate the results on the first diagonal of C. We perform vertical rotations upward of B, and repeat $\sqrt{P}$ times. Snyder's algorithm in pseudo-code is given in Algorithm 4. It is illustrated on the 3×3 torus in Fig. 5.11.

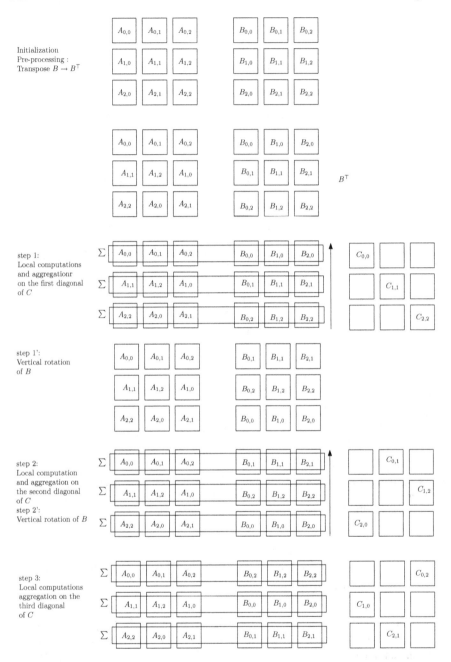

Fig. 5.11 Illustrating Snyder's algorithm for the matrix product $C = A \times B$: we first start by transposing matrix B. At stage i, we compute all local products accumulate by summing the results on all the process rows to obtain definitively all the matrix blocks of C of the ith diagonal. We then rotate upward B. After completing the matrix product, we transpose again B to find back its original configuration

---

Data: A, B, C matrices `array`$[0..d - 1, 0..d - 1]$
Result: Matrix product $C = A \times B$
```
// Preskewing
```
Transpose B;
```
// Computation stages
```
for $k = 1$ *to* $\sqrt{P}$ **do**
> ```
> // Row-wise inner product of A and B
> ```
> Local matrix block computation: $C = A \times B$;
> ```
> // We compute the definitive C block matrix for the k-th
>    diagonal
> // Global sum (reduce)
> ```
> Parallel prefix with $\sum$ on C on the processor rows to get the k-th diagonal block element of C;
> Vertical shift of B;

end
```
// We transpose B to get back its original layout
```
Transpose B;

Algorithm 4: Snyder's algorithm in pseudo-code for computing the matrix product.

Table 5.1 Comparing the three matrix product algorithms on the torus

Algorithm	Cannon	Fox	Snyder
Pre-processing	Pre-skewing of A and B	None	Transposing $B \leftarrow B^{\mathsf{T}}$
Matrix product	Locally	Locally	$\sum$ on all rows
Communication on A	Left $\rightarrow$ right	Horizontal broadcast	None
Communication on B	Bottom $\rightarrow$ top	Bottom $\rightarrow$ top	Bottom $\rightarrow$ top

5.4.4 Comparisons of Cannon's, Fox's and Snyder's Algorithms

We have concisely described the three main matrix product algorithms on the topology of the 2D torus. Let us quickly compare those methods in Table 5.1.

5.5 Notes and References

For a celebrated textbook on matrices and linear algebra, we recommend the "Golub" book [1]. Matrix calculus extends vectors and scalar calculus, and can furthermore be generalized using the multi-dimensional tensor calculus (that is at the core of differential geometry). The matrix product of Cannon [3] dates back to 1969, the algorithm from Fox is from a 1987 paper [4], and Snyder's algorithm [5] has been reported in 1992. We recommend the textbook of Casanova et al. [6] for a gentle introduction to parallel algorithms, including the aforementioned three matrix multi-plication algorithms. High performance parallel scientific computation is often done by blending multi-core shared memory *OpenMP* programming language with the computer cluster distributed-memory MPI programming paradigm.

5.6 Summary

In linear algebra, the fundamental primitives are (1) the scalar products of vectors, (2) the matrix–vector products and (3) the matrix–matrix products. The vector-matrix product and matrix–matrix product can be easily reinterpreted in terms of scalar products. For distributed memory parallel algorithms, we assume that matrix data are initially distributed on the different computer nodes, and we seek to minimize the communication costs while performing local products. Depending on the chosen topology, we may either choose the column-block decomposition of matrices (for example, for the oriented rings) or the checkerboard matrix-block decompositions for the torus topology. Although the matrix product is one of the cornerstone of many algorithms, the complexity of this problem has not yet been settled, and often the naive cubic time algorithm or a parallel implementation is used instead of more sophisticated algorithm like the Winograd–Coppersmith algorithm [2].

5.7 Exercises

Exercise 1 *Product of symmetric matrices*
How can one optimize the matrix product on the torus when input matrices are symmetric?

Exercise 2 *Matrix product on the ring*
Propose parallel algorithms for the matrix product on the ring topology.

References

1. Golub, G.H., Van Loan, C.F.: Matrix Computations. Johns Hopkins University Press, Baltimore (1996)
2. Le, F.-G.: Powers of tensors and fast matrix multiplication. arXiv preprint arXiv:1401.7714 (2014)
3. Elliot, L.C.: A cellular computer to implement the Kalman filter algorithm. Ph.D. thesis, Montana State University, Bozeman (1969) AAI7010025
4. Fox, G.C., Otto, S.W., Hey, A.J.G.: Matrix algorithms on a hypercube I: Matrix multiplication. Parallel Comput. **4**(1), 17–31 (1987)

5. Calvin, L., Lawrence, S.: A matrix product algorithm and its comparative performance on hypercubes. In: Proceedings of the Scalable High Performance Computing Conference, SHPCC-92, IEEE, pp. 190–194 (1992)
6. Casanova, H., Legrand, A., Robert, Y.: Parallel Algorithms. Chapman & Hall/CRC Numerical Analysis and Scientific Computing. CRC Press, Boca Raton (2009)

Chapter 6
The MapReduce Paradigm

6.1 The Challenge of Processing Big Data Fast!

The system of *MapReduce* (or *Hadoop* for an equivalent open source in Java) offers a simple framework to parallelize and execute parallel algorithms on *massive data sets*, commonly called Big Data (with size ranging from a few gigabytes to a few terabytes or even petabytes). This dedicated MapReduce paradigm of data-intensive parallel programming was originally developed by Google in 2003. MapReduce is an abstract model of parallel programming for processing massive data sets on a cluster of computers, and a platform to execute and monitor jobs. MapReduce is straightforward to use, can be easily extended, and even more importantly MapReduce is prone to both hardware and software failures.[1]

Back to 2007, Google processed 20 *Petabytes* (PB) per day, and this figure exponentially increases every year. If the volume capacity of your notebook hard disk is 1 TB today, can you imagine how to process 20,000 times this volume per day on your machine? That is truly challenging. Moreover, in many scientific areas, data-sets often come from high-throughput scientific instruments and it becomes increasingly challenging to process those massive data-sets. Such kind of applications abound for example in particle physics, astronomy, genome analytics, etc. Human/machines are also producing many data-sets that are log files of web applications on the Internet that need to be finely analyzed. For example, one would like to segment the user clicks of a site to discover what pages are browsed during a session. Knowing users' behaviors allows one to further tailor the website to the different user profiles, by adding advertising panels for example! Click stream analysis further pushes the parallel algorithms to deliver the output online as flows of clicks are constantly recorded on a log file. Search engines also need to index the faster possible way all documents

---

[1] When one uses several hundreds of interconnected cheap machines, failures happen quite often in practice, and need to be addressed.

© Springer International Publishing Switzerland 2016   147
F. Nielsen, *Introduction to HPC with MPI for Data Science*, Undergraduate
Topics in Computer Science, DOI 10.1007/978-3-319-21903-5_6

accessible from the Internet: the page contents are first retrieved using a crawler. Not to mention the various agencies in the world screening the individual digital activities.

Nowadays, one of the key challenge is to batch process those Big Data. We continually seek to push the envelope on the volume that can be processed. This is an endeavor quest. Moreover, we even require to analyze online in real-time (and not any more in batch mode) these data streams (like news feeds, tweets and other information from social networks). Therefore it is not surprising to see many renown global companies to contribute to platform development of tools to satisfy their needs. For example, let us cite the *Apache storm*,[2] or the *Apache Spark*[3] for processing streams, or *Hive*[4] for a SQL-like language tailored to very large databases, etc.

To give a flavor on how massive are these Big Data, let us say that 1 petabyte (PB) allows to store about 10 billions (10^{10}) of photos (Facebook, Flickr, Instagram, etc.) or equivalently 13 years of HD video (YouTube, DailyMotion, etc.). Processing linearly 20 PB on a common PC would require over 7 years. Thus one has to develop efficient parallel algorithms with sub-linear running time complexity. MapReduce is such a framework that allows to perform these computing tasks easily: it becomes easy for common (and casual) developers to process several terabytes of data on small-size computer clusters. And this is very useful for small to mid-size companies.

6.2   The Basic Principle of MapReduce

6.2.1   Map and Reduce Processes

Although MapReduce is a very simple model of parallel programming, it nevertheless offers a flexible way to program highly versatile applications. Indeed, many problems can be solved by using these two fundamental steps:

1. Step 1 (MAP): A function is evaluated on a sequence of data, producing thereby new elements associated with keys,
2. Step 2 (REDUCE): We aggregate the new elements having the same key, and reduce them with another user-defined function.

For example, to compute the word count in a large collection of documents (called a *text corpus*), we associate to each word w_i of the texts, the pair $w_i \mapsto (k_i, v_i)$, where $k_i = k(w_i) = w_i$ denotes the key for the data element w_i, and $v_i = v(w_i) = 1$ is the value of the evaluated function (one count per word). Then we reduce those pairs by considering groups of words $G(k) = \{w_i \mid k(w_i) = k\}$ having the same key k by computing the corresponding cumulative sum. Let us notice that the map function can be computed in parallel using *independent processes* on the data properly distributed

---

[2]https://storm.apache.org/.

[3]https://spark.apache.org/streaming/.

[4]https://hive.apache.org/.

on a computer cluster. However, the processes `reduce` that take as input the output results of the `map` processes are not independent. The `map` procedure transforms input data into intermediate data that are (key,value) pairs.

Since we manipulate large-scale data sets, both the functions `map` and `reduce` will be implemented by fast processes of a computer cluster. Therefore MapReduce targets a *fine-grained parallelism* where local computations are elementary operations. The processes implementing the *user-defined function* `map` are called *mappers*, and the ones implementing the `reduce` functions are called *reducers*.

6.2.2 A Historical Perspective: Map and Reduce in Functional Programming Languages

For readers familiar with functional programming, let us remark that these two fundamental notions of `map` and `reduce` are already part of functional languages. For example, in Lisp (Common Lisp/Scheme) or in OCaml,[5] we can implement these two basic operations as follows:

- `map` :

$$(x_1, \ldots, x_n) \xrightarrow{f} (f(x_1), \ldots, f(x_n))$$

- `reduce` :

$$(x_1, \ldots, x_n) \xrightarrow{r(\sum)} \sum_{i=1}^{n} x_i$$

For the `reduce` primitive, we require a binary operator that can be commutative like the sum, or not (like the product of matrices, or the scalar division).

In Lisp,[6] these two functions can be used as follows:

- `map`

```
CL-USER  > (mapcar #'sqrt '(3 4 5 6 7))
(1.7320508 2.0 2.236068 2.4494899 2.6457513)
```

- `reduce`

```
CL-USER  > (reduce #'+ '(1 2 3 4 5))
15
```

---

[5]http://caml.inria.fr/ocaml/.
[6]One can download the Common Lisp from http://www.lispworks.com/.

In OCaml, we implement the map as a *unary operator* (that is, an operator taking a single argument):

```
# let square x=x*x;;
val square : int -> int = <fun>
# let maplist = List.map square;;
val maplist : int list -> int list = <fun>
# maplist [4;4;2];;
- : int list = [16; 16; 4]
#
```

Similarly, reduce in OCaml has the following calling syntax for a *binary operator f* (that is, an operation taking two arguments):

```
fold_right f [e1;e2; ... ;en] a = (f e1 (f e2  (f en a))
fold_left f a [e1;e2; ... ;en]=(f .. (f (f a e1) e2) ... en)
```

For example:

```
List.fold_left ( + ) 0 [1;2;3;4] ;;
List.fold_right ( + )   [1;2;3;4] 0 ;;
```

Since in functional programming we do not use variables like in traditional imperative languages (say, C/C++/Java), one can easily parallelize those operations. Furthermore, MapReduce provides monitoring tools to control the MapReduce jobs.

6.3   Data Types and the MapReduce Mechanism

In the MapReduce framework, the map and reduce operations are semantically typed as follows:

- Mapper:

$$\boxed{\text{map}(k_1, v_1) \rightarrow \text{list}(k_2, v_2)}$$

- Reducer:

$$\boxed{\text{reduce}(k_2, \text{list}(v_2)) \rightarrow \text{list}(v_2)}$$

A MapReduce task has three different stages:

1. *Mapper*: emit from input data a set of (key, value) pairs,
2. *Sorter*: group the intermediate pairs according to the value of their key,
3. *Reducer*: on intermediate pairs grouped by keys, we perform a *parallel prefix operation* (reduce, or aggregation) on all the values associated to a same key, and this for all different key values.

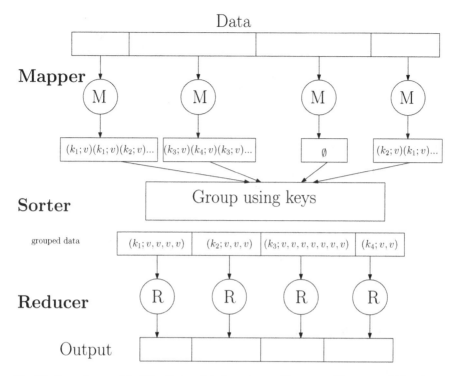

Fig. 6.1 Execution model of MapReduce into three stages: (*1*) mapper, (*2*) sorter and (*3*) reducer

Only the *mapper* and the *reducer* stages depend on user-defined functions (*UDFs*). The sorter stage is automatically managed by the MapReduce system. Thus a MapReduce algorithm is simple since it consists in applying the mapper on the input data, to group the results into lists of pairs (key2,value2), and re-order that list into lists of pairs (key2,list of value2) for each distinct value of key2, and finally to call the reducer on each element of these novel lists, and aggregate the results.

Figure 6.1 illustrates these three fundamental stages of MapReduce.

Let us now give two other examples of parallelizing programs using the MapReduce framework:

- the renown UNIX command `grep` that can be computed in parallel.[7] In Unix, we count in decreasing order all the lines that have matched a given regular expression for the files of a directory with the following command line:

```
grep -Eh regularexpression repertoire/* | sort |
uniq -c | sort -nr
```

---

[7]http://wiki.apache.org/hadoop/Grep.

For example, this is very useful for analyzing the log files of a web site to know which pages matching a given regular expression is the most viewed. With the MapReduce formalism, we can easily implement the distributed *grep* functionality as follows:

- `map`: emit value '1' when a line matches the regular expression.
- `reduce`: cumulative sum function (prefix parallel operation with the binary associative and commutative operator "+").

• reversed list of references on the web:

- `map`: emit (target,source) pairs for each URL (Uniform Resource Location) target found in a source page, and
- `reduce`: concatenate all those URLs associated to a given URL.

In order to be general when processing (key,value) pairs, MapReduce only considers *strings of characters* for storing the values. Thus numerical elements need to be converted explicitly to strings and conversely data must be retrieved from these character strings.

6.4   A Complete Example of MapReduce in C++

We shall describe a complete working example that counts the occurrences of words in documents. First, let us write in pseudo-code the two user-defined functions `map` and `reduce`, with input, values and output all encoded into strings of characters:

User-defined function `map`.

```
    map(String input_key, String input_value)
for each word w in input_value
                   EmitIntermediate(w, "1");
```

User-defined function `reduce`.

```
reduce(String output_key, Iterator
   intermediate_values)

int result = 0;

for each v in intermediate_values
           {result += ParseInt(v);}

Emit(AsString(result));
```

For illustration purpose, the full source code corresponding to the C++ MapReduce program is given below. Function f that maps data is the following (for `map` processes):

```cpp
#include "mapreduce/mapreduce.h"
// User Defined Function (UDF)

class WordCounter :
public Mapper {
public:
  virtual void Map(const MapInput& input) {
    const string& text = input.value();
    const int n = text.size();

    for (int i = 0; i < n; ) {
      // Skip past leading whitespace
      while ( (i < n) && isspace(text[i]))
        i++;

      // Find word end
      int start = i;
      while ( (i < n) && !isspace(text[i]))
        i++;
      if (start < i)
        EmitIntermediate(text.substr(start, i-start)
          , "1");
    }
  }
};

REGISTER_MAPPER(WordCounter);
```

The code snippet for the *Reducer* is:

```cpp
// fonction utilisateur de réduction

class Adder :
public Reducer {
  virtual void Reduce(ReduceInput* input) {
    // Iterate over all entries with the
    // same key and add the values
    int64 value = 0;
    while (!input->done()) {
      value += StringToInt(input->value());
      input->NextValue();
    }

    // Emit sum for input->key()
    Emit(IntToString(value));
  }
};

REGISTER_REDUCER(Adder);
```

We can then use these functions into a MapReduce program as follows:

```cpp
int main(int argc, char** argv) {
  ParseCommandLineFlags(argc, argv);
  MapReduceSpecification spec;
```

```
for (int i = 1; i < argc; i++) {
  MapReduceInput* input = spec.add_input();
  input->set_format("text");
  input->set_filepattern(argv[i]);
  input->set_mapper_class("WordCounter");
}

// Define output
MapReduceOutput* out = spec.output();
out->set_filebase("/gfs/test/freq");
out->set_num_tasks(100);
out->set_format("text");
out->set_reducer_class("Adder");

// Optional
  // (combine) on each process
out->set_combiner_class("Adder");

// set various parameters of MapReduce
spec.set_machines(2000);
spec.set_map_megabytes(100);
spec.set_reduce_megabytes(100);

// Now run it!
MapReduceResult result;

if (!MapReduce(spec, &result)) abort();
return 0;
}
```

6.5   Launching MapReduce Jobs and Overview of the MapReduce Architecture

The MapReduce system works on large computer clusters, and is fault-tolerant to various problems that can occur while running MapReduce jobs. Indeed, when one uses thousands to millions or even hundreds of millions of cores,[8] it is quite frequent to face hardware failures like a hard disk drive (HDD) that suddenly fails, or the network that becomes congested and very slow on a group of machines (potentially due also to failures of network cards), etc. Some computers can also become very slow due to their overload: they are called *stragglers*. MapReduce is fault-tolerant and implement a master-slave architecture. MapReduce re-launches automatically tasks that have not been completed within a prescribed time by implementing a *time-out* mechanism. Figure 6.2 illustrates the task scheduler of MapReduce that can

---

[8]Those figures are usually trade secrets of companies, and are not disclosed publicly.

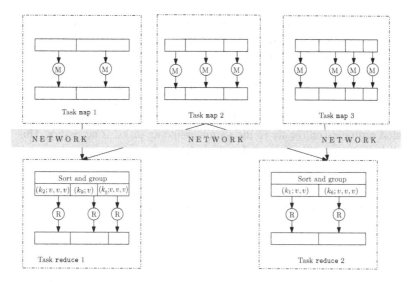

Fig. 6.2 Execution model of MapReduce: data and map processes are independently allocated by MapReduce on processes that preferentially already stored data locally. The reduce processes collect the (key,value) pairs to compute the reduction operation

decide to execute a same task on several machines (in order to provide redundancy by replication), and obtain results when the fastest task has been completed.

Data transfer on the network is costly as latency cannot be improved and bandwidth is limited in practice. Therefore, the task schedule allocate tasks preferentially to machines that already locally store data. MapReduce also offers a control interface that allows to visualize various statistics on the executed tasks, to predict the duration time of ongoing tasks, etc. It is a very useful monitoring tool to observe the workload of MapReduce tasks on a computer cluster.

Since MapReduce relies on a master-slave architecture, it is also prone to failure when the *master machine* fails. Thus the master node periodically writes all its data structures and states into a safe copy in order to resume MapReduce tasks in case it fails (restoration points). Data are stored on the *Google File System* (*GFS*) that splits files into blocks of 64 MBs, and save several copies of these pieces on different computers in order to be robust and fault-tolerant. We have explained the very basic underlying principles of MapReduce. Let us mention that there exist many optimizations of MapReduce that we omitted for sake of conciseness. For example, the combiner combines locally the intermediate keys when they are equal in order to optimize the network traffic by downsizing the data to transfer to the reducer. Sometimes, this implies to modify slightly the MapReduce code. For example, if we wish to compute the mean, the combiner not only requires to send the mean but also the number of elements that yielded that mean.

The success story of MapReduce is mainly due to its automatic parallelization from two simple user-defined functions. MapReduce fully handles the traditionally cumbersome data distribution, task monitoring, etc. MapReduce takes care of sending data transfer orders and manages the load balancing of computers. It offers a parallel programming framework that is fault-tolerant (which is not the case of MPI where one has to take care manually of all those details). Its model abstraction is simple and yet powerful enough to implement a rich set of applications like sorting, parallel machine learning algorithms, data mining algorithms, and so on. Moreover MapReduce provides monitoring tools that allow the cluster administrators to adjust allocated resources on the fly to the various ongoing tasks, if necessary. This last capability is very much appreciated in the industry.

6.6   Using MapReduce in MPI with the MR-MPI Library

So far, we have explained the model of computation of MapReduce. We can also implement by hand a MapReduce algorithm using MPI. In fact, there exists a software library readily available for this: MR-MPI.[9] The documentation[10] of *MR-MPI* is available online too.

For example, the collate method aggregates on all processes an object of type KeyValue and converts it to an object KeyMultiValue. This method returns the total number of unique (key,value) pairs.

The program below shows how to compute the frequency of occurrence of words in a collection of files. It displays in its output the 2015 most frequent words.

```
#include "mpi.h"
#include "stdio.h"
#include "stdlib.h"
#include "string.h"
#include "sys/stat.h"
#include "mapreduce.h"
#include "keyvalue.h"

using namespace MAPREDUCE_NS;

void fileread(int, KeyValue *, void *);
void sum(char *, int, char *, int, int *, KeyValue*,
    void *);
int ncompare(char *, int, char *, int);
void output(int, char*, int, char *, int, KeyValue*,
    void *);

struct Count {int n, limit, flag;};

/* Syntax : wordfreq file1 file2  */

int main(int narg, char **args)
```

[9]http://mapreduce.sandia.gov/.

[10]http://mapreduce.sandia.gov/doc/Manual.html.

```
{
  MPI_Init(&narg, &args);
  int me, nprocs;

    MPI_Comm_rank(MPI_COMM_WORLD, &me);
  MPI_Comm_size(MPI_COMM_WORLD, &nprocs);

  MapReduce *mr = new MapReduce(MPI_COMM_WORLD);

  int nwords = mr->map(narg-1, &fileread, &args[1]);
  mr->collate(NULL);
  int nunique = mr->reduce(&sum, NULL);
  mr->sort_values(&ncompare);

  Count count;
  count.n = 0;
  count.limit = 2015;
  count.flag = 0;
  mr->map(mr->kv, &output, &count);
  mr->gather(1);
  mr->sort_values(&ncompare);

  count.n = 0;
  count.limit = 10;
  count.flag = 1;
  mr->map(mr->kv, &output, &count);

  delete mr;
  MPI_Finalize();
}

/* For each word, emit (key=word,valeur=NULL) */
void fileread(int itask, KeyValue *kv, void *ptr)
{
  char **files = (char **) ptr;

  struct stat stbuf;
  int flag = stat(files[itask], &stbuf);
  int filesize = stbuf.st_size;

  FILE *fp = fopen(files[itask], "r");
  char *text = new char[filesize+1];
  int nchar = fread(text, 1, filesize, fp);
  text[nchar] = '\0';
  fclose(fp);

  char *whitespace = " \t\n\f\r\0";
  char *word = strtok(text, whitespace);

  while (word) {
    kv->add(word, strlen(word)+1, NULL, 0);
    word = strtok(NULL, whitespace);
  }
```

```
  delete [] text;
}

/* emit ppairs (key=word, valeur=count) */
void sum(char *key, int keybytes, char *multivalue,
int nvalues, int *valuebytes, KeyValue *kv, void *
   ptr)
{
  kv->add(key, keybytes, (char *) &nvalues, sizeof(
     int));
}

/* for sorting, comparison function */

int ncompare(char *p1, int len1, char *p2, int len2)
{
  int i1 = *(int *) p1;
  int i2 = *(int *) p2;
  if (i1 > i2) return -1;
  else if (i1 < i2) return 1;
  else return 0;
}

/* output: display the selected words */

void output(int itask, char *key, int keybytes, char
     *value,
int valuebytes, KeyValue *kv, void *ptr)
{
  Count *count = (Count *) ptr;
  count->n++;
  if (count->n > count->limit) return;

  int n = *(int *) value;
  if (count->flag) printf("%d %s\n", n, key);
  else kv->add(key, keybytes, (char *) &n, sizeof(
     int));
}
```

6.7   Notes and References

One can install MapReduce on its own machine (single node mode) using a virtual
machine.[11] The MapReduce implementation depends on the environment like multi-
core computers with shared memory, or NUMA (*Non-uniform memory access*) multiprocessors, architectures with distributed memory and interconnection network, etc.

---

[11] http://www.thecloudavenue.com/2013/01/virtual-machine-for-learning-hadoop.html.

For example, a MapReduce implementation[12] is available in MPI, and its efficient implementation is discussed in [1].

MapReduce applications on graphs using MPI are covered in [2]. One can use Hadoop on its own computer (without requiring to have access to a computer cluster) to compile and debug programs before launching them on big clusters. That is, one can define and rent configurations on clusters using the various cloud academic or industrial computing platforms (Amazon EC2, Microsoft Azure, Google, etc.). *Out-of-core processing* is the field of parallel algorithms that need to access data that cannot be all stored in the RAM, and need external access. Similarly, out-of-core visualization is an area of computer graphics that handles massive data sets that cannot be stored on a single local memory. Handling big data also requires to visualize big information. Another computing paradigm are streaming algorithms. Streaming algorithms [3] consider data read from streams. Data are processed eventually in one or several passes.

6.8 Summary

MapReduce is a paradigm of parallel programming to deal with Big Data on large-scale clusters of machines. A MapReduce program includes two user-defined functions (UDFs), called `map` and `reduce`, that calculates on (key,value) pairs. The MapReduce system executes a parallel program in three stages:

1. mapper stage that emits (key,value) pairs from data using the user-defined function `map`,
2. sorter stage that gathers the (key,value) pairs into groups of keys, and
3. reducer stage that aggregates all values attached to the same key using the user-defined function `reduce`.

The MapReduce system relies on a master-slave architecture, and takes care of allocating the various resources, distributing data, launching `map` processes (all independent processes), and performing `reduce` operations according to the current resource workload (CPU, network traffic, etc.). MapReduce also provides various tools for controlling tasks, and periodically saves its state in case the master machine crashes (restoration point). In order to optimize the network traffic, an optional optimization stage, called `combiner` allows one to perform locally on machines reduce operations before sending these results out on the network for further inter-machine reductions. The MapReduce paradigm was originally developed in C++ at Google and relied on the Google File System, GFS. A widely popular open source alternative implementation in Java is called Hadoop. Hadoop relies on its own parallel file system: HDFS.

---

[12]http://mapreduce.sandia.gov/.

References

1. Hoefler, T., Lumsdaine, A., Dongarra, J.: Towards efficient MapReduce using MPI. In: Ropo, M., Westerholm, J., Dongarra, J. (eds.) Recent Advances in Parallel Virtual Machine and Message Passing Interface. Lecture Notes in Computer Science, vol. 5759, pp. 240–249. Springer, Berlin (2009)
2. Plimpton, S.J., Devine, K.D.: Mapreduce in MPI for large-scale graph algorithms. Parallel Comput. **37**(9), 610–632 (2011)
3. Kaur, S., Bhatnagar, V., Chakravarthy, S.: Stream clustering algorithms: a primer. In: Ella Hassanien, A., Taher Azar, A., Snasael, V., Kacprzyk, J., Abawajy, J.H. (eds.) Big Data in Complex Systems. Studies in Big Data, vol. 9, pp. 105–145. Springer International Publishing, Switzerland (2015)

Part II
High Performance Computing (HPC) for Data Science (DS)

Chapter 7
Partition-Based Clustering with k-Means

7.1 Exploratory Data Analysis and Clustering

Nowadays, huge size data-sets are commonly publicly available, and it becomes increasingly important to efficiently process them to discover worthwhile structures (or "patterns") in those seas of data. *Exploratory* data analysis is concerned with this challenge of finding such structural information without any prior knowledge: in this case, those techniques that consist in learning from data without prior knowledge are called generically *unsupervised machine learning*.

Let $X = \{x_1, \ldots, x_n\}$ denote a data-set like a collection of images (often static, that is given once for all when we begin with the analysis). We seek for compact subsets of data, called clusters, that represent *categories* of data (say, the *cluster* of the car images or the cluster of the cat images, etc.). Each datum $x_i \in \mathbb{X}$ (with $\mathbb{X}$ denoting the space of data, usually $\mathbb{X} \subset \mathbb{R}^d$) is described as an *attribute vector* $x_i = (x_i^1, \ldots, x_i^d)$, called a *feature vector*. We adopt the following notation x_i^j (meaning $x_i^{(j)}$) to describe the jth coordinate of vector x_i. Vector attributes can either be *numerical quantities* or *categorical values* (that is qualitative attributes) like the fixed set of words of a dictionary, or *ordered categorical data* (like the ordered ranking A < B < C < D < E), or a mix of those different data types.

Exploratory analysis differs from *supervised classification* that consists in a first stage to learn a *classifier function* $C(\cdot)$ from labeled data of a *training data set* $Z = \{(x_1, y_1), \ldots, (x_n, y_n)\}$, with the x_i's the attributes and the y_i's the class labels, in order in a second stage to classify new unlabeled observations x_j belonging to a *testing set*: $\hat{y}_j = C(x_j)$. The hat notation in $\hat{y}_j$ indicates that one has *estimated* the class, a so-called *inference task* performed from a training data set.

Clustering is a set of techniques that consists in detecting subsets of data that define groups or clusters. Those groups should ideally represent *semantic categories* of data: for example, the flower groups organized by species from a database of flower images. One such famous public data-set is available from the *UCI repository*[1] as

---

[1] Available online at https://archive.ics.uci.edu/ml/datasets.html.

© Springer International Publishing Switzerland 2016
F. Nielsen, *Introduction to HPC with MPI for Data Science*, Undergraduate
Topics in Computer Science, DOI 10.1007/978-3-319-21903-5_7

Fig. 7.1 Exploratory analysis consists in finding intrinsic structures in data sets like groups of data called cluster. Clustering is a set of techniques that seek to find homogeneous clusters in data-sets. In this 2D toy example, the Human eye perceives three well-formed clusters for the digits: '4', '4', '2'. In practice, data-sets are living in high dimensions, and thus cannot be visually inspected: Therefore we require clustering algorithms to automatically find those groups

filename Iris[2]: it contains $n = 150$ numerical data in dimension 4 (with attributes describing the length and the width of both the sepals and petals, in centimeters), classified in $k = 3$ botanical groups: Setosa iris, Virginica iris, and Versicolor iris.

To summarize, classification enables to label new observations while clustering allows one to discover those classes as clusters (Fig. 7.1).

7.1.1 Hard Clustering: Partitioning Data Sets

Partition-based clustering consists in dividing a data set $X = \{x_1, \ldots, x_n\}$ into k *homogeneous groups* $G_1 \subset X, \ldots, G_k \subset X$ (the non-overlapping clusters G_i) such that we have:

$$X = \cup_{i=1}^{k} G_i, \quad \forall i \neq j, \ G_i \cap G_j = \emptyset,$$
$$X := \uplus_{i=1}^{k} G_i$$

Notation $a := b$ indicates that the equality sign should be understood by definition (that is, it is not an equality resulting from some mathematical calculation). Thus a data element (datum) is allocated to a unique group $G_{l(x_i)}$: Partition-based clustering is a *hard clustering technique*, and differentiates itself from other *soft clustering techniques* that gives a positive membership weight $l_{i,j} > 0$ for all the x_i's and the groups $G_{l(x_i)}$'s with $\sum_{j=1}^{k} l_{i,j} = 1$ (normalization constraint): $l_{i,j} = 1$ if and only if (iff.) $j = l(x_i)$. We denote by $L = [l_{i,j}]$ the *membership matrix* of size $n \times k$.

---

[2]http://en.wikipedia.org/wiki/Iris_flower_data_set.

7.1.2 Cost Functions and Model-Based Clustering

Finding a good partitioning of the data $X = \biguplus_{i=1}^{k} G_i$ requires to be able to evaluate the clustering *fitness* of partitions. However, we often proceed the other way around! From a given *cost function*, we seek an efficient algorithm that partitions X by minimizing this prescribed cost function. A generic cost function $e_k(\cdot; \cdot)$ (also synonymously called *energy function*, *loss function* or *objective function*) is written as the sum of the costs of each group as follows:

$$e_k(X; G_1, \ldots, G_k) = \sum_{i=1}^{k} e_1(G_i),$$

with $e_1(G)$ the cost function for a single group.

We can also associate for each group G_i a *model* c_i that defines the "center" of that cluster. The collection of centers, the c_i's, are called the *prototypes*, and those prototypes allow one to define a distance between any data $x \in X$ and any cluster G (with corresponding prototype c) as follows:

$$D_M(x, G) = D(x, c).$$

Function $D_M(x, G)$ denotes the distance between an element x and a cluster using the prototype of that cluster. Function $D(p, q)$ is a *base distance* to properly define according to nature of the data set. That is, we have $D_M(x, G) = D(x, c)$ where c is the prototype of G.

Given the set of k prototypes $C = \{c_1, \ldots, c_k\}$, one can define the overall cost of a partition-based clustering by:

$$e_k(X; C) = \sum_{i=1}^{n} \min_{j \in \{1, \ldots, k\}} D(x_i, c_j),$$

and the cost of a single cluster is defined by $e_1(G, c) = \sum_{x \in G} D(x, c)$. Model-based clustering with a single center associated to each cluster induces a partition of the data set X: $G(C) = \biguplus_{j=1}^{k} G_j$, with $G_j = \{x_i \in X \ : \ D(x_i, c_j) \leq D(x_i, c_l), \ \forall l \in \{1, \ldots, k\}\}$.

There exists many clustering cost/loss functions that gives rise to many different kinds of partitions. Next, we shall introduce the most celebrated such a function called *k-means*, and explain why the minimization of this loss function provides good clustering partitions in practice.

7.2 The k-Means Objective Function

The k-means cost function asks to minimize the sum of squared Euclidean distances of data points to their closest prototype centers:

$$e_k(X; C) = \sum_{i=1}^{n} \min_{j \in \{1, \dots, k\}} \|x_i - c_j\|^2.$$

Although that the squared Euclidean distance $D(x, c) = \|x - c\|^2$ is a symmetric dissimilarity measure equals to zero if and only if $x = c$, it is *not* a metric because it fails to satisfy the triangular inequalities of the ordinary Euclidean distance: $\|x - c\|_2 = \sqrt{\sum_{j=1}^{d}(x^i - c^j)^2}$. In fact, there is a good reason to choose the squared Euclidean distance instead of the Euclidean distance: Indeed, the cost of a single cluster $e_1(G) = e_1(G, c)$ is minimized when we choose for the cluster prototype its center of mass c, called the *centroid*:

$$c(G) := \operatorname{argmin}_c \sum_{x \in G} \|x - c\|^2 = \frac{1}{|G|} \sum_{x \in G} x,$$

where $|G|$ denotes the cardinality of G, that is the number of elements contained in group G. We use the following notation $\operatorname{argmin}_x f(x)$ to denote the argument that yields the minimum in case this minimum value is unique.[3]
Thus the minimal cost is $e_1(G, c) = \sum_{x \in G} \|x - c(G)\|^2 := v(G)$, the normalized variance of cluster G. Indeed, the normalized variance of X is defined in statistics as:

$$v(X) = \frac{1}{n} \sum_{i=1}^{n} \|x_i - \bar{x}\|^2,$$

with $\bar{x} = \frac{1}{n} \sum_{i=1}^{n} x_i$ the center of mass. Technically speaking, we often meet in the literature the unbiased variance formula $v_{\text{unbiased}}(X) = \frac{1}{n-1} \sum_{i=1}^{n} \|x_i - \bar{x}\|^2$, but for fixed n the minimizer of the biased/unbiased variance does not change.
We can rewrite the variance of a d-dimensional point cloud X as:

$$\boxed{v(X) = \left(\frac{1}{n} \sum_{i=1}^{n} x_i^2\right) - \bar{x}^\top \bar{x}}$$

This formula is mathematically the same as the variance for a random variable X:

$$\mathbb{V}[X] = \mathbb{E}[(X - \mu(X))^2] = \mathbb{E}[X^2] - (\mathbb{E}[X])^2$$

---

[3]Otherwise, we can choose the "smallest" x that yields the minimum value according to some lexicographic order on $\mathbb{X}$.

where $\mu(X) = \mathbb{E}[X]$ denotes the expectation of the random variable X.

We can define a positive weight attribute $w_i = w(x_i) > 0$ for each element x_i of X such that $\sum_{i=1}^{n} w_i = 1$ (data weights normalized).

The following theorem characterizes the prototype c_1 as the center for a single cluster (case $k = 1$ with $X = G_1$):

Theorem 3 *Let $X = \{(w_1, x_1), \ldots, (w_n, x_n)\} \subset \mathbb{R}^d$ be a weighted data-set with $w_i > 0$ and $\sum_{i=1}^{n} w_i = 1$. The center c that minimizes the weighted variance $v(X) = \sum_{i=1}^{n} w_i \|x_i - c\|^2$ is the unique barycenter: $c = \bar{x} = \sum_{i=1}^{n} w_i x_i$.*

Proof Let $\langle x, y \rangle$ denote the *scalar product*: $\langle x, y \rangle = x^\top y = \sum_{j=1}^{d} x^j y^j = \langle y, x \rangle$. The scalar product is a symmetric bi-linear form: $\langle \lambda x + b, y \rangle = \lambda \langle x, y \rangle + \langle b, y \rangle$ for $\lambda \in \mathbb{R}$. Now, the squared Euclidean distance $D(x, y) = \|x - y\|^2$ can be rewritten using scalar producs as $D(x, y) = \langle x - y, x - y \rangle = \langle x, x \rangle - 2\langle x, y \rangle + \langle y, y \rangle$.

We seek to minimize $\min_{c \in \mathbb{R}^d} \sum_{i=1}^{n} w_i \langle x_i - c, x_i - c \rangle$. We can mathematically rewrite this optimization problem as:

$$\min_{c \in \mathbb{R}^d} \sum_{i=1}^{n} w_i \langle x_i - c, x_i - c \rangle$$

$$\min_{c \in \mathbb{R}^d} \sum_{i=1}^{n} w_i (\langle x_i, x_i \rangle - 2\langle x_i, c \rangle + \langle c, c \rangle)$$

$$\min_{c \in \mathbb{R}^d} \left(\sum_{i=1}^{n} w_i \langle x_i, x_i \rangle \right) - 2\left\langle \sum_{i=1}^{n} w_i x_i, c \right\rangle + \langle c, c \rangle$$

We can remove the term $\sum_{i=1}^{n} w_i \langle x_i, x_i \rangle$ from the minimization since it is independent of c. Thus we seek to minimize equivalently:

$$\min_{c \in \mathbb{R}^d} E(c) := -2\left\langle \sum_{i=1}^{n} w_i x_i, c \right\rangle + \langle c, c \rangle.$$

A *convex function* $f(x)$ satisfies $f(\alpha x + (1 - \alpha)y) \le \alpha f(x) + (1 - \alpha)f(y)$ for any $\alpha \in [0, 1]$. It is a *strictly convex function* iff. $f(\alpha x + (1 - \alpha)y) < \alpha f(x) + (1 - \alpha)f(y)$ for any $\alpha \in (0, 1)$. Figure 7.2 plots the graph of a strictly convex function. Note that the *epigraph* defined as the geometric object $\mathcal{F} = \{(x, f(x)) : x \in \mathbb{R}\}$ is a geometric convex object. A *geometric convex object* satisfies the property that any line segment joining two points of the object shall fully lie inside the object.

For univariate convex functions, there exists at most one global minimum x^* (for example, $\exp(-x)$ is strictly convex without a minimum), and it can be found by setting the derivative to zero: $f'(x^*) = 0$. For a multi-variate real-valued function, we denote by $\nabla_x F(x)$ its *gradient* (the vector of partial derivatives), and by $\nabla_x^2 F(x)$ the *Hessian matrix* (of second-order derivatives). A smooth function F is strictly convex if and only if $\nabla^2 F \succ 0$ where $M \succ 0$ denotes that the matrix M is positive-definite:

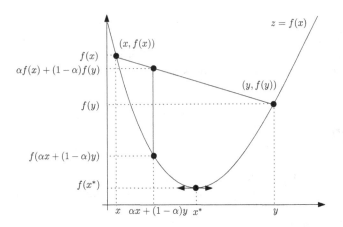

Fig. 7.2 Plot of a strictly convex function satisfying $f(\alpha x + (1 - \alpha)y) < \alpha f(x) + (1 - \alpha)f(y)$ for any $\alpha \in (0, 1)$

$\forall x \neq 0$, $x^\top M x > 0$. A strictly convex function admits at most a global unique minimum x^* such that $\nabla F(x^*) = 0$.

We get the following d partial derivatives to set to zero:

$$\frac{d}{dc^j} E(c) = -2 \sum_{i=1}^{n} w_i x_i^j + 2c^j, \quad \forall j \in \{1, \ldots, d\},$$

Consider the d^2 second derivatives (for proving the convexity of the objective function) as:

$$\frac{d^2}{dc^j c^l} E(c) = 2, \quad \text{for } l = j, \forall j \in \{1, \ldots, d\}.$$

The cost function $E(c)$ is strictly convex and admits a unique minimum. This minimum is obtained by zeroing all partial derivatives:

$$\frac{d}{dc^j} E(c) = 0 \Leftrightarrow c^j = \sum_{i=1}^{n} w_i x_i^j.$$

Thus we have shown that the minimizers of the weighted sum of squared Euclidean distance of the center to the points is the unique barycenter:

$$c = \bar{x} = \sum_{i=1}^{n} w_i x_i.$$

The centroid is also called *isobarycenter* when $w_i = \frac{1}{n}$.   □

Fig. 7.3 The k-means cost function tend to find globular-shaped clusters that minimize the weighted sum of the cluster variances. k-Means clustering is a model-based clustering where each cluster is associated to a prototype: its center of mass, or centroid. Here, we have choosen $k = 4$ groups for the k-means: Cluster prototypes, centroids, are illustrated with large disks

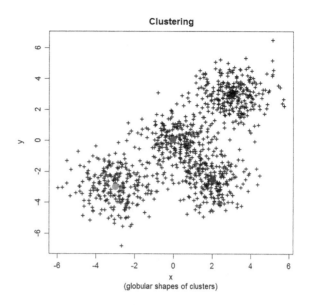

If instead of choosing the squared Euclidean distance, we had chosen the ordinary Euclidean distance, one obtains the so-called *Fermat-Weber point* that generalizes the notion of median. It is thus also called the *geometric median*.[4] Although the Fermat-Weber point is unique and often used in operations research for facility location problems, it does not admit a closed-form solution, but can be arbitrarily finely approximated. The *k-median clustering* is the clustering obtained by minimizing the cost function $\min_C \sum_{i=1}^n \min_{j\in\{1,\dots,k\}} \|x_i - c_j\|$ (observe that the squared Euclidean distance of k-means has been replaced by the regular Euclidean distance). Note that the obtained partitions from k-means and k-medians can be very different from each other. Indeed, the centroid location can be different to the median for a single cluster. Moreover, centroids can be easily corrupted by adding a single outlier point. We say that the *breakdown point* of the centroid is 0: A single outlier p_0 diverging to infinity will impact the centroid to be diverging to infinity too. But the median is provably more robust since it requires $\lfloor \frac{n}{2} \rfloor$ outliers (that is, about 50% of outliers) to steer the median point to ∞. Therefore k-median clustering is often preferred when there are many outliers in data-sets.

Let us remark that finding the center of a single cluster is a particular case of clustering with $k = 1$ cluster. With the squared Euclidean distance cost, we find that the center is the mean of the attributes, hence its naming: k-means. Figure 7.3 displays the clustering result on a given data-set. This figure has been produced using the following code in the *R language*[5]:

---

[4]http://en.wikipedia.org/wiki/Geometric_median.

[5]Freely available online at https://www.r-project.org/.

> WWW source code: Example-kMeans.R

```
# filename:  Example–kMeans.R
# k–means clustering using the R language
N <- 100000
x <- matrix(0, N, 2)
x[seq(1,N,by = 4),]  <- rnorm(N/2)
x[seq(2,N,by = 4),]  <- rnorm(N/2, 3, 1)
x[seq(3,N,by = 4),]  <- rnorm(N/2, -3, 1)
x[seq(4,N,by = 4),1] <- rnorm(N/4, 2, 1)
x[seq(4,N,by    = 4),2] <- rnorm(N/4, -2.5, 1)
start.kmeans <- proc.time()[3]
ans.kmeans <- kmeans(x, 4, nstart=3, iter.max=10, algorithm="Lloyd")
ans.kmeans$centers
end.kmeans <- proc.time()[3]
end.kmeans - start.kmeans
these <- sample(1:nrow(x), 1000)
plot(x[these,1], x[these,2], pch="+", xlab="x", ylab="y")
title(main="Clustering", sub="(globular shapes of clusters)", xlab="x",
      ylab="y")
points(ans.kmeans$centers, pch=19, cex=2, col=1:4)
```

7.2.1 Rewriting the k-Means Cost Function for a Dual Interpretation of Clustering: Group Intra-cluster or Separate Inter-cluster Data

The k-means cost function seeks compact globular clusters of small variances. Indeed, the cost function can be reinterpreted as the minimization of the weighted sum of cluster variances as follows:

$$\min_{C=\{c_1,\ldots,c_k\}} \sum_{i=1}^{n} \min_{j\in\{1,\ldots,k\}} w_i \|x_i - c_j\|^2,$$

$$\min_{C=\{c_1,\ldots,c_k\}} \sum_{j=1}^{k} \sum_{x\in G_j} w(x)\|x - c_j\|^2$$

$$\min_{C=\{c_1,\ldots,c_k\}} \sum_{j=1}^{k} W_j v(G_j),$$

where $W_j := \sum_{x\in G_j} w(x)$ denotes the cumulative weight of the elements in cluster G_j (see Sect. 7.12).

We can also show that clustering data into homogeneous groups correspond equivalently to separate data of X into groups: Indeed, let $A := \sum_{i=1}^{n} \sum_{j=i+1}^{n} \|x_i - x_j\|^2$

denote the *constant* that is the sum of the inter-point squared Euclidean distances (fixed for a given data-set, and independent of k). For a given partition, we can decompose A into two terms: the sum of the intra-distances inside a same cluster, and the sum of the inter-distance among two distinct clusters:

$$A = \sum_{i=1}^{l} \left(\sum_{x_i, x_j \in G_l} \|x_i - x_j\|^2 + \sum_{x_i \in G_l, x_j \notin G_l} \|x_i - x_j\|^2 \right).$$

Thus to minimize the sum of the intra-cluster squared Euclidean distances $\sum_{i=1}^{l} \sum_{x_i, x_j \in G_l} \|x_i - x_j\|^2$ is equivalent to maximize the sum of the inter-cluster squared Euclidean distances since A is a constant (for a given X):

$$\min_{C} \sum_{i=1}^{l} \sum_{x_i, x_j \in G_l} \|x_i - x_j\|^2$$

$$= \min_{C} A - \sum_{i=1}^{l} \sum_{x_i \in G_l, x_j \notin G_l} \|x_i - x_j\|^2$$

$$\equiv \max_{C} \sum_{i=1}^{l} \sum_{x_i \in G_l, x_j \notin G_l} \|x_i - x_j\|^2$$

Therefore, we have a dual description to define a good clustering:

- *cluster* data into *homogeneous groups* in order to minimize the weighted sum of cluster variances, or
- *separate* data in order to maximize the inter-cluster squared Euclidean distances.

7.2.2 Complexity and Tractability of the k-Means Optimization Problem

Finding the minimum of a k-means cost function is a *NP-hard problem* as soon as the dimension $d > 1$ and the number of clusters $k > 1$. When $k = 1$, we have shown that we can compute the optimal solution (the centroid) in linear time (computing the mean of the group). When $d = 1$, we can compute an optimal k-means solution using *dynamic programming*: Using $O(nk)$ memory, we can solve the k-means for n scalar values in time $O(n^2 k)$ (see the exercises at the end of this chapter for further details).

Theorem 4 (k-means complexity) *Finding a partition that minimizes the k-means cost function is NP-hard when $k > 1$ and $d > 1$. When $d = 1$, we can solve for the exact k-means using dynamic programming in $O(n^2 k)$ time using $O(nk)$ memory.*

We quickly recall that P is the class of decision problems (that is, answering yes/no questions) that can be solved in polynomial time, and NP is the class of problems for which one can verify the solution in *polynomial time* (like for example, 3-SAT[6]). The NP-complete class is that class of problems that can be solved one from another by using a polynomial-time reduction scheme: $X \propto_{\text{polynomial}} Y, \forall Y \in$ NP. The NP-hard class is the class of problems, not necessarily in NP, such that $\exists Y \in \text{NP} - \text{Complete} \propto_{\text{polynomial}} X$.

Since the k-means problem is theoretically NP-hard, we seek efficient heuristics to approximate the cost function. We distinguish two classes of such heuristics:

1. *global heuristics* that do not depend on initialization, and
2. *local heuristics* that iteratively starts from a solution (a partition) and iteratively improves this partition using "pivot rules."

Of course, one need to initialize local heuristics with a global heuristic. This yields many strategies for obtaining in practice a good k-means clustering! Finding novel k-means heuristics is still an active research topic 50 years after its inception!

7.3 Lloyd's Batched k-Means Local Heuristic

We now present the celebrated Lloyd's heuristic (1957) that consists from a given initialization to iteratively repeat until convergence the following two steps:

Assign points to clusters.   For all $x_i \in X$, let $l_i = \text{argmin}_l \|x_i - c_l\|^2$, and define the k cluster groups as $G_j = \{x_i : l_i = j\}$ with $n_j = |G_j|$, the number of elements of X falling into the jth cluster.

Update centers.   For all $j \in \{1, \ldots, k\}$, update the centers to their cluster centroids : $c_j = \frac{1}{n_j} \sum_{x \in G_j} x$ (or the barycenters $c_j = \frac{1}{\sum_{x \in G_j} w(x)} \sum_{x \in G_j} w(x)x$ for weighted data-sets).

Figure 7.4 illustrates a few iterations of Lloyd's algorithm.

Theorem 5 *Lloyd's k-means heuristics converge monotonically into a local minimum after a finite number of iterations, upper bounded by $\binom{n}{k}$.*

Proof Let $G_1^{(t)}, \ldots, G_k^{(t)}$ denote the partition of X at time t, with cost $e_k(X, C_t)$. Let $G(C_t) = \uplus_{j=1}^{k} G_i^{(t)}$ denote the clusters induced by the k centers C_t. At stage $t + 1$, since we assign points to clusters that have the nearest squared euclidean distance, we minimize:

$$e_k(X; G^{(t+1)}) \leq e_k(X, G(C_t)).$$

---

[6]The 3-*SAT problem* consists in answering whether a boolean formula with n clauses of 3 literals can be satisfiable or not. 3-SAT is a famous NP-complete problem (Cook's theorem, 1971), a corner stone of theoretical computer science.

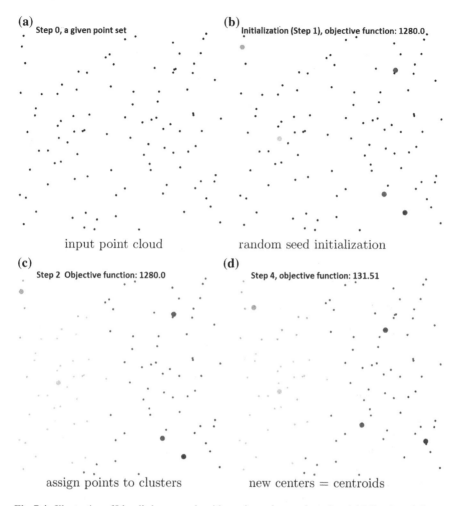

(a) Step 0, a given point set

input point cloud

(b) Initialization (Step 1), objective function: 1280.0.

random seed initialization

(c) Step 2 Objective function: 1280.0

assign points to clusters

(d) Step 4, objective function: 131.51

new centers = centroids

Fig. 7.4 Illustration of Lloyd's k-means algorithm: **a** input data set, **b** random initialization of cluster centers, **c** assigning points to clusters, **d** center relocations, etc. until the algorithm convergences into a local minimum of the cost function

Now, recall that the k-means cost function is equal to the weighted sum of the intra-cluster variances: $e_k(X; G^{(t+1)}) = \sum_{j=1}^{k} v(G_j^{(t+1)}, c_j)$. When we update the cluster centers to their centroids (that are the points that minimize the squared Euclidean distance in these groups), we have for each group $v(G_j^{(t+1)}, c(G_j^{(t+1)})) \leq v(G_j^{(t+1)}, c_j)$. Thus we deduce that:

$$e_k(X; C_{t+1}) \leq e_k(G^{(t+1)}; C_t) \leq e_k(X; C_t).$$

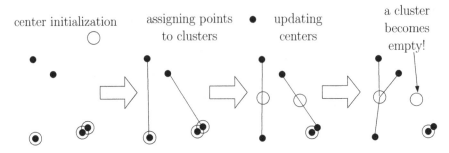

Fig. 7.5 Empty cluster exceptions in Lloyd's heuristic: Cluster centers are depicted with large circles. Initialization followed by an assignment step with a center relocation step, and new assignment step. One of the cluster becomes empty

Since $e_k(X; C) \geq 0$ and that we can never repeat twice the same partitions among the $O(\binom{n}{k})$ potential partitions,[7] we necessarily converge into a local minimum after a finite number of iterations.   □

Let us now present a few remarkable observations on the k-means clustering:

Observation 1 Although that Lloyd's heuristic perform remarkably well in practice, it has been shown that in the worst-case we can have an exponential number of iterations, even in the planar case $d = 2$ [1, 2]. In 1D, Lloyd's k-means can require $\Omega(n)$ iterations until convergence [2]. But recall that the 1D case can be solved polynomially using dynamic programming.

Observation 2 Even if the k-means cost function as a unique global minimum, there can be exponentially many partition solutions that yield this minimum value (one single min but many argmin): For example, let us consider the 4 vertices of a square. For $k = 2$, we have two optimal solutions (from the vertices of the parallel edges). Let us now clone $\frac{n}{4}$ copies of this square, each square located very far away to each other, and consider $k = \frac{n}{4}$: In that case, there exists 2^k optimal clusterings.

Observation 3 In some cases, after assigning points to clusters in Lloyd's batched heuristic, we can obtain *empty clusters*: This case happens rarely in practice but its probability increases with the dimension. Thus one has to take care when implementing Lloyd's k-means of these potential empty cluster exceptions. One such configuration is illustrated in Fig. 7.5. Note that this problem is in fact a blessing, since we can choose new center points in order to reinitialize those empty clusters while ensuring that the sum of cluster variances decreases.

Lloyd's k-means are a local heuristic that starts from a given initialization (either induced by an initial set of k prototypes, or by a given starting partition that induces the

---

[7] The number of distinct partitions of a set of n elements into k non-empty subsets is defined by the *second kind of Stirling number*: $\begin{Bmatrix} n \\ k \end{Bmatrix} = \frac{1}{k!} \sum_{j=0}^{k} (-1)^{k-j} \binom{k}{j} j^n$.

centroid prototypes) and guarantees monotonous convergence to a local minimum. We shall now describe a few initialization methods: That is, global heuristics for k-means.

7.4 Initializing k-Means with Global Heuristics

7.4.1 Random Seed Initialization (as Known as Forgy's Initialization)

Let us choose the k distinct seeds randomly from X (for example, by sampling uniformly the k indices from $[n] = \{1, \ldots, n\}$). There are $\binom{n}{k}$ such different random drawings. Then we create the group partition $G(C) = \{G_1, \ldots, G_k\}$ from the seed variates $C = \{c_1, \ldots, c_k\}$. There is no theoretical guarantee that $e_k(X, G)$ is close to the global minimum $e_k^*(X, G) = \min_C e_k(X, G)$. Thus in order to increase the chance of finding a good initialization, not too far from $e_k^*(X, G)$, we can initialize l times to get the seed sets $C_1, \ldots, C_l$ and keep the best seeds that yielded the best k-means cost so far: That is, keep C_{l^*} with $l^* = \mathrm{argmin}_l e_k(X; G(C_l))$. This method is sometimes called *Forgy's initialization* with l restarts in software packages.

7.4.2 Global k-Means: The Best Greedy Initialization

In the *global k-means*, we first choose randomly the first seed c_1, then greedily choose the seeds c_2 to c_k. Let $C_{\leq i} = \{c_1, \ldots, c_i\}$ denote the set of the first i seeds. We choose $c_i \in X$ in order to minimize $e_i(X, C_{\leq i})$ (there are only $n - i + 1$ possible choices that can be exhaustively tested). Finally, we consider for c_1 all the n potential choices $c_1 = x_1, \ldots, c_1 = x_n$, and we keep the best seed set.

7.4.3 k-Means++: A Simple Probabilistically-Guaranteed Initialization

Let us now consider a probabilistic initialization that guarantees with high probability a good initialization. Denote by $e_k^*(X) = \min_C e_k(X; C) = e_k(X, C^*)$ the global minimum value of the k-means cost, with $C^* = \mathrm{argmin}_C e_k(X; C)$. A $(1 + \epsilon)$-approximation of the k-means is defined by a set of prototypes C such that:

$$e_k^*(X) \leq e_k(X, C) \leq (1 + \epsilon)e_k^*(X).$$

In other words, the ratio $\frac{e_k(X,C)}{e_k^*(X)}$ is at most $1 + \epsilon$.

The k-means++ *initialization* choose iteratively the seeds by weighting the elements x_i's according to the squared Euclidean distance of x_i to the already chosen seeds. Let $D^2(x, C)$ denote the minimum squared Euclidean distance of x to an element of C: $D^2(x, C) = \min_{c \in C} \|x - c\|^2$.

For a weighted set X, the k-means++ initialization procedure writes as follows:

- Choose c_1 uniformly randomly in X. If we had shuffled X beforehand, we set $C_{++} = \{c_1\}$.
- For $i = 2$ to k

Draw $c_i = x \in X$ with probability:

$$p(x) = \frac{w(x)D^2(x, C_{++})}{\sum_y w(y)D^2(y, C_{++})}$$

$C_{++} \leftarrow C_{++} \cup \{c_i\}$.

Theorem 6 (k-means++ [3]) k-Means++ *probability initialization guarantee with high probability that* $\mathbb{E}[e_k(X, C_{++})] \leq 8(2 + \ln k)e_k^*(X)$.

That is, the k-means++ are $\tilde{O}(\log k)$ competitive. The notation $\tilde{O}(\cdot)$ emphasizes the fact that the analysis is probabilistic in expectation. The technical proof is reported in the paper [3]. Here, to give a flavor of the tools used in the proof, we shall give an elementary proof in the case of $k = 1$ cluster. That is, we choose randomly a point $x_0 \in X$. Let c^* denote the center of mass of X.

We have:

$$\mathbb{E}[e_1(X)] = \frac{1}{|X|} \sum_{x_0 \in X} \sum_{x \in X} \|x - x_0\|^2.$$

We shall use the following *variance-bias decomposition* for any z:

$$\sum_{x \in X} \|x - z\|^2 - \sum_{x \in X} \|x - c^*\|^2 = |X|\|c^* - z\|^2.$$

Thus we deduce that

$$\mathbb{E}[e_1(X)] = \frac{1}{|X|} \sum_{x_0 \in X} \left(\sum_{x \in X} \|x - c^*\|^2 + |X|\|x_0 - c^*\|^2 \right),$$

$$= 2 \sum_{x \in X} \|x - c^*\|^2,$$

$$= 2e_1^*(X).$$

Hence, in the case of $k = 1$ cluster, by randomly choosing the first seed c_1 uniformly in X, we guarantee in expectation a 2-approximation.

7.5 Application of k-Means to Vector Quantization (VQ)

7.5.1 Vector Quantization

In *vector quantization* (VQ for short), we are given a set $X = \{x_1, \ldots, x_n\}$ that we seek to encode with words $c_1, \ldots, c_k$. This dictionary of words is called a *codebook*. We define the encoding and decoding functions as follows:

- quantization function $i(\cdot)$: $x \in \mathbb{R}^d \to \{1, \ldots, k\}$
- decoding function: $c(\cdot)$

To compress and code a message $(t_1, \ldots, t_m)$ of m elements of an alphabet X of n characters $(t_i \in X)$, we associate to each t_i its code $i(t_i)$ via the encoding function $i(\cdot)$ that belongs to the k words of the code book. For example, we may quantize the 24-bit colors of an image (encoded using 3 color channels, 'R' for red, 'G' for green, and 'B' for blue) into k distinct color levels using vector quantization (the k-prototypes of the k-means ran on all the pixel colors). Thus instead of coding an image of dimension $m = w \times h$ pixels using $24\,m$ bits, we rather code the (R, G, B) colors of a *palette* of size k, and then encode the pixel colors using $m \times \log k$ bits (the contents of the image). Thus we save memory storage or shrink communication time for sending an image over a digital channel.

The distortion error introduced by the quantization of colors into an alphabet of k letters is $E = \frac{1}{n} \sum_{i=1}^{n} \|x - c(i(x))\|^2$, the *Mean Square Error (MSE)*.

k-Means clustering allows one to find a code book minimizing (locally) the MSE: $e_k(X, C) = v(X) - v(C)$. Here, the variance denotes the information spread, and we seek to minimize this loss of information. Indeed, we can rewrite the k-means cost function as follows:

$$e_k(X, C) = \sum_{i=1}^{n} \min_{j=1}^{k} \|x_i - c_j\|^2,$$

$$= v(X) - v(C), \text{ with } C = \{(n_j, c_j)\}_{j=1}^{k}$$

Thus, k-means can be reinterpreted as the minimization of the difference between the variances of X and its quantization by k centers C. In other words, quantization asks to minimize the difference between the variance of a discrete random variable on n letters and the variance of a discrete random variable on k letters. The variance plays the role of information, and we seek to minimize this difference of information between these two random variables. In *Information Theory* (IT), this is related to rate distortion theory.

7.5.2 Lloyd's Local Minima and Stable Voronoi Partitions

For all $x_i \in X$, we associate a *label* in $\mathbb{N}$:

$$l_C(x) = \arg\min_{j \in \{1,\dots,k\}} \|x - c_j\|^2$$

We can extend this labeling function to the full space $\mathbb{X}$, and we obtain a partition of $\mathbb{X}$ called a *Voronoi diagram*. This partition of space is illustrated in Fig. 7.6. A *Voronoi cell* V_j of the Voronoi diagram is defined by:

$$V_j = \left\{ x \in \mathbb{R}^d \; : \; \|x - c_j\| \leq \|x - c_l\| \; \forall l \in \{1, \dots, n\} \right\}.$$

Here, let us remark that the squared Euclidean distance or the ordinary Euclidean distance yields to the same Voronoi diagram that decomposes the space into proximity cells. In fact, Voronoi cells do not change if we apply any strictly monotonous function on the base distance. The square function is such an example of a monotonous function on $\mathbb{R}_+$.

Now, let us note that once Lloyd's k-means heuristic has converged, the cluster groups G_i make a Voronoi partition, and have the *convex hulls* (co) of their groups pairwise disjoint: $\forall i \neq j, \quad \mathrm{co}(G_i) \cap \mathrm{co}(G_j) = \emptyset$ where:

$$\mathrm{co}(X) = \{x : x = \sum_{x_i \in X} \lambda_i x_i, \sum_{i=1}^{n} \lambda_i = 1, \lambda_i \geq 0\}.$$

Fig. 7.6 Voronoi diagram induced by k centers C, called generators, and Voronoi partition of X induced by C

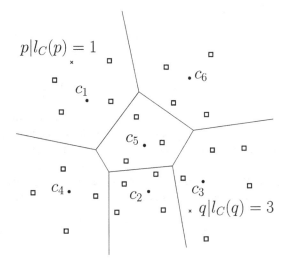

$p | l_C(p) = 1$

7.6 A Physical Interpretation of k-Means: The Inertia Decomposition

Let us consider $X = \{(x_i, w_i)\}_i$ as n body masses located at positions x_i's with respective weights w_i's. In Physics, the concept of *inertia* measures the resistance of a body when we move it around a given point. We measure the *total inertia* $I(X)$ of a point cloud X as the sum of squared Euclidean distances of points of X with respect to its center of mass $c = \sum_{i=1}^{k} w_i x_i$:

$$I(X) := \sum_{i=1}^{n} w_i \|x_i - c\|^2.$$

Thus, when we increase the masses on points, inertia increases too (i.e., it becomes more difficult to rotate the point set around its center of mass). Similarly, when we consider points getting farther away of the center of mass, it also becomes harder to rotation this point cloud around its center of mass c. Therefore k-means can be reinterpreted physically as the task to identify k groups such that the sum of inertia of these groups with respect to their barycenters is minimal. *Huygens' formula* report an invariant or a mathematical identity between the total inertia of the system and its decomposition into the sum of the intra-group inertia plus the inertia of the inter-groups:

Theorem 7 (Huygens' formula: Inertia decomposition) *The total inertia* $I(X) = \sum_{i=1}^{n} w_i \|x_i - \bar{x}\|^2$ *equals to* $I_{\text{intra}}(G) + I_{\text{inter}}(C)$ *with the intra-group inertia* $I_{\text{intra}}(G) = \sum_{i=1}^{k} I(G_i) = \sum_{i=1}^{k} \sum_{x_j \in \mathcal{G}_i} w_j \|x_j - c_i\|^2$ *and the inter-group inertia* $I_{\text{inter}}(C) = \sum_{i=1}^{k} W_i \|c_i - c\|^2$ *(a unique centroid c) with* $W_i = \sum_{x \in G_i} w(x)$.

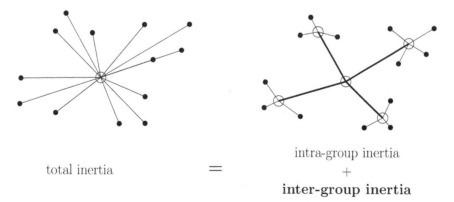

total inertia   =   intra-group inertia
                                      +
                                      inter-group inertia

Fig. 7.7 The total inertia of a system of point masses is invariant by group decomposition. k-Means optimizes the decomposition that minimizes the intra-group inertia

Figure 7.7 illustrates two decompositions of inertia that have the same total inertia. Since the total inertia is invariant, minimizing the intra-group inertia amounts to maximize the inter-group inertia.

7.7 Choosing k in k-Means: Model Selection

Until so far, we have considered that the number of clusters k was prescribed, and known beforehand. This is not true in practice when one performs exploratory data analysis, and k has to be guessed as well. Finding the right value of k is an important problem referred to as *model selection* in the literature. For any value of k, we can consider the optimal k-means cost function $e_k^*(X)$ (that can be estimated empirically in practice, say using Lloyd's heuristics on several initializations). Let us notice that $e_k(X)$ decreases monotonically until reaching $e_n(X) = 0$ (in that case, each point is trivially allocated to its own cluster).

7.7.1 Model Selection via the Elbow Method

To choose a correct value for k, one can use the so-called *elbow method*. This is a visual procedure: First, we plot the function $(k, e_k(X))$ for $k \in [n] = \{1, \ldots, n\}$, and we choose k that defines the inflexion point: the elbow (separating the forearm from the arm). The reason to choose this value of k is that for small k values, the sum of cluster variances decreases quickly and then starting from some value, the sum of variances describes *a plateau*. This visual inspection method is called the "elbow method" because the function $f(k) = e_k(X)$ looks like an arm on practical data-sets (with the plateau being the forearm): The elbow returns the optimal number of clusters (Fig. 7.8). One drawback of this method is that it is computationally very expensive, and sometimes (depending on the data-sets), the inflexion point between the sharp decrease and the plateau is not so well defined!

7.7.2 Model Selection: Explaining Variance Reduction with k

We calculate the *proportion of variance* that is explained by k classes:

$$R^2(k) = \frac{I_{\text{inter}}(k)}{I_{\text{total}}}.$$

We have $0 < R^2(k) \leq 1$. We then choose k^* that minimizes the ratio $\frac{R^2(k)}{R^2(k+1)}$:

$$k^* = \arg\min_k \left(\frac{R^2(k)}{R^2(k+1)} \right).$$

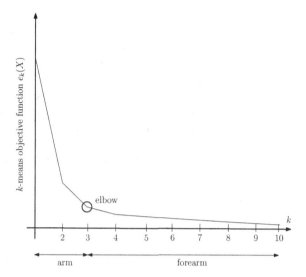

Fig. 7.8 Choosing k with the elbow method: the elbow defines the value of k that separates the area of high decrease (the arm) to the plateau area (the forearm)

We have presented two essential methods to choose the right value of k, the number of clusters. In machine learning, k denotes the *complexity of the model*, and choosing k is therefore called the *model selection* problem. There exists some algorithms that perform clustering without requiring to know beforehand k. For example, *affinity propagation* [4] is such a popular algorithm, or a fast convex relaxation minimization of k-means [5].

7.8 Parallel k-Means Clustering on a Cluster of Machines

There are many ways to design a parallel version of Lloyd's k-means heuristic on a cluster of computers: That is, on a set of interconnected machines that we consider as a "super-computer" with distributed memory (one local memory for each machine). As usual, for sake of simplicity, we consider that each computer has a single processing core (a processing unit) and associates a node to each machine to describe the communication links by a graph. Those different processors communicate with each other by sending and receiving messages using the MPI interface: The *Message Passing Interface*. Sending a message has a communication cost that is split into two terms: one for the latency of initialization the communication and one that is proportional to the length of the message. Sending structured data requires first to *serialize* it into a universal "string" before sending (encoding) at the sender node and to reconstruct it (de-serialize the string to reconstruct the structure) at the receiver node.

A k-means clustering problem can be characterized by the number of attributes (that is, the dimension of the data point cloud), the number of data elements n, and the number of clusters, k. We consider $k \ll n$ (that is, $k = o(n)$) so that all cluster centers requiring a memory space $O(dk)$ can be stored into the local memory of each machine. Since in practice the memory (RAM) is fixed (that is, $O(1)$), that means that we consider theoretically the special case of $k = O(1)$ here. However, the number of elements n is considered (very) large compared to k, so that the full data-set X need to be distributed among the P processors (since X cannot be fully contained in the RAM of a single computer).

In order to design a simple but efficient parallel k-means heuristic, we rely on the following composability/decomposability theorem:

Theorem 8 (Composability of barycenters) *Let X_1 and X_2 be two weighted data-sets with respective overall weights $W_1 > 0$ and $W_2 > 0$. We have:*

$$\boxed{\bar{x}(X_1 \cup X_2) = \frac{W_1}{W_1 + W_2}\bar{x}(X_1) + \frac{W_2}{W_1 + W_2}\bar{x}(X_2)}$$

where $\bar{x}(X_i)$ denotes the barycenter for X_i, for $i \in \{1, 2\}$.

This property turns out to be essential for distributed the centroid computation on a partition of X into P subsets $X_1, \ldots, X_P$ where P is the number of processors (or machines of the cluster). The parallel algorithm is described in pseudo-code in Algorithm 5.

At run time, each processor knows the overall number of processors of the cluster, P, by using the function MPI_Comm_size(), and its rank number indexed between 0 and $P - 1$ by using the standard MPI function MPI_Comm_rank(). It is the task of processor P_0 (the root machine) to initialize the k cluster prototypes and to broadcast them to all other processors using the primitive MPI_Bcast(C, root processor). Then we loop until convergence using a while structure: Each processor P_l computes the labeling of its group of data X_l, and the cumulative sum of the vectors of the k groups corresponding to P_l with the local cardinality of each cluster. Then we aggregate and broadcast all those group cardinals using the MPI primitive MPI_Allreduce. The aggregation operation (that is associative and commutative) can be chosen among a set of binary operators like $+$ or min, etc. We specify this binary operation as an argument of the MPI primitive MPI_Allreduce: Here, it is MPI_SUM to indicate the cumulative sum operation. Since some clusters in some partial data-sets associated to machines may be empty, we take of those cases when computing the local centroids (see the $\max(n_j, 1)$ operation in Algorithm 5).

A complete source code using the C API of OpenMPI is syntactically different from the Algorithm 5 written in the pseudo-code as the arguments in the MPI primitives ask for the length of the message, the type of data to be communicated, etc.

```
/* Distributed k-means clustering in MPI                    */
p = MPI_Comm_size();
r = MPI_Comm_rank();
previousMSE = 0;
/* Mean Square Error, the cost function for the k-means      */
MSE = ∞;
if r = 0 then
    /* Initialize randomly the cluster seeds               */
    Initialize C = (c₁, ..., cₖ);
    MPI_Bcast(C, 0);
end
while MSE ≠ previousMSE do
    previousMSE = MSE;
    MSE' = 0;
    for j = 1 to k do
        m'ⱼ = 0;
        n'ⱼ = 0;
    end
    for i = r(n/p) to (r + 1)(n/p) - 1 do
        for j = 1 to k do
            Calculate dᵢ,ⱼ = d²(xᵢ, mⱼ) = ‖xᵢ - mⱼ‖²;
        end
        Find the closest centroid mₗ to xᵢ: l = arg minⱼ dᵢ,ⱼ;
        /* Update stage                                     */
        m'ₗ = m'ₗ + xᵢ;
        n'ₗ = n'ₗ + 1;
        MSE' = MSE' + d²(xᵢ, mₗ);
    end
    /* Aggregate: make use of the composability property of
       centroids                                            */
    for j = 1 to k do
        MPI_Allreduce(n'ⱼ, nⱼ, MPI_SUM);
        MPI_Allreduce(m'ⱼ, mⱼ, MPI_SUM);
        /* To prevent dividing by zero                      */
        nⱼ = max(nⱼ, 1);
        mⱼ = mⱼ/nⱼ;
    end
    /* Update the cost function                             */
    MPI_Allreduce(MSE', MSE, MPI_SUM);
end
```

Algorithm 5: Lloyd's parallel k-means heuristic using MPI.

In this distributed implementation of k-means, we optimize the sequential code by an optimal speed-up P.

7.9　Evaluating Clustering Partitions

In order to evaluate the performances of the various clustering techniques (like the various k-means local/global heuristics), it is important to have *ground-truth data-sets* that tell us for each data element is true cluster membership. Without these ground-truth data sets, we could only perform a subjective or qualitative evaluation of the clustering methods. Although that in 2D, Human eyes can amazingly evaluate whether the obtained clustering is good or not, it becomes impossible to visualize in dimensions $d > 3$.

When ground-truth data-sets are available (say, data-sets annotated by experts), we can compute various metrics that are quantitative values that measure the *similarity of two partitions*: the one induced by the labels in the ground-truth data-set (assumed to be the optimal clustering by definition!) and the one reported by an automatic clustering algorithm.

7.9.1　The Rand Index

The *Rand index* (1971) computes the similarity of two partitions as follows: Let $G = \uplus G_i$ and $G' = \uplus G'_i$ be the cluster decomposition of the k-means heuristic and of the ground-truth data-set, respectively.

We compare all the $\binom{n}{2}$ pairs (x_i, x_j) of points, and count those that belong to the same cluster (a) from those that are found to belong to different clusters (b). Thus we obtain the Rand index that belongs to the interval $[0, 1]$:

$$\text{Rand}(G, G') = \frac{a + b}{\binom{n}{2}}$$

with

- a: $\#\{(i, j)\ :\ l(x_i) = l(x_j) \land l'(x_i) = l'(x_j)\}$,
- b: $\#\{(i, j)\ :\ l(x_i) \neq l(x_j) \land l'(x_i) \neq l'(x_j)\}$,

where $l(\text{cot})$ and $l'(\text{cot})$ are the two cluster labeling functions of the ground-truth clustering and the automatic clustering.

Notation: $\text{condition}_1 \land \text{condition}_2$ denotes that both conditions have to be true in order to be true (logic AND operator). Let us remark that the Rand index avoids us to relabel the k groups in order to make the two partitions compatible with each other: Indeed, there are $k!$ such permutation relabeling that we should take into account otherwise, and it is therefore not computationally-tractable (since $k!$ grows exponentially with k) to consider them in practice! A more sophisticated implementation of the Rand index often used in practice is called the *adjusted Rand index* [6].

7.9.2 Normalized Mutual Information (NMI)

The *Normalized Mutual Information* (*NMI*) is a notion that is well-defined in Information Theory. Let $n_{j,j'} = \{x \in G_j \ \wedge \ x \in G'_{j'}\}$. Then the NMI is defined as:

$$\mathrm{NMI}(G, G') = \frac{\sum_j^k \sum_{j'}^{k'} n_{j,j'} \log \frac{n \times n_{j,j'}}{n_j n_{j'}}}{\sqrt{\left(\sum_j^k n_j \log \frac{n_j}{n}\right)\left(\sum_{j'}^{k'} n'_j \log \frac{n'_j}{n}\right)}}$$

NMI is an estimation of the information-theoretic quantity:

$$\frac{I(X; Y)}{\sqrt{H(X)H(Y)}},$$

where $I(X; Y)$ denotes the *mutual information* between two random variables, and $H(\cdot)$ denotes the *Shannon entropy* of a random variable.

7.10 Notes and References

We described a way to cluster data by minimizing a cost function: the sum of intra-cluster variances of the k clusters. Historically, the methodology of the k-means has been first introduced by Hugo Steinhaus [7] (by studying the inertia of a body), and has been rediscovered many times independently later on (like in vector quantization, VQ), etc. In this chapter, we have described the usual k-means techniques. A full description of k-means requires its own textbook! Depending on the cost function, one can obtain more or less efficient optimization algorithms, and the obtained clustering can be more or less adapted to the data-sets. In fact, when one describes axiomatically the properties of a good clustering, it can be shown that there *does not* exist any cost function to optimize that fulfills those properties [8] (see also [9, 10]).

Lloyd's batched heuristic has been first reported in details in [11]. In practice, Hartigan's single-swap heuristic (described in the Sect. 7.12) is getting again more and more popular since it is more efficient and provably reaches better local minima than Lloyd's method. The k-means++ probabilistic initialization dates back from 2007. A deterministic initialization for k-means is described in [12]: One get a $(1 + \epsilon)$-approximation in time $O(\epsilon^{-2k^2 d} n \log^k n)$. Among the NP-hard problems, k-means is rather "easy" to approximate because it admits a *Polynomial Time Approximation Scheme* (or *PTAS* for short) [13]: That is, for any $\epsilon > 0$, one gets a $(1 + \epsilon)$-approximation of the k-means cost function in polynomial time.

Fig. 7.9 Example of a
data-set for which k-means
fails to cluster appropriately
into two clusters. Indeed,
k-means is limited to report
Voronoi partitions with
disjoint group convex hull. In
practice, such a data-set is
clustered using a kernel
method

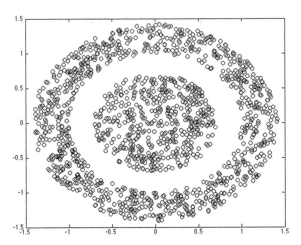

k-Means have been reported on a distributed memory parallel architecture using
the MPI interface in [14]. Lloyd's heuristic is updating the point assignment to clusters
at each stage (batched k-means): one can also update after each point relocation by
considering the points one by one. This is precisely the MacQueen's heuristic [15]
that is mentioned in Sect. 7.12. k-Means++ is intrinsically a sequential algorithm
and its generalization to parallel architectures, termed k-means||, has been proposed
in [16]. Nowadays, with the wide availability of big size data-sets, one even seeks to
cluster large data-sets with billions (k) of clusters [17]. The *core-sets* approximation
techniques [18] allows one to reduce very large data-sets into tiny data-sets by trading
the exact cost function minimization by a controlled approximation of it. Another
construction method of such core-sets in parallel has been reported in [19]. Another
hot topic in data clustering is to be able to cluster data among different entities
while preserving the privacy of data elements. In [20], a method is given to perform
privacy-preserving data clustering on *vertically partitioned data*[8] with Lloyd's k-
means heuristic.

We have emphasized on the fact that the k-means objective function seek to detect
globular-shaped clusters. Although the k-means is often used in practice, it is not (by
far!) a universal solution for clustering. For example, Fig. 7.9 depicts a data-set that is
easy to cluster by Human eye-brain systems; However, the k-means optimization will
not obtain a desired partitioning. This is because k-means report Voronoi partitions
However, this kind of data-set is handled using kernel[9] k-means [21].

---

[8] Vertical partitioning means that each entity has only a block of attributes.

[9] It is mathematically always possible to separate data by increasing by lifting the features into
higher dimensions using a *kernel mapping*.

7.11 Summary

Exploratory data analysis consists in finding structures in data-sets that bring knowledge of these data-sets. Clustering is a set of techniques that partitions data into homogeneous groups, and thus allows one to discover classes, with potential semantic meaning for each class. Clustering by k-means asks to minimize the weighted sum of intra-cluster variances by assigning to each group a center: its prototype that plays the role of the model for that cluster. That is, k-means clustering belongs to the family of *model-based clustering*. Minimizing the k-means objective function is a NP-hard problem in general, and the celebrated Lloyd's heuristic consists in repeating until convergence the following two steps: (1) assignment of data points to their closest cluster center, and (2) update the cluster centers by setting the centers (prototypes) to their cluster centroids. Lloyd's heuristic is guaranteed to converge monotonically to a local minimum that is characterized by a Voronoi partition induced by the cluster centers. Since we do not know a priori the number of clusters k, we need to estimate it by performing a *model selection*: a usual rule of thumb consists in choosing the value of k that minimizes the ratio of the sum of intra-cluster variances for k and $k + 1$, and that can be visually interpreted as the elbow (hence the name, elbow method), the inflexion point in the graph plot of the cost function $e_k(\cdot)$. Lloyd's k-means can be easily parallelized on a distributed memory architecture by using the MPI interface and by using the *decomposition property of centroids*: The centroid (or barycenter) of a data set partitioned into groups amounts to equivalently compute the barycenter of the centroids (or barycenters) of the groups.

Processing Code for Lloyd's k-Means Algorithm

Figure 7.10 displays a snapshot of the `processing.org` program.

> WWW source code: `kmeansLloydProcessing.pde`

7.12 Exercises

Exercise 1 (*Barycenter and variance with non-normalized positive weights*)

- For a positive vector $w = (w_1, \ldots, w_n) \in \mathbb{R}_+^d$ (not normalized to one) on data-set $X = \{x_1, \ldots, x_n\}$, prove that weighted sum of squared Euclidean distance to the center $\sum_{i=1}^n w_i \|x_i - c\|^2$ is minimized for the barycenter $\bar{x}$:

$$\bar{x} = \sum_{i=1}^n \frac{w_i}{W} x_i,$$

where $W = \sum_{i=1}^n w_i$ is the total sum of weights and that the non-normalized variance can be written as:

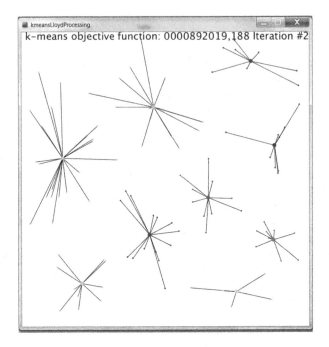

Fig. 7.10 Snapshot of the `processing` code for Lloyd's k-means heuristic

$$v(X, w) = \sum_{i=1}^{n} w_i \|x_i - \bar{x}\|^2 = \sum_{i=1}^{n} w_i \|x_i\|^2 - W\bar{x}^2.$$

- Observe that this formula amounts to take normalized weights $\tilde{w}_i = \frac{w_i}{W}$ in the classic (normalized weight) formula.
- What happens when some weights are negative? Can we still guarantee the uniqueness of the minimizer?
- Deduce the composability formula of barycenters: Let $\{X_i\}_{i \in \{1,...,k\}}$ be k weighted data-sets with respective total weights W_i. Prove that:

$$\bar{x}(\uplus_{i=1}^{k} X_i) = \sum_{i=1}^{k} \frac{W_i}{\sum_{j=1}^{k} W_j} \bar{x}(X_i),$$

where $\bar{x}(X_i)$ are the barycenters of the X_i's.

Exercise 2 (*Center of mass for scalars* $(d = 1)$) Prove that the *arithmetic mean* $c = \frac{1}{n} \sum_{i=1}^{n} x_i$ is also an equilibrium centers since we have the following property:

$$\sum_{x_i < c} (c - x_i) = \sum_{x_i \geq c} (x_i - c).$$

Exercise 3 (*Bias-variance decomposition*) Let $v(X, z) = \sum_{x \in X} \|x - z\|^2$ and $v(X) = v(X, \bar{x})$ with $\bar{x} = \frac{1}{n} \sum_i x_i$.

- Prove that $v(X, z) = v(X) + n\|\bar{x} - z\|^2$. Deduce that the center of mass $\bar{x}$ minimizes $v(X, z)$.
- Generalize this decomposition to weighted point sets $X = \{(x_i, w_i)\}_i$.
- Interpret X as a discrete random variable, and prove the bias-variance decomposition formula for an arbitrary random variable.

Exercise 4 (*k-Medoids (as known as discrete k-means)*) Let us minimize the k-means cost function by constraining the prototypes c_j to belong to the data-elements, the x_i's.

- Prove using the bias-variance decomposition that the best cost of the *k-medoids* is at most twice the best cost of k-means.
- Deduce a heuristic for the k-means where prototype are constrained to belong to the initial data-set (batched assignment).
- Provide an upper bound on the maximal number of iterations of your heuristic.

Exercise 5 (*Intra-cluster distance minimization and inter-cluster distance maximization*) Let $X = \{x_1, \ldots, x_n\}$ be a data-set of n elements (quantitative or categorical attributes), and $D(x_i, x_j) \geq 0$ a dissimilarity function between any two arbitrary elements $x_i \in X$ and $x_j \in X$. Prove that for a given partition of X into k clusters $C_1, \ldots, C_k$ that minimizing the intra-cluster pairwise distances $\sum_{l=1}^{k} \sum_{x_i \in C_l} \sum_{x_j \in C_l} D(x_i, x_j)$ is equivalent to maximize the pairwise inter-cluster distances $\sum_{l=1}^{k} \sum_{x_i \in C_l} \sum_{x_j \notin C_l} D(x_i, x_j)$. For categorical attribute data-sets, one can consider the *Jaccard distance*, $D(x_i, x_j) = \frac{|x_i \cap x_j|}{x_i \cup x_j}$, and cluster with the k-medoid technique described in the Sect. 7.12.

Exercise 6 (*MacQueen's local k-means heuristic [15]*) *MacQueen's local k-means heuristic* updates iteratively the cluster prototypes by assigning the points one by one to clusters until it converges:

- Initialize $c_j = x_j$ for $j = 1, \ldots, k$
- Assign incrementally data elements $x_1, \ldots, x_n$ in a cyclic sequence until convergence: Assign x_i to its nearest cluster center c_j of C, and update this center: we remove x_i from its current center and assign it to its new center.

- Prove the following update formula:

$$c_{l(x_i)} \leftarrow \frac{n_{l(x_i)} c_{l(x_i)} - x_i}{n_{l(x_i)} - 1}, \quad n_{l(x_i)} \leftarrow n_{l(x_i)} - 1$$

$$l(x_i) = \operatorname{argmin}_j \|x_i - c_j\|^2$$

$$c_{l(x_i)} \leftarrow \frac{n_{l(x_i)} c_{l(x_i)} + x_i}{n_{l(x_i)} - 1}, \quad n_{l(x_i)} \leftarrow n_{l(x_i)} + 1$$

- Prove that local minima match the local minima of Lloyd's batched k-means.
- What is the complexity of MacQueen's heuristic?

Exercise 7 (*Hartigan's k-means heuristic: Swap a point from a cluster to another cluster* [22]) We propose the following iterative k-means local heuristic: Consider in a cyclic order the elements x_i, one by one. For a given x_i currently belonging to cluster $G_{l(x_i)}$ with $l(x_i) = \text{argmin}_{j\in\{1,\dots,k\}}\|x_i - c_j\|^2$ its membership, we move x_i into another cluster G_l iff. the k-means cost function decreases.

1. Write mathematically $\Delta(x_i, l)$: the gain of the cost function when x_i is swapped from $G_{l(x_i)}$ to G_l. For x_i being swapped from a source cluster G_s to a target cluster G_t, prove the following formula:

$$\Delta(x_i; s \to t) = \frac{n_t}{n_t + 1}\|c_t - x_i\|^2 - \frac{n_s}{n_s - 1}\|c_s - x_i\|^2$$

2. Prove that Hartigan's local minima are a proper subset of Lloyd's local minima.
3. Give in pseudo-code the Hartigan's k-means local heuristic. What is the complexity of this algorithm?
4. Observe that this heuristic always guarantees non-empty clusters at any time (and behaves differently from Lloyd's heuristic that may procedure empty cluster exceptions).

Exercise 8 (Horizontally versus vertically separated *k-means parallel clustering* [20]) Consider clustering n data of d attributes using a cluster of P machines. Assume that $d \gg n$ and propose a parallel implementation of the k-means algorithm by distributing the features among the machines (thus a portion of each datum is stored on each machine). Compare your *vertically separated* implementation of k-means with the *horizontally separated* parallel k-means (when data elements are partitioned and distributed among the machines).

Exercise 9 (**k-Means clustering with Bregman divergences* [23]) The k-means cost function can be generalized to *Bregman divergences* as follows: $e_k(X, G) = \sum_{i=1}^{n} \min_{j\in\{1,\dots,k\}} D_F(x_i, c_j)$. Bregman divergences are defined for a strictly convex and differentiable generator $F(x)$ by:

$$D_F(x, y) = F(x) - F(y) - (x - y)^\top \nabla F(y),$$

where $\nabla F(y) = (\frac{d}{dy^1} F(y), \dots, \frac{d}{dy^d} F(y))$ denotes the gradient operator (vector of partial derivatives).

1. Prove that the squared Euclidean distance is a Bregman divergence but not the Euclidean distance.
2. Prove that the minimizer of $\min_c \sum_{i=1}^{n} w_i D_F(x_i, c)$ is the barycenter $\bar{x} = \sum_{i=1}^{n} w_i x_i$. (In fact, one can prove that the only distortion measures that ensure barycenters as minimizers are the Bregman divergences.)

3. Deduce the corresponding Bregman batches k-means and Bregman Hartigan's k-means heuristics.
4. Prove that the composability property of barycenters still holds for Bregman divergences.

Exercise 10 (*k-Modes* [24]) To cluster categorical data (that is, non-numerical data), one can use the *Hamming distance* between any two d-dimensional attribute vectors x and y: $D_H(x, y) = \sum_{j=1}^{d} 1_{x^j \neq y^j}$ where $1_{a \neq b} = 1$ iff. $a \neq b$ and zero otherwise. Hamming distance is a metric satisfying the triangular inequality. Let $t_{l,m}$ be the mth category of the lth dimension of an element.

1. Prove that the mode $m = (m^1, \ldots, m^d)$ with $m^j = t_{j,m^*}$ and $m^* = \text{argmax}_m \#$ $\{x_i^j = t_{j,m}\}$ maximizes $\sum_{i=1}^{n} w_i D_H(x_i, m)$ where $\#\{\cdot\}$ denotes the cardinality of a data-set. That is, in other words, for each dimension, we choose the dominant category for the mode.
2. Prove that the barycenter may not be necessarily unique by reporting a counter example.
3. Design a *k-mode clustering heuristic* that is inspired from k-means heuristics, and show how one can use it to cluster a collection of text documents.
4. Show how to combine k-means and k-modes to cluster mixed attribute vectors (with some dimensions being numerical, and some other dimensions categorical).

Exercise 11 (*Hegselmann-Krause model for opinion dynamics* [25]) Consider a set of n individuals $p_1, \ldots, p_n$, represented as points of the d-dimensional space $\mathbb{R}^d$. At a given iteration, each individual updates its position as the center of mass of all individuals falling within a distance less than a prescribed threshold r (say, radius $r = 1$; thus including itself too), and repeat this process until convergence (when individuals do not move anymore). At convergence, there are at most $k \leq n$ distinct individuals (distinct opinions). Implement in MPI this algorithm. What is the complexity of your algorithm? How does this algorithm differ from the Lloyd's k-means algorithm?

Exercise 12 (**Barycenters for an arbitrary convex distance*) Let $D(\cdot, \cdot)$ be a strictly convex and twice differentiable distance function (not necessarily symmetric nor satisfying the triangular inequality). We define the barycenter $\bar{x}$ of a weighted point cloud $X = \{(x_i, w_i)\}_i$ as the minimizer of $\bar{x} = \arg\min_c \sum_{i=1}^{n} w_i D(x_i, c)$.

• Prove that this barycenter is unique.
• Provide a geometric interpretation when zeroing the gradient $\nabla_c(\sum_{i=1}^{n} w_i D(x_i, c))$: The barycenter is the unique point that cancels the vector field $V(x) = \sum_{i=1}^{n} w_i \nabla_x D(x_i, x)$.

Exercise 13 (**$1D$ k-means using dynamic programming* [26]) Although that k-means in a NP-hard problem, in 1D, one can get a polynomial-time algorithm using dynamic programming. First, one starts by sorting the n scalars of $X = \{x_1, \ldots, x_n\}$ in increasing order, in $O(n \log n)$ time. Therefore we assume that $x_1 \leq \cdots \leq x_n$.

- We seek for a relationship between the optimal clustering for k clusters from the optimal clustering for $k - 1$ clusters. Let $X_{i,j} = \{x_i, \ldots, x_j\}$ denote the subset of scalars $x_i, \ldots, x_j$. Write the mathematical recurrence equation of the best clustering $e_k(X_{1,n})$ using the terms $e_{k-1}(X_{1,j-1})$ and $e_1(X_{j,n})$.
- Show how to find the optimal partition from the dynamic programming table using backtracking. What is the complexity of your algorithm?
- By preprocessing the n scalars into three cumulative sums $\sum_{l=1}^{j} w_l$, $\sum_{l=1}^{j} w_l x_i$ and $\sum_{l=1}^{j} w_l x_i^2$, show how to calculate $v(X_{i,j}) = \sum_{l=i}^{j} w_i \|x_l - \bar{x}_{i,j}\|$ in constant time, where $\bar{x}_{i,j} = \frac{1}{\sum_{l=i}^{j} w_l} \sum_{l=i}^{j} w_l x_l$. Deduce that an optimal k-means partitioning can be exactly calculated in 1D in $O(n^2 k)$ time.

References

1. Vattani, A.: k-means requires exponentially many iterations even in the plane. Discret. Comput. Geom. **45**(4), 596–616 (2011)
2. Har-Peled, S., Sadri, B.: How fast is the k-means method? Algorithmica **41**(3), 185–202 (2005)
3. Arthur, D., Vassilvitskii, S.: k-means++: The advantages of careful seeding. In: Proceedings of the Eighteenth Annual ACM-SIAM Symposium on Discrete Algorithms, pp. 1027–1035. Society for Industrial and Applied Mathematics, USA (2007)
4. Frey, B.J., Dueck, D.: Clustering by passing messages between data points. Science **315**, 972–976 (2007)
5. Lashkari, D., Golland, P.: Convex clustering with exemplar-based models. In: Advances in Neural Information Processing Systems, pp. 825–832 (2007)
6. Hubert, L., Arabie, P.: Comparing partitions. J. classif. **2**(1), 193–218 (1985)
7. Steinhaus, H.: Sur la division des corps matériels en parties. Bull. Acad. Polon. Sci. Cl. **III**(4), 801–804 (1956)
8. Kleinberg, J.: An impossibility theorem for clustering. In: Becker, S., Thrun, S., Obermayer, K. (eds.) Advances in Neural Information Processing Systems, pp. 446–453. MIT Press, USA (2002)
9. Zadeh, R., Ben-David, S.: A uniqueness theorem for clustering. In: Bilmes, J., Ng, A.Y. (eds) Uncertainty in Artificial Intelligence (UAI), pp. 639–646. Association for Uncertainty in Artificial Intelligence (AUAI) Press, USA (2009)
10. Carlsson, G., Mémoli, F.: Characterization, stability and convergence of hierarchical clustering methods. J. Mach. Learn. Res. (JMLR) **11**, 1425–1470 (2010)
11. Lloyd, S.P.: Least squares quantization in PCM. IEEE Trans. Inf. Theory, IT-28(2):129–137, Mar (1982). First appeared as a technical report in 1957
12. Matousek, J.: On approximate geometric k-clustering. Discret. Comput. Geom. **24**(1), 61–84 (2000)
13. Awasthi, P., Blum, A., Sheffet, O.: Stability yields a PTAS for k-median and k-means clustering. In: FOCS, pp. 309–318. IEEE Computer Society, USA (2010)
14. Dhillon, I.S., Modha, D.S.: A data-clustering algorithm on distributed memory multiprocessors. In: Revised Papers from Large-Scale Parallel Data Mining, Workshop on Large-Scale Parallel KDD Systems, SIGKDD, pp. 245–260, Springer, London (2000)
15. James, B.: MacQueen. Some methods of classification and analysis of multivariate observations. In: Le Cam, L.M., Neyman, J. (eds.) Proceedings of the Fifth Berkeley Symposium on Mathematical Statistics and Probability. University of California Press, Berkeley (1967)
16. Bahmani, B., Moseley, B., Vattani, A., Kumar, R., Vassilvitskii, S.: Scalable k-means+. In: Proceedings of the VLDB Endowment **5**(7) (2012)

17. Babenko, A., Lempitsky, V.S.: Improving bilayer product quantization for billion-scale approximate nearest neighbors in high dimensions. CoRR, abs/1404.1831, 2014
18. Feldman, D., Schmidt, M., Sohler, C.: Turning big data into tiny data: Constant-size coresets for k-means, PCA and projective clustering. In: Symposium on Discrete Algorithms (SODA), pp. 1434–1453 (2013)
19. Balcan, M-F., Ehrlich, S., Liang, Y.: Distributed k-means and k-median clustering on general topologies. In: Advances in Neural Information Processing Systems, pp. 1995–2003 (2013)
20. Vaidya, J., Clifton, C.: Privacy-preserving k-means clustering over vertically partitioned data. In: Proceedings of the Ninth ACM SIGKDD International Conference on Knowledge Discovery and Data Mining, pp. 206–215, ACM, New York (2003)
21. Dhillon, I.S., Guan, Y., Kulis, B.: Kernel k-means: spectral clustering and normalized cuts. In: Proceedings of the Tenth ACM SIGKDD International Conference on Knowledge Discovery and Data Mining, KDD '04, pp. 551–556, ACM, New York (2004)
22. Telgarsky, M., Vattani, A.: Hartigan's method: k-means clustering without Voronoi. In: International Conference on Artificial Intelligence and Statistics, pp. 820–827 (2010)
23. Banerjee, A., Merugu, S., Inderjit S.D., Joydeep G.: Clustering with Bregman divergences. J. Mach. Learn. Res. **6**, 1705–1749 (2005)
24. Huang, Z.: Extensions to the k-means algorithm for clustering large data sets with categorical values. Data Min. Knowl. Discov. **2**(3), 283–304 (1998)
25. Hegselmann, R., Krause, U.: Opinion dynamics and bounded confidence models, analysis, and simulation. J. Artif. Soc. Soc. Simul. (JASSS), **5**(3) (2002)
26. Nielsen, F., Nock, R.: Optimal interval clustering: Application to Bregman clustering and statistical mixture learning. IEEE Signal Process. Lett. **21**(10), 1289–1292 (2014)

Chapter 8
Hierarchical Clustering

8.1 Agglomerative Versus Divisive Hierarchical Clustering, and Dendrogram Representations

Hierarchical clustering is yet another technique for performing data exploratory analysis. It is an unsupervised technique. In the former clustering chapter, we have described at length a technique to partition a data-set $X = \{x_1, \ldots, x_n\}$ into a collection of groups called clusters $X = \uplus_{i=1}^{k} G_i$ by minimizing the k-means objective function (i.e., the weighted sum of cluster intra-variances): in that case, we dealt with flat clustering that delivers a non-hierarchical partition structure of the data-set. To contrast with this flat clustering technique, we cover in this chapter another widely used clustering technique: namely, *hierarchical clustering*.

Hierarchical clustering consists in building a binary merge tree, starting from the data elements stored at the leaves (interpreted as singleton sets) and proceed by merging two by two the "closest" sub-sets (stored at nodes) until we reach the root of the tree that contains all the elements of X. We denote by $\Delta(X_i, X_j)$ the distance between any two sub-sets of X, called the *linkage distance*. This technique is also called *agglomerative hierarchical clustering* since we start from the leaves storing singletons (the x_i's) and merge iteratively subsets until we reach the root.

The graphical representation of this binary merge tree is called a *dendrogram*. This word stems from the greek *dendron* that means *tree* and *gramma* the means *draw*. For example, to draw a dendrogram, we can draw an internal node $s(X')$ containing a subset $X' \subseteq X$ at height $h(X') = |X'|$, where $|\cdot|$ denotes the cardinality of X', that is, its number of elements. We then draw edges between this node $s(X')$ and its two sibling nodes $s(X_1)$ and $s(X_2)$ with $X' = X_1 \cup X_2$ (and $X_1 \cap X_2 = \emptyset$). Figure 8.1 depicts conceptually the process of drawing a dendrogram. There exists several ways to visualize the hierarchical structures obtained by hierarchical clustering. For example, we may use special Venn diagrams using nested convex bodies, as depicted in Fig. 8.2.

Figure 8.3 shows such an example of a dendrogram that has been drawn from a agglomerative hierarchical clustering computed on a data-set provided in the free

© Springer International Publishing Switzerland 2016
F. Nielsen, *Introduction to HPC with MPI for Data Science*, Undergraduate
Topics in Computer Science, DOI 10.1007/978-3-319-21903-5_8

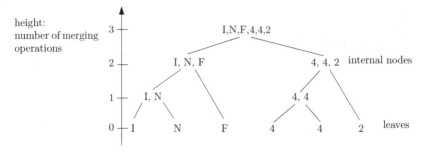

Fig. 8.1 Drawing a dendrogram by embedding the nodes on the plane using a height function

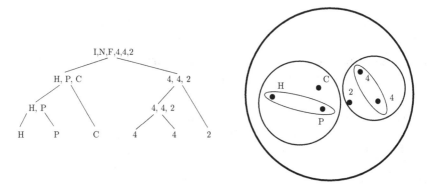

Fig. 8.2 Several visualizations of a dendrogram: dendrogram (*left*) and equivalent Venn diagram (*right*) using nested ellipses (and *disks*)

multi-platform R language[1] (GNU General Public License). The (short) R code for producing this figure is the following:

```
d <- dist(as.matrix(mtcars))     # find distance matrix
hc <- hclust(d,method="average" )
plot(hc, xlab="x", ylab="height", main="Hierarchical clustering (average
    distance)", sub="(cars)")
```

We have chosen the *Euclidean distance* $D(x_i, x_j) = \|x_i - x_j\|$ as the basic distance between any two elements of X, and the minimum distance as the linkage distance for defining the *sub-set distance* $\Delta(X_i, X_j) = \min_{x \in X, y \in X_j} D(x, y)$. Here is an excerpt of that data-set that describes some features for the car data-set:

	mpg	cyl	disp	hp	drat	wt	qsec	vs	am	gear	carb
Mazda RX4	21.0	6	160.0	110	3.90	2.620	16.46	0	1	4	4
Mazda RX4 Wag	21.0	6	160.0	110	3.90	2.875	17.02	0	1	4	4
Datsun 710	22.8	4	108.0	93	3.85	2.320	18.61	1	1	4	1
Hornet 4 Drive	21.4	6	258.0	110	3.08	3.215	19.44	1	0	3	1

---

[1]Download and install R from the following URL: http://www.r-project.org/.

Hierarchical clustering (average distance)

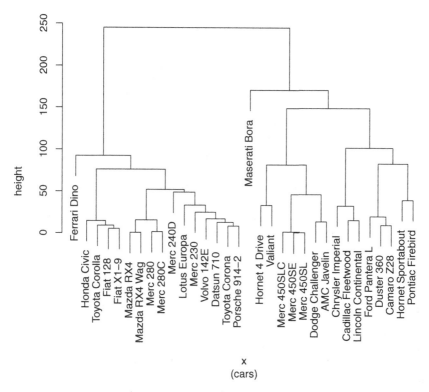

x
(cars)

Fig. 8.3 Example of a dendrogram for a car data-set: the data elements are stored at the leaves of the binary merge tree

Hornet Sportabout	18.7	8	360.0	175	3.15	3.440	17.02	0	0	3	2
Valiant	18.1	6	225.0	105	2.76	3.460	20.22	1	0	3	1
Duster 360	14.3	8	360.0	245	3.21	3.570	15.84	0	0	3	4
Merc 240D	24.4	4	146.7	62	3.69	3.190	20.00	1	0	4	2
Merc 230	22.8	4	140.8	95	3.92	3.150	22.90	1	0	4	2
Merc 280	19.2	6	167.6	123	3.92	3.440	18.30	1	0	4	4
Merc 280C	17.8	6	167.6	123	3.92	3.440	18.90	1	0	4	4
Merc 450SE	16.4	8	275.8	180	3.07	4.070	17.40	0	0	3	3
Merc 450SL	17.3	8	275.8	180	3.07	3.730	17.60	0	0	3	3
Merc 450SLC	15.2	8	275.8	180	3.07	3.780	18.00	0	0	3	3
Cadillac Fleetwood	10.4	8	472.0	205	2.93	5.250	17.98	0	0	3	4
Lincoln Continental	10.4	8	460.0	215	3.00	5.424	17.82	0	0	3	4
Chrysler Imperial	14.7	8	440.0	230	3.23	5.345	17.42	0	0	3	4
Fiat 128	32.4	4	78.7	66	4.08	2.200	19.47	1	1	4	1
Honda Civic	30.4	4	75.7	52	4.93	1.615	18.52	1	1	4	2
Toyota Corolla	33.9	4	71.1	65	4.22	1.835	19.90	1	1	4	1
Toyota Corona	21.5	4	120.1	97	3.70	2.465	20.01	1	0	3	1
Dodge Challenger	15.5	8	318.0	150	2.76	3.520	16.87	0	0	3	2
AMC Javelin	15.2	8	304.0	150	3.15	3.435	17.30	0	0	3	2

Camaro Z28	13.3	8	350.0	245	3.73	3.840	15.41	0	0	3	4
Pontiac Firebird	19.2	8	400.0	175	3.08	3.845	17.05	0	0	3	2
Fiat X1-9	27.3	4	79.0	66	4.08	1.935	18.90	1	1	4	1
Porsche 914-2	26.0	4	120.3	91	4.43	2.140	16.70	0	1	5	2
Lotus Europa	30.4	4	95.1	113	3.77	1.513	16.90	1	1	5	2
Ford Pantera L	15.8	8	351.0	264	4.22	3.170	14.50	0	1	5	4
Ferrari Dino	19.7	6	145.0	175	3.62	2.770	15.50	0	1	5	6
Maserati Bora	15.0	8	301.0	335	3.54	3.570	14.60	0	1	5	8
Volvo 142E	21.4	4	121.0	109	4.11	2.780	18.60	1	1	4	2

Notice that the visual drawing of hierarchical clusterings, dendrograms, conveys rich information for both qualitative and quantitative evaluations of various hierarchical clustering techniques that we shall present below.

To contrast with agglomerative hierarchical clustering, we also have *divisive hierarchical clustering* that starts from the root containing all the data-set X, and splits this root node into two children nodes containing respectively X_1 and X_2 (so that $X = X_1 \cup X_2$ and $X_1 \cap X_2 = \emptyset$), and so on recursively until we reach leaves that store in singletons the data elements. In the remainder, we concentrate on agglomerative hierarchical clustering (AHC) that is mostly used in applications.

8.2   Strategies to Define a Good Linkage Distance

Let $D(x_i, x_j)$ denote the elementary distance between any two elements of X (for example, the Euclidean distance). In order to select at each stage of the hierarchical clustering the closest pair of sub-sets, we need to define a sub-set distance $\Delta(X_i, X_j)$ between any two sub-sets of elements. Of course, when both sub-sets are singletons $X_i = \{x_i\}$ and $X_j = \{x_j\}$, we should have $\Delta(X_i, X_j) = D(x_i, x_j)$. We present below three such common *linkage functions*:

1. *Single Linkage* (SL):

$$\Delta(X_i, X_j) = \min_{x_i \in X_i, x_j \in X_j} D(x_i, x_j)$$

2. *Complete Linkage* (CL) (or diameter):

$$\Delta(X_i, X_j) = \max_{x_i \in X_i, x_j \in X_j} D(x_i, x_j)$$

3. *Group Average Linkage* (GAL):

$$\Delta(X_i, X_j) = \frac{1}{|X_i||X_j|} \sum_{x_i \in X_i} \sum_{x_j \in X_j} D(x_i, x_j)$$

Figure 8.4 visualizes pictorially those three different linkage functions.

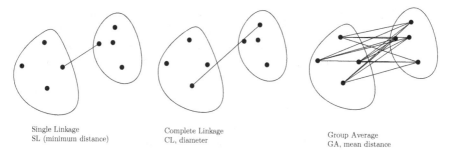

| Single Linkage | Complete Linkage | Group Average |
| SL (minimum distance) | CL, diameter | GA, mean distance |

Fig. 8.4 Illustrating the common linkage functions defining distances between sub-sets: single linkage, complete linkage and group average linkage

There exist many other sub-set distances Δ that are commonly called linkage distances because they literally allow one to *link sub-trees* representing the sub-sets in the dendrogram representation.

8.2.1 A Generic Algorithm for Agglomerative Hierarchical Clustering

We summarize below the principle of the generic agglomerative hierarchical clustering (AHC) for a prescribed linkage distance $\Delta(\cdot, \cdot)$ (user-defined and relying on yet another used-defined element distance):

Algorithm **AHC**

- Initialize for each data element $x_i \in X$ its cluster singleton $G_i = \{x_i\}$ in a list
- While there remains two elements in the list, do:

  - Choose G_i and G_j so that $\Delta(G_i, G_j)$ is minimized among all pairs,
  - Merge $G_{i,j} = G_i \cup G_j$, and
      add $G_{i,j}$ to the list, and
      remove G_i and G_j from the list.

- Return the remaining group in the list ($G_{\text{root}} = X$) as the dendrogram root.

Since we start from $n = |X|$ leaves to finish with a root containing the full set X, we perform exactly $n - 1$ merge operations. A straightforward implementation of this AHC algorithm yields a cubic time complexity, in $O(n^3)$. Depending on the linkage distance, we can optimize this naive algorithm and obtain far better time complexities.

Observation 4 Notice that in general the dendrogram may not be unique for a link-age distance function: Indeed, there can be *several* "closest" pairs of subsets, but we choose only one pair at each iteration and reiterate (thus breaking the symmetry, say, by introducing a lexicographic order on the pairs). In other words, if we had applied a permutation σ on the elements of X, and re-run the AHC algorithm, we could have obtained another dendrogram in output. For numerical data, we can slightly perturbate the initial data-set by adding some small random noise drawn uniformly in $(0, \epsilon)$ to bypass this problem. However, for *categorical data*, the problem still remains and therefore careful attention should be given to handle this problem.

The standard optimized AHC algorithm is called SLINK [1], and has a quadratic complexity, in $O(n^2)$ time. Single-linkage AHC yields a *"chaining phenomenon"* in dendrograms as depicted in Fig. 8.5. The AHC algorithm with complete linkage (also called diameter linkage) is called CLINK [2], and can be computed in $O(n^2 \log n)$ time. One disadvantage of complete linkage is that it is very sensitive to *outliers* (that is, artifact data that should have been removed beforehand when possible—the cleaning stage of data-sets). At first glance, the group average AHC is more computationally costly to compute but can also be optimized as well to get a sub-cubic time complexity. Usually, we recommend in applications the group average AHC algorithm that does not produce chaining phenomena and is more robust to noisy input.

8.2.2 Choosing the Appropriate Elementary Distance Between Elements

The *base distance function* $D(\cdot, \cdot)$ plays a crucial role on the shape of dendrograms. This distance function is a *dissimilarity measure* that evaluates how different element x_i is from element x_j (for any pair of elements). Although we often use the Euclidean distance, we can also choose other *metric distances*[2] like the *city block distance* (called the *Manhattan distance* or the L_1-norm induced distance[3]):

$$\boxed{D_1(p, q) = \sum_{j=1}^{d} |p^j - q^j|}$$

Recall that we use the super-script notation $x = (x^1, \ldots, x^j, \ldots, x^d)$ for an attribute vector x with d components: the x^j's are the coordinates of a d-dimensional vector x.

---

[2]Satisfying the symmetry ($D(p, q) = D(q, p)$), the law of indiscernibility ($D(p, q) = 0$ if and only if $p = q$), and the triangular inequality (for all triples $D(p, q) \leq D(p, r) + D(q, r)$). See Sect. 8.5 that introduces ultra-metrics.

[3]A norm $\|.\|$ induces a distance $D(p, q) = \|p - q\|$.

Fig. 8.5 Comparisons of
dendrograms obtained from
agglomerative hierarchical
clustering for three
commonly used linkage
functions: single linkage
(*top*), complete linkage
(*middle*) and group average
linkage (*bottom*)

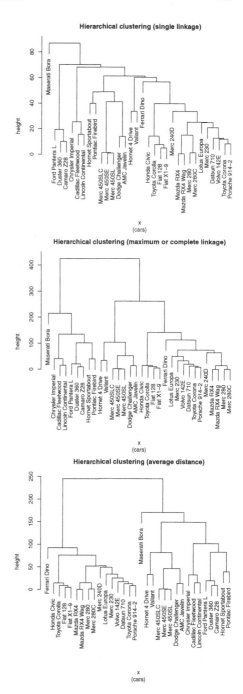

We can also use the *Minkowski distances* that generalize both the Euclidean distance (for $m = 2$) and the Manhattan distance (for $m = 1$):

$$D_m(p, q) = \left(\sum_{j=1}^{d} |p^j - q^j|^m \right)^{\frac{1}{m}} = \|p - q\|_m, m \geq 1$$

When the data coordinates have different scale factors, or are correlated, we better use the *Mahalanobis distance*[4]:

$$D_\Sigma(p, q) = \sqrt{(p - q)^\top \Sigma^{-1}(p - q)} = D_2(L^\top p, L^\top q)$$

with the *precision matrix* (inverse of the *covariance matrix*) $\Sigma^{-1} = L^\top L$ being factorized by the *Cholesky matrix* (matrix L is a *lower triangular matrix*). That is, the Mahalanobis distance $D_\Sigma(p, q)$ amounts to compute a traditional Euclidean distance $D_2(L^\top p, L^\top q)$ after an *affine change of variable*: $x \leftarrow L^\top x$. Matrix Σ is called the covariance matrix, and its inverse matrix Σ^{-1} is called the precision matrix. We can estimate the covariance matrix from a data-set sample $x_1, \ldots, x_n$ by computing:

$$\Sigma = \frac{1}{n-1} \sum_{i=1}^{n} (x_i - \bar{x})(x_i - \bar{x})^\top,$$

with $\bar{x} = \frac{1}{n} \sum_{i=1}^{n} x_i$ the empirical mean, also called the *sample mean*.

For categorical data (that is non-numerical), we often use an *agreement distance* like the *Hamming distance*:

$$D_H(p, q) = \sum_{j=1}^{d} 1_{[p^j \neq q^j]}$$

where $1_{[a \neq b]} = 1$ if and only if $a \neq b$, and zero otherwise. That is, the Hamming distance counts the number of times corresponding attributes are different from each other. The Hamming distance is a metric distance.

Often, we can link a *similarity* measure to a *dissimilarity* measure, and vice-versa. For example, considering the Hamming distance on d-dimensional binary vectors, we can define the corresponding similarity measure by $S_H(p, q) = \frac{d - D_H(p,q)}{d}$ (with $0 \leq S_H(p, q) \leq 1$, and maximal similarity when $p = q$).

There exist many other distance functions that have been used in a broad panel of applications. Let us cite the *Jaccard distance* $D_J(A, B) = \frac{|A \cap B|}{A \cup B}$ defined on sets,

---

[4]A metric distance that is symmetric and satisfies the triangle inequality.

the *edit distance* for finding distance between combinatorial structures (like texts or DNA sequences), the *cosine distance* $D_{\cos}(p, q) = 1 - \frac{p^\top q}{\|p\|\|q\|}$ (very useful when analyzing a corpus of texts with documents represented by a frequency histogram of word occurrences), etc.

8.3 Ward Merging Criterion and Centroids

One can also take a sub-set distance Δ according to the centroids of the sub-sets. This criterion allows us to implement a variance minimization process. This yields the *Ward linkage* function: to merge X_i ($n_i = |X_i|$) with X_j ($n_j = |X_j|$), we consider the following Ward criterion:

$$\Delta(X_i, X_j) = \frac{n_i n_j}{n_i + n_j} \|c(X_i) - c(X_j)\|^2$$

where $c(X')$ denotes the centroid of subset $X' \subseteq X$: $c(X') = \frac{1}{|X'|} \sum_{x \in X'} x$ (we may consider weighted points too). Observe that the distance between two elements induced from the sub-set distance Δ is merely half of the squared Euclidean distance: $\Delta(\{x_i\}, \{x_j\}) = D(x_i, x_j) = \frac{1}{2} \|x_i - x_j\|^2$. Figure 8.6 illustrates visually the difference between the dendrograms obtained from the group average AHC and from the Ward AHC (of minimal variance).

Notice that we can always define the similarity $S(X_i, X_j)$ between two sub-sets by defining $S(X_i, X_j) = -\Delta(X_i, X_j)$. The merging steps of a path sequence of length l in the tree dendrogram are said monotonous when we have the property that $S_1 \geq S_2 \geq \cdots \geq S_l$. A hierarchical clustering is said *non-monotonous* when

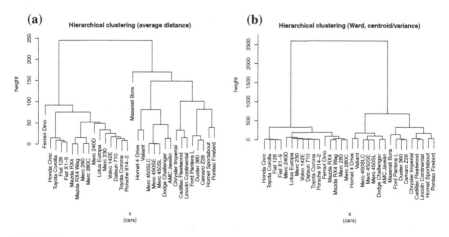

Fig. 8.6 Comparing dendrograms obtained for (**a**) the group average linkage, and (**b**) Ward linkage

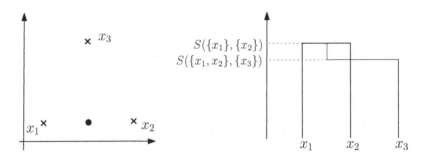

Fig. 8.7 Example of an inversion phenomenon in a dendrogram obtained when using Ward's criterion for hierarchical clustering on a toy data-set of a triple of elements

there exists at least one *inversion*, say $S_i < S_{i+1}$, on a path from the leaves to the root of the dendrogram. The Ward AHC is not monotonous because there can exist inversions. However, the single linkage, complete linkage and group average linkage are all guaranteed to be monotonous.

When we draw the nodes of the merge tree (i.e., nodes of the dendrogram) using a height function defined as the similarity, an inversion in a dendrogram can be noticed graphically by the fact that one horizontal height line can be lower than another horizontal height line for a former merging operation. Indeed, this contradicts the fact the nodes on a path from a leaf to the root should be y-monotonous. Figure 8.7 illustrates an inversion in a dendrogram.

8.4   Retrieving Flat Partitions from Dendrograms

From a dendrogram, we can extract many different flat partitions. Figure 8.8 illustrates this concept by displaying two constant-height cuts that induce respective partitions of the data sets. Note that the cutting path on the dendrogram *does not need* to be at constant height in general (see Sect. 8.8).

8.5   Ultra-metric Distances and Phylogenetic Trees

A distance function $D(\cdot, \cdot)$ is called *a metric* if it satisfies the following three axioms:

Law of indiscernibility. $D(x, y) \geq 0$ with equality iff. $x = y$,
Symmetry. $D(x, y) = D(y, x)$
Triangular inequality. $D(x, y) \leq D(x, z) + D(z, y)$,

The Euclidean distance and the Hamming distance are two examples of metric distances. Beware that the squared Euclidean distance is not a metric although it is

Hierarchical clustering

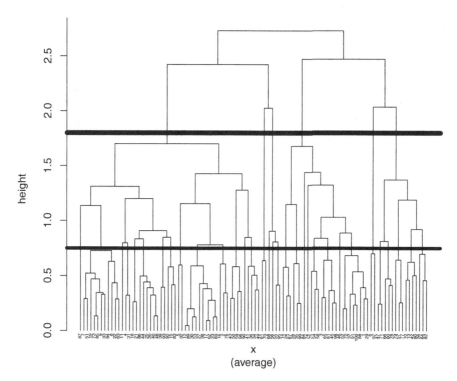

x
(average)

Fig. 8.8 Retrieving flat partitions from a dendrogram: we choose the height for cutting the dendrogram. At a given height, we obtain a flat clustering (that is a partition of the full data-set). The cut path does not need to be at a constant height. Thus a dendrogram allows one to obtain many flat partitions. Here, we show two different cuts at constant height, for $h = 0.75$ and $h = 1.8$

symmetric and satisfies the law of indiscernibility. Indeed, the triangular inequality is not anymore satisfied when we take the square of the Euclidean distance (however, recall that the squared Euclidean distance is used to define the potential function of the k-means in flat clustering in order to get centroids and minimizes of cluster variances). The law of indiscernibility can further be split into two sub-axioms: The law of non-negativity $D(p, q) \geq 0$, and the law of reflexivity: $D(p, q) = 0 \Leftrightarrow p = q$.

Hierarchical clustering is tightly linked to a class of distances called the class of *ultra-metrics*. A distance is said ultra-metric if it is a metric and further ensures that:

$$D(x, y) \leq \max_z(D(x, z), D(z, y)).$$

Let us now explain the link between ultra-metrics and hierarchical clustering: In evolution theory, species evolve with time, and the distance between species is represented by a so-called *phylogenetic tree*. Let us write for short $D_{i,j} = D(x_i, x_j)$. A tree is said *additive* if and only if we can attach to each edge a weight so that for each pair of leaves, the distance between them is equal to the sum of the distances of the edges linking them. A tree is said ultra-metric when the distance between two leaves, say i and j, and their *common ancestor*, say k, is equal: $D_{i,k} = D_{j,k}$. We can draw an ultra-metric tree by choosing the height distance $\frac{1}{2} D_{i,j}$ for visualizing a dendrogram. This distance can be interpreted s a clock time among all the elements of X (for species, it represents the biological time).

The group average AHC guarantees to produce an ultra-metric tree. We shall call this hierarchical clustering that embeds the nodes of the tree with its height the *Unweighted Pair Group Method using arithmetic Averages* algorithm (or UPGMA, for short). We write in pseudo-code this algorithm below:

Algorithm **UPGMA** :

- For all i, initialize x_i to its cluster $C_i = \{x_i\}$, and set this node leaf to height 0.
- While there remains at least two clusters:

    - Find the closest pair of clusters C_i and C_j that minimizes the group average distance $\Delta_{i,j}$,
    - Define a new cluster $C_k = C_i \cup C_j$ and compute the distance $\Delta_{k,l}$ for all l,
    - Add a node k to the children C_i and C_j, and set the height of that node to $\frac{1}{2} \Delta(C_i, C_j)$,
    - Remove both C_i and C_j from the cluster list, and reiterate until we get two remaining clusters.

- For the last two clusters C_i and C_j, set the root node at height $\frac{1}{2} \Delta(C_i, C_j)$.

Theorem 9 *When the matrix distance* $M = [D_{i,j}]_{i,j}$ *with* $D_{i,j} = D(x_i, x_j)$ *of a data-set* X *satisfies the ultra-metric property, then there exists a unique ultra-metric tree that can be built with the UPGMA algorithm.*

Phylogenetic trees are often used when modeling the evolution of species: We associate to the vertical axis the chronological time of evolution, as depicted in Fig. 8.9. The UPGMA allows to build such an ultra-metric tree. However let us emphasize that data-sets are often noisy and therefore the matrix distance is often not ultra-metric since corrupted. Another drawback is that we need to consider the matrix of pairwise distances that requires a quadratic memory space, and can therefore only be limited to reasonable size data-sets (but not big data as is!).

8.6   Notes and References

There exist many hierarchical clustering algorithms. Let us cite *SLINK* [1] (Single Linkage, 1973), *CLINK* [2] (Complete Linkage, 1977), and a general survey [3] providing a high-level abstraction of hierarchical clustering. Although that flat clustering minimizing the k-means objective function is NP-hard (even in the plane), it has been

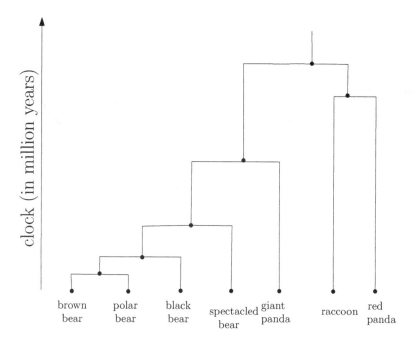

Fig. 8.9 Dendrograms and phylogenetic trees for visualizing the evolution of species

recently proved (2012) that we can extract from a single linkage hierarchical clustering the optimal k-means clustering provided that some stability criterion is satisfied, see [4] (the extraction of the flat partition is performed using dynamic programming to find the best non-constant height dendrogram cut). The hierarchical clustering that minimizes Ward's variance criterion and its related criteria have been thoroughly investigated in [5, 6]. Various hierarchical clustering algorithms (including SLINK, CLINK and Ward) can be unified in the generic Lance-Williams framework, see [7] and Sect. 8.8. Uniqueness and monotonic properties of hierarchical clustering have been studied in [8]. Although that hierarchical clustering algorithms are a priori harder to parallelize compare to flat clustering techniques (like k-means), let us mention this work [9] that reports an efficient parallel algorithm. We refer to [10] for an explanation of the divisive hierarchical clustering technique that maximizes the notion of modularity. Distances is at the core of many algorithms: we recommend the encyclopedia of distances [11] for a compact review of main distances.

8.7 Summary

Agglomerative hierarchical clustering differs from partition-based clustering since it builds a binary merge tree starting from leaves that contain data elements to the root that contains the full data-set. The graphical representation of that tree that embeds the nodes on the plane is called a dendrogram. To implement a hierarchical clustering algorithm, one has to choose a linkage function (single linkage, average linkage, complete linkage, Ward linkage, etc.) that defines the distance between any two sub-sets (and rely on the base distance between elements). A hierarchical clustering is monotonous if and only if the similarity decreases along the path from any leaf to the root, otherwise there exists at least one inversion. The single, complete, and average linkage criteria guarantee the monotonic property, but not the often used Ward's criterion. From a dendrogram, one can extract many data-set partitions that correspond to flat clustering output. Phylogenetic trees used to model the evolution of species are ultra-metric trees. Hierarchical clustering using the average linkage guarantees to build an ultra-metric tree when the base distance between any two elements is ultra-metric.

8.8 Exercises

Exercise 1 (*Checking the ultra-metric property of a distance matrix*) Let M denote a square matrix of dimension $n \times n$ that stores at index (i, j) the distance $D(x_i, x_j)$ between element x_i and element x_j.

- Design an algorithm that checks whether the distance matrix satisfies the ultra-metric property or not,
- What is the time complexity of your algorithm?

Exercise 2 (*Euclidean metric distance and Hamming metric distance*)

- Prove that the Euclidean distance is a metric, but not the squared Euclidean distance.
- Prove that the Hamming distance satisfies the axioms of a metric.
- Prove that the distance $D(p, q) = \left(\sum_{j=1}^{d} |p^j - q^j|^m \right)^{\frac{1}{m}}$ for $0 < m < 1$ is not a metric (when $m \geq 1$, recall that it is the m-norm induced Minkowski metric distance).

Exercise 3 (*Combining flat clustering with hierarchical clustering*) Let $X = \{x_1, \ldots, x_n\}$ be n data elements, each datum has d attributes.

- Give an algorithm that clusters hierarchically the data, and retrieve a partition of at most l elements (for large l, it produces an over-clustering), and use after a k-means algorithm on the centroids of these groups. What kind of applications can you think of that strategy?
- What is the complexity of your algorithm? Explain its advantages compare to only hierarchical clustering or to only partition-based clustering?

Exercise 4 (*Hierarchical clustering of Lance and Williams* [7])

- State the hierarchical clustering algorithm using the following shortcut notations $D_{ij} = \Delta(C_i, C_j)$ and $D_{(ij)k} = \Delta(C_i \cup C_j, C_k)$ for disjoint groups C_i, C_j and C_k.
- A hierarchical clustering belongs to the Lance-Williams family if and only if it can be written canonically as:

$$D_{(ij)k} = \alpha_i D_{ik} + \alpha_j D_{jk} + \beta D_{ij} + \gamma |D_{ik} - D_{jk}|,$$

with $\alpha_i, \alpha_j, \beta$, and γ parameters depending on the size of clusters. Prove that Ward minimum variance criterion ($D(x_i, x_j) = \|x_i - x_j\|^2$) for disjoint groups C_i, C_j and C_k yields the following formula:

$$D(C_i \cup C_j, C_k)$$
$$= \frac{n_i + n_k}{n_i + n_j + n_k} D(C_i, C_k) + \frac{n_j + n_k}{n_i + n_j + n_k} D(C_j, C_k) - \frac{n_k}{n_i + n_j + n_k} D(C_i, C_j).$$

- Deduce that Ward's algorithm is a particular case Lance-Williams's generic hierarchical clustering with the following parameterization:

$$\alpha_l = \frac{n_l + n_k}{n_i + n_j + n_k}, \qquad \beta = \frac{-n_k}{n_i + n_j + n_k}, \qquad \gamma = 0.$$

- Prove that Lance-Williams' algorithm unify single linkage, complete linkage and group average linkage.

Exercise 5 (*Centroid-based hierarchical clustering for an arbitrary convex distance function*) For a convex distance $D(\cdot, \cdot)$, let us define the centroid of X as the unique minimizer of $\min_c \sum_{x \in X} D(x, c)$. Prove that the inversion phenomenon that can happen for Ward criterion does not happen for the Euclidean distance nor for the Manhattan distance (two examples of convex distances).

Exercise 6 (* *Retrieving the best k-means flat partition from a hierarchical clustering* [4]) Given a dendrogram, one can extract many different partitions:

- How many distinct partitions can be retrieved from a dendrogram?
- For a sub-set X', let us denote by $c(X')$ the centroid of X' and by $v(X')$ its variance: $v(X') = \frac{1}{|X'|} \sum_{x \in X'} x^\top x - (c(X')^\top c(X'))^2$. Give a dynamic programming code for retrieving the best k-means flat clustering from a dendrogram. What is the time complexity of your algorithm?

Exercise 7 (* *Cosine distances between documents and spherical k-means*) Let p and q be two vectors of d attributes, and consider the cosine distance: $D(p, q) = \cos(\theta_{p,q}) = 1 - \frac{p^\top q}{\|p\|\|q\|}$. The cosine distance is an angular distance that does not account for the magnitude of vectors. For a collection of text documents, we model a text t by its word frequency/counting vector $f(t)$ (given a word dictionary).

- Prove that the cosine distance is a metric,
- Design an agglomerative hierarchical clustering that allows one to cluster text documents,
- Generalize the k-means flat clustering to a partition-based clustering algorithm relying on the cosine distance. We shall consider attribute vector as a point set lying on the unit sphere, and prove that the spherical centroid is the Euclidean centroid projected back to the unit sphere (when all points are enclosed into the same hemisphere). How to define the spherical centroid of two antipodal points on the unit sphere centered at the origin?

Exercise 8 (* *Hierarchical clustering for Bregman divergences* [12]) Bregman divergences are non-metric distances that are defined according to a strictly convex and differentiable generator function $F(x)$ by:

$$D_F(x, y) = F(x) - F(y) - (x - y)^\top \nabla F(y),$$

where $\nabla F(y) = \left(\frac{\mathrm{d}}{\mathrm{d}y^1} F(y), \ldots, \frac{\mathrm{d}}{\mathrm{d}y^d} F(y) \right)$ denotes the gradient vector.

- Prove that for $F(x) = x^\top x$, the Bregman divergence amounts to the squared Euclidean distance.
- Prove that Bregman divergences can never be a metric, and that the squared Mahalanobis distance is a symmetric Bregman divergence.
- Generalize Ward's criterion for Bregman divergences as follows:

$$\Delta(X_i, X_j) = |X_i| \times D_F(c(X_i), c(X_i \cup X_j)) + |X_j| \times D_F(c(X_j), c(X_i \cup X_j)),$$

where $c(X_l)$ is the center of mass of X_l. Check that for the Bregman generator $F(x) = \frac{1}{2} x^\top x$, we get the usual Ward's criterion.
- Report a Bregman hierarchical clustering algorithm. Can inversion phenomena happen?

Exercise 9 (** *Single linkage hierarchical clustering and minimum spanning tree* [13]) Give a naive implementation of the single linkage hierarchical clustering. What is the time complexity of your naive algorithm? Given a planar point set $X = \{x_1, \ldots, x_n\}$, the Euclidean Minimum Spanning Tree (MST) is a tree with nodes anchored at all points of X so that the sum of all tree edge lengths is minimized. Prove that the MST is a subgraph of the Delaunay triangulation (the dual structure of the Voronoi diagram). Prove that the edge information contained in the Euclidean minimum spanning tree allows one to easily deduce the structure of the single linkage dendrogram. As a byproduct, report a quadratic time algorithm for the single linkage hierarchical clustering.

References

1. Sibson, R.: SLINK: An optimally efficient algorithm for the single-link cluster method. Comput. J. **16**(1), 30–34 (1973)
2. Defays, D.: An efficient algorithm for a complete link method. Comput. J **20**(4), 364–366 (1977)
3. Murtagh, F.: A survey of recent advances in hierarchical clustering algorithms. Comput. J. **26**(4), 354–359 (1983)
4. Awasthi, P., Blum, A., Sheffet, Or.: Center-based clustering under perturbation stability. Inf. Process. Lett. **112**(1–2), 49–54 (2012)
5. Ward, J.H.: Hierarchical grouping to optimize an objective function. J. Am. Stat. Assoc. **58**(301), 236–244 (1963)
6. Murtagh, F., Legendre, P.: Ward's hierarchical agglomerative clustering method: Which algorithms implement Ward's criterion? J. Classif. **31**(3), 274–295 (2014)
7. Lance, G.N., Williams, W.T., A general theory of classificatory sorting strategies. Comput. J. **10**(3), 271–277 (1967)
8. Byron J. T. Morgan., Andrew P.G. Ray.: Non-uniqueness and inversions in cluster analysis. Appl. Stat. pp. 117–134 (1995)
9. Olson, C.F.: Parallel algorithms for hierarchical clustering. Parallel Comput. **21**(8), 1313–1325 (1995)
10. Mark E.J. Newman.: Modularity and community structure in networks. In: Proceedings of the National Academy of Sciences (PNAS), 103(23):8577–8582 (2006)
11. Deza, M.M., Deza, E.: Encyclopedia of Distances. Springer, Berlin (2014). Third Edition
12. Telgarsky, M., Dasgupta, S.: Agglomerative Bregman clustering. In International Conference on Machine Learning (ICML). icml.cc / Omnipress (2012)
13. Gower, J.C., Ross, G.J.S.: Minimum spanning trees and single linkage cluster analysis. Appl. Stat. pp. 54–64 (1969)

Chapter 9
Supervised Learning: Practice and Theory of Classification with the k-NN Rule

9.1 Supervised Learning

In supervised learning, we are given a labeled *training set* $Z = \{(x_i, y_i)\}_i$ with $y_i \in \pm 1$ (the ground truth labeled data) and the task is to learn a *classifier* so that we can classify new unlabeled observations of a *testing set* $Q = \{x_i'\}_i$. We shall see in this chapter a very simple algorithm that is nonetheless provably good to classify data: the *k-Nearest Neighbor rule*, or *k-NN rule* for short. When the training set has only two classes, we deal with *binary classification*, otherwise it is a multi-class classification problem. Statistical learning assumes that both the training set and the testing set are independently and identically sampled for an arbitrary but fixed unknown distribution.

9.2 Nearest Neighbor Classification: NN-Rule

The *nearest neighbor classification rule* assigns a label to an element x as the class $l(x) \in \{-1, +1\}$ where $l(x)$ is the label of the closest labeled point $\mathrm{NN}(x)$ in the training set: $l(x) = l(\mathrm{NN}_Z(x))$. That is, we have $l(x) = y_e$ for $e = \arg\min_{i=1}^n D(x, x_i)$ where $D(\cdot, \cdot)$ is an appropriate distance function (usually taken as the Euclidean distance). Let us notice that in case there exist several points yielding the same minimal distance, we choose arbitrarily one of those points. For example, we may use the *lexicographic order* on Z, and report the lowest index point of Z in case of nearest neighbor ties. Thus the notion of "nearest neighbor" is defined according to an appropriate distance function $D(\cdot, \cdot)$ between any two elements. For example, we have already surveyed in the previous chapters, the Euclidean distance $D(p, q) = \sqrt{\sum_{j=1}^d (p^j - q^j)^2}$ or a generalization called the Minkowski distances $D_l(p, q) = \left(\sum_{j=1}^d |p^j - q^j|^l \right)^{\frac{1}{l}}$ (metrics when $l \geq 1$) for numerical attributes (Fig. 9.1), and the

© Springer International Publishing Switzerland 2016
F. Nielsen, *Introduction to HPC with MPI for Data Science*, Undergraduate
Topics in Computer Science, DOI 10.1007/978-3-319-21903-5_9

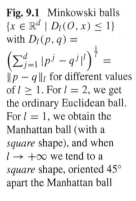

Fig. 9.1 Minkowski balls $\{x \in \mathbb{R}^d \mid D_l(O, x) \leq 1\}$ with $D_l(p, q) =$ $\left(\sum_{j=1}^{d} |p^j - q^j|^l\right)^{\frac{1}{l}} =$ $\|p - q\|_l$ for different values of $l \geq 1$. For $l = 2$, we get the ordinary Euclidean ball. For $l = 1$, we obtain the Manhattan ball (with a *square* shape), and when $l \to +\infty$ we tend to a *square* shape, oriented $45°$ apart the Manhattan ball

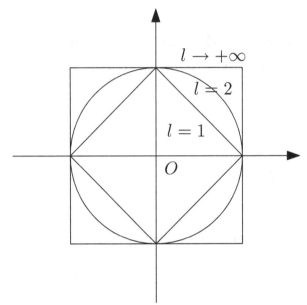

Hamming distance $D_H(p, q) = \sum_{j=1}^{d}(1 - \delta_{p^j}(q^j)) = \sum_{j=1}^{d} 1_{[p^j \neq q^j]}$ for categorical attributes (agreement distance). We denote by $\delta_x(y) = 1$ the *Dirac function* that is equal to 1 if and only if $y = x$, and 0 otherwise.

We classify $t = |Q|$ new unlabeled observations of the testing set by answering t nearest neighbor (NN) queries in X. It is crucial to answer these queries as fast as possible, at least in sub-linear time so that we can beat the naive algorithm that scans all the points of X. There exists many data-structures to answer such NN queries but as the dimension d increases, it becomes (provably) difficult to beat significantly the naive algorithm. This is the phenomenon that bears the name of the *curse of dimensionality*! Historically, this curse of dimensionality was introduced by Bellman, the founder of the dynamic programming paradigm.

9.2.1 Optimizing Euclidean Distance Computation for Nearest Neighbor Queries

We often choose the Euclidean distance as the underlying distance, and the NN queries can be optimized in practice. Indeed, let us first notice that a distance or a monotonically increasing function of this distance, like the square function, does not change the *relative ordering* of points according to a query point q. That is, we have $l = \arg\min_{i=1}^{n} D(q, x_i) = \arg\min_{i=1}^{n} D^2(q, x_i)$. This is useful observation as the squared Euclidean distance is easier to handle mathematically. Indeed,computing the squared Euclidean distance between two vector attributes of d dimensions amounts to compute d subtractions, d square operations, and $d - 1$ sums. That is $3d - 1$ elementary arithmetic operations. We can also interpret the squared Euclidean distance (or any other norm-based induced distance) as $D^2(q, x_i) = \langle q - x_i, q - x_i \rangle$, where $\langle x, y \rangle = x^\top y$ is the *scalar product* (technically, the Euclidean space can also be interpreted as a Hilbert space equipped with the dot product). Computing a scalar product between two d-dimensional vectors requires $2d - 1$ operations. Now, if we preprocess the computation of the squared norms $\text{norm}^2(p) = \langle p, p \rangle = \sum_{j=1}^{d} (p^j)^2$ in $(2d - 1)n$ time for the points of the training set Z, with $|Z| = n$, then we can compute $D^2(p, q)$ as $D^2(p, q) = \text{norm}^2(p) + \text{norm}^2(q) - 2\langle p, q \rangle$: that is, it amounts to perform t scalar products for each query of the test set Q with $|Q| = t$. To classify the t unlabeled data, the naive method requires $(3d - 1)nt$ while the method that preprocess by computing the $n + t$ norms in $(2d - 1)(n + t)$ time requires an overall time $(2d - 1)(n + t) + t(2 + 2d - 1)$. Therefore for $t \ll n \ll d$, the obtained speed-up is $\frac{3dnt}{4dt} = 3n$. In practice, one can use the *Graphical Processing Units* (*GPUs*) of modern PCs that allows to quickly compute scalar product internally.

9.2.2 Nearest Neighbor (NN) Rules and Voronoi Diagrams

For a given training set Z with $n = |Z|$ d-dimensional numerical data elements, the space $\mathbb{R}^d$ is partitioned into n equivalence classes for the nearest neighbor labeling function (where the arg min is constant). These are precisely the *Voronoi cells* that decompose the space into proximity cells. We have already introduced the Voronoi diagrams in the k-means clustering chapter. We quickly recall that Voronoi diagram of a finite set of points $X = \{p_1, \ldots, p_n\}$ of $\mathbb{R}^d$ (called the Voronoi generators) partitions the space into Voronoi cells that are proximity cells. A Voronoi cell $V(x_i)$ is defined as the set of points of $\mathbb{R}^d$ that is closed to x_i than to any other generator x_j (with $j \neq i$). That is, $V(x_i) = \{x \in \mathbb{R}^d \mid \|x - x_i\| \leq \|x - x_j\| \ \forall j \neq i\}$. Figure 9.2 depicts a planar Voronoi diagram (observe that there are unbounded cells).

Here, we consider only bi-chromatic generators (two classes '-1' and '$+1$', or red/blue sites) for the Voronoi diagram. Thus the bichromatic Voronoi diagram decomposes the space into two types of colored cells, and the boundary between these color changes indicates the *decision boundary* of the *NN classifier*. Figure 9.3 illustrates these geometric aspects. Note that in practice one cannot compute Voronoi diagrams in high dimension because of their exponential combinatorial complexity. Nevertheless, the facets of the bi-chromatic Voronoi diagrams that support cells of different colors define precisely the decision boundary. Thus the NN-rule has a piecewise linear decision boundary since bisectors (i.e., the locii of points at equidistance to two generators) are hyperplanes.

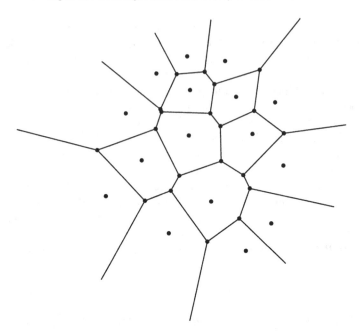

Fig. 9.2 Example of a planar Voronoi diagram that partitions the space into proximity cells

9.2.3 Enhancing the NN-Rule with the k-NN Rule by Voting!

In order for the classifier to be resilient to noisy data-sets (say, imprecise input and outliers), we may class a new observation q by choosing among the first k nearest neighbors of X, the dominant class. For binary classification, it is useful to choose an odd value for k in order to avoid vote ties. In practice, increasing k allows one to be tolerant to outliers in the data-set, but the drawback is that the decision boundary becomes more fuzzy as k increases. There exit many techniques or rules of thumbs to choose the most appropriate value of k for this k-NN rule. For example, the *cross-validation* method that uses part of the training set to train, and the remaining part to test. Note that the k-NN voting rule generalizes the NN-rule (by choosing $k = 1$, NN = 1-NN). When dealing with multi-classes, the rule consists in choosing the dominant class inside the k-NNs. Technically speaking, the space $\mathbb{R}^d$ can also be decomposed into elementary cells, the k-order Voronoi cells (see Sect. 9.9), where inside a cell, the k closest neighbor sites does not change. The k-order Voronoi diagram is an affine diagram and the k-NN decision boundary is also piecewise linear.

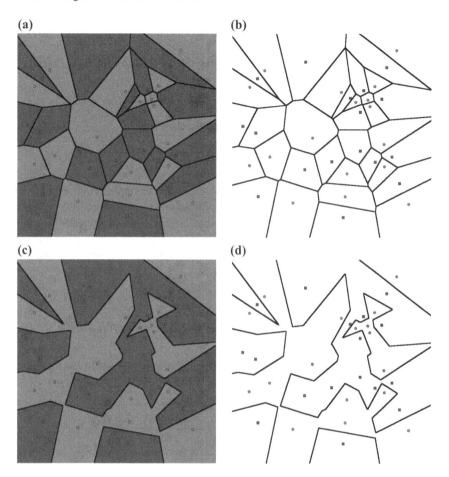

Fig. 9.3 k-NN classification rules and bi-chromatic Voronoi diagrams: **a** bichromatic Voronoi diagram, **b** voronoi bi-chromatic bisectors, **c** classifier using the 1-NN rule (classes are monochromatic union of Voronoi cells), and **d** boundary decision defined as the interface of these two classes

9.3 Evaluating the Performance of Classifiers

We described a family of piecewise linear classifier based on the k-NN rule to classify observations using the labeling function $l_k(x)$ that returns the majority class of the k nearest neighbor in the training set Z of point to classify, x. In order to choose the best classifier in that family, one needs to be able to assess the performance of classifiers.

9.3.1   Misclassification Error Rate

The *misclassification rate* or *error rate* on a testing set Q with t unlabeled observations to classify is simply defined by:

$$\tau_{\text{Error}} = \frac{\#\text{misclassified}}{t} = 1 - \frac{\#\text{correctly classified}}{t} = \tau_{\text{misclassification}}$$

This indicator is not discriminative when the class label proportions are unbalanced (in the testing set or even in the training set). For example, when we classify email messages into C_{spam} for spam and C_{ham} for non-spam (good emails), we notice that we often have far less spams than regular emails. Thus if we seek to minimize the misclassification error rate, then it would suffice to classify non-spam all emails, and thus achieve a good error rate! This highlights the problem of taking into consideration the relative proportion of classes.

9.3.2   Confusion Matrices and True/False Positive/Negative

The *confusion matrix* $M = [m_{i,j}]_{i,j}$ stores its coefficients $m_{i,j}$ of well-classified rates when x is classified as C_i (estimated class) with the ground-truth class being C_j:

$$M = [m_{i,j}]_{i,j}, \quad m_{i,j} = \tau_{(x \text{ predicted as } C_i | x \in C_j)}$$

For binary classification (i.e., two classes), consider the following 2×2 array that indicates the four cases with

True	prediction is correct
False	prediction is wrong
Positive	predicted label is class C_{+1}
Negative	predicted label is class C_{-1}

	Predicted label	
	C_{+1}	C_{-1}
true label C_{+1}	True Positive (TP)	False Negative (FN)
C_{-1}	False Positive (FP)	True Negative (TN)

The diagonal of the confusion matrix M indicates the successful rate for all classes. This misclassified data can either by *false positive* (FP) or *false negative* (FN):

- A false positive (FP) is an observation x misclassified as C_1 (positive class) albeit it is C_{-1} (negative class). "Positive" means '+1' in this context.
- Similarly, a false negative (FN), is an observation x misclassified as C_{-1} (negative class) albeit it is C_{+1} (positive class). In this context, "negative" means '−1'.

The false positive are also called *type I error*, and the false negative are called *type II error*. Similarly, we define the *true negative* (TN) and the *false negative* (TP). Thus, the error rate can be rewritten as:

$$\tau_{\text{error}} = \frac{\text{FP} + \text{FN}}{\text{TP} + \text{TN} + \text{FP} + \text{FN}} = 1 - \frac{\text{TP} + \text{TN}}{\text{TP} + \text{TN} + \text{FP} + \text{FN}},$$

since $\text{TP} + \text{TN} + \text{FP} + \text{FN} = t = |Q|$, the number of queries to classify.

9.4 Precision, Recall and F-Score

We define the *precision* as the proportion of true positive in the true class (the TP and FP data):

$$\tau_{\text{Precision}} = \frac{\text{TP}}{\text{TP} + \text{FP}}.$$

We can easily check that $0 \leq \tau_{\text{Precision}} \leq 1$. The precision is the percentage of correctly classified elements in the positive class.

The *recall rate* is the proportion of true +1 (TP) in the data classified +1 (TP and FN):

$$\tau_{\text{recall}} = \frac{\text{TP}}{\text{TP} + \text{FN}}.$$

The *F-score* is a rate that is constructed in order to give as much weight to the false positive as to the false negative. It is defined as the harmonic mean,[1] and is often used in practice:

$$\tau_{\text{F-score}} = \frac{2 \times \tau_{\text{Precision}} \times \tau_{\text{Recall}}}{\tau_{\text{Precision}} + \tau_{\text{Recall}}}$$

In practice, we choose classifiers that yield the best F-scores. For example, for several odd values of k, one can evaluates the k-NN classification rule using the F-score, and finally choose the best value of k that gave the best F-score.

---

[1] The harmonic mean is defined by $h(x, y) = \frac{1}{\frac{1}{2}\frac{1}{x} + \frac{1}{2}\frac{1}{y}} = \frac{2xy}{x+y}$. It is often used to average ratio quantities.

9.5   Statistical Machine Learning and Bayes' Minimal Error Bound

Nowadays, in the era of big data, it is reasonable to assume that both the training set Z and the test set Q can be modeled by statistical distributions (from generative models having probability densities). Classifier performances can then be studied mathematically. Let us assume that X (from $Z = (X, Y)$) and Q are two data sets, called observations, that are identically and independently distributed (*iid*) samples from random variables X, Y and Z. We write $X \sim_{\text{iid}} \mathcal{D}$ to state that X has been sampled iid. from a probability law $\mathcal{D}$ (say, a Gaussian distribution). An *univariate distribution* has its support in $\mathbb{R}$, the real line. Otherwise, we have *multivariate distributions* (say, with support in $\mathbb{R}^d$). We can interpret X as a random vector of dimension $n \times d$. Let us recall the probability fact that two random variables X_1 and X_2 are *independent* iff. $\Pr(X_1 = x_1, X_2 = x_2) = \Pr(X_1 = x_1) \times \Pr(X_2 = x_2)$. Statistical modeling allows to consider X as a statistical mixture. The density of a statistical mixture can mathematically be written as: $m(x) = w_1 p_1(x) + w_2 p_2(x)$ with w_1 and w_2 *a priori probabilities* of belonging to classes C_1 and C_2 ($w_1 = 1 - w_2$), and $p_1(x) = \Pr(X_1 | Y_1 = C_1)$ and $p_2(x) = \Pr(X_2 | Y_2 = C_2)$ the *conditional probabilities*. We seek for a classifier that yields a good performance in the large sample limit: That is, asymptotically when $n \to +\infty$.

9.5.1   Non-parametric Probability Density Estimation

Given an iid observation set $X = \{x_1, \ldots, x_n\}$ that we assume sampled from a fixed but unknown density $p(x)$, we seek to model the underlying distribution. For a parametric law $p(x|\theta)$ (that belongs to a family of distributions indexed by a parameter vector θ), this amounts to estimate the parameter θ of this distribution (Fig. 9.4). For example, for a Gaussian distribution $p(x|\theta = (\mu, \sigma^2))$, we estimate with the *maximum likelihood estimator* (MLE) the mean as $\hat{\mu} = \frac{1}{n} \sum_{i=1}^{n} x_i$ and the (unbiased) variance as $v = \sigma^2$ with $\widehat{\sigma^2} = \frac{1}{n-1} \sum_{i=1}^{n} (x_i - \hat{\mu})^2$. When the distributions is not indexed by a fixed-dimensional parameter, we say that the distribution is non-parametric. The parametric distributions are often (but not necessarily) unimodal[2] and these models lack flexibility to model complex *multimodal density*. The *non-parametric density modeling* method is far more flexible since it allows to model any smooth density, including all multimodal smooth distributions. We state a key theorem in non-parametric statistical modeling.

Theorem 10 *The balloon estimator allows to approximate a smooth density $p(x)$ with support in $\mathbb{R}^d$ by $p(x) \approx \frac{k}{nV(B)}$, where k is the number of samples of X that is contained in the ball B, and $V(B)$ its volume.*

---

[2]The modes of a density function are its local maxima.

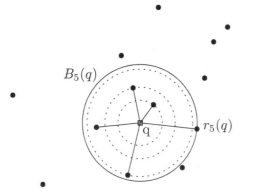

Fig. 9.4 Illustration of a k-NN query for $k = 5$. The *ball* covering the k-NN has radius $r_k(q)$. The radius allows to estimate locally the underlying distribution of X by $p(x) \approx \frac{k}{nV(B_k(x))} \propto \frac{k}{nr_k(x)^d}$

Proof Let P_R denote the probability that a sample x falls inside a region R: $P_R = \int_{x \in R} p(x)\mathrm{d}x$. The probability that k of n samples fall inside R is thus given by the binomial law:

$$P_R^{(k)} = \binom{n}{k} P_R^k (1 - P_R)^{n-k},$$

and the expectation of k is $\mathbb{E}[k] = nP_R$. Thus the maximum likelihood estimator $\widehat{P_R}$ for P_R is $\frac{k}{n}$. Assume the density is continuous and the that region R is small enough so that $p(x)$ can be assumed to be constant in R. Then, we have:

$$\int_{x \in R} p(x)\mathrm{d}x \approx p(x)V_R,$$

with $V_R = \int_{x \in R} \mathrm{d}x$ the region volume. Thus the estimator of the density is $p(x) \approx \frac{k}{nV}$. □

We can apply this *ballon estimator* theorem in two ways:

- First, we fix the ball B radius (and henceforth its volume $V(B)$), and we count the number of points falling inside B for a given position x (this generalizes the 1D histogram method for approximating smooth univariate densities), or
- Second, we fix the value of k, and we seek the smallest ball centered at X that exactly contains k points. This approach is called the non-parametric estimation by k-NNs. Notice that for each different value of k, we have a different ballon estimator.

Let $r_k(x)$ denote the radius of the covering ball $B_k(x)$. The volume $V_k(x)$ is proportional to $r_k(x)^d$ up to a multiplicative constant that only depends on the dimension: $V_k(x) = c_d r_k(x)^d \propto r_k(x)^d$.

9.5.2 Probability of Error and Bayes' Error

First, let us observe that *any* classifier will necessarily have a non-zero misclassification rate since the distributions $X_{\pm 1}$ of the two classes share the same support: thus we can never be 100% sure that we have correctly labeled a sample: a misclassification error always exist! In Bayesian decision theory (i.e., assuming class a priori probabilities and class conditional probabilities), the *probability of error* is the minimal error of a classifier:

$$P_e = \text{Pr(error)} = \int p(x) \text{Pr(error}|x)\mathrm{d}x,$$

with

$$\text{Pr(error}|x) = \begin{cases} \text{Pr}(C_{+1}|x) & \text{rule decided } C_{-1}, \\ \text{Pr}(C_{-1}|x) & \text{rule decided } C_{+1} \end{cases}$$

The *Bayesian error* generalize the error probability by taking into account a *cost matrix* $[c_{i,j}]_{i,j}$ for each potential classification scenario: matrix coefficient $c_{i,j}$ denotes the cost of classifying a new observation x in class C_j knowing that x belongs to class C_i. The Bayesian error minimizes the expected risk, and coincides with the probability or error P_e when one chooses $c_{i,i} = 0$ (no penalty when correctly classified) and $c_{i,j} = 1$ (unit penalty cost for misclassification) for all $j \neq i$.

Recall that Bayes' fundamental identity (as known as *Bayes's rule* or *Bayes's theorem*) is:

$$\boxed{\text{Pr}(C_i|x) = \frac{\text{Pr}(x|C_i)\,\text{Pr}(C_i)}{\text{Pr}(x)}}$$

This can be easily shown using the *chain rule property* of probabilities:

$$\text{Pr}(A \wedge B) = \text{Pr}(A)\,\text{Pr}(B|A) = \text{Pr}(B)\,\text{Pr}(A|B) \Rightarrow \text{Pr}(B|A) = \frac{\text{Pr}(B)\,\text{Pr}(A|B)}{\text{Pr}(A)}.$$

The optimal rule for Bayesian classification that minimizes the probability of error is the *maximum* a posteriori (*MAP* for short) rule: we classify x to class C_i if and only if:

$$\text{Pr}(C_i|x) \geq \text{Pr}(C_j|x).$$

In other words, we choose the class that maximizes the a posteriori probability. By using Bayes' identity and by canceling the common denominator term $\text{Pr}(x)$, this amounts to choose class C_i such that:

$$w_i\,\text{Pr}(x|C_i) \geq w_j\,\text{Pr}(x|C_j), \ \forall j \neq i.$$

Since we neither know the conditional probability laws $\Pr(x|C_i)$ nor the a priori laws, we need to estimate them from observations in practice. We can estimate non-parametrically these distributions by using the balloon estimator that uses the nearest neighbor structures as follows: first, let us consider without loss of generality, the case of two classes $C_{\pm 1}$. We calculate the prior probabilities from the class frequencies of the observations:

$$\Pr(C_{\pm 1}) = w_{\pm 1} = \frac{n_{\pm 1}}{n}.$$

Then we compute the class-conditional probabilities as follows:

$$\Pr(x|C_{\pm 1}) = \frac{k_{\pm 1}}{n_{\pm 1} V_k},$$

with V_k the volume of the ball that cover the k-NNs of x.

Similarly, the non-conditional density (mixture of two distributions) can be estimated using the k-NNs by:

$$m(x) \approx \frac{k}{n V_k(x)}$$

We deduce the a posteriori probabilities using the MAP Bayesian's rule:

$$\Pr(C_{\pm 1}|x) = \frac{\Pr(x|C_{\pm 1}) \Pr(C_{\pm 1})}{\Pr(x)} = \frac{\frac{k_{\pm 1}}{n_{\pm 1} V_k} \frac{n_{\pm 1}}{n}}{\frac{k}{n V_k}} = \frac{k_{\pm 1}}{k}.$$

Hence, we have proved that the voting rule of the k-NN classification rule is sound! We shall now quantify the relative performance of the k-NN classifier compared to the minimum error probability P_e.

9.5.3 Probability of Error for the k-NN Rule

When both the size of the training set and the size of the testing set become large enough, asymptotically tending to infinity ($t, n \to +\infty$), the probability of error $P_e(k\text{-NN})$ of the k-NN rule is a worst twice the minimum probability of error P_e (induced by the MAP rule if one truly knew the class a priori probabilities $w_{\pm 1}$ and class-conditional probabilities $p_{\pm 1}(x)$):

$$\boxed{P_e \le \tau_{\text{error}}(\text{NN}) \le 2 P_e}$$

For the the multi-class case ($m \ge 2$ classes) and the NN-rule, one can further prove that we have the following guaranteed upper-bound:

$$P_e \leq \tau_{\text{error}}(\text{NN}) \leq P_e \left(2 - \frac{m}{m-1} P_e\right).$$

Theorem 11 *The optimal Bayesian MAP rule can be approximated by the k-NN voting rule within a multiplicative error factor of 2 when we estimate non-parametrically the class probabilities using the k-NN balloon estimator.*

Let us notice that when the dimension is large, we need in practice many samples to get this theoretical bound. Once again, this is the phenomenon of the curse of dimensionality that explains that in high-dimensional spaces, problems become exponentially more difficult to solve!

9.6   Implementing Nearest Neighbor Queries on a Computer Cluster

Let us consider P units of computation (UCs, or Processing Elements, PEs) with distributed memory. To classify a new query q, we shall use the *decomposable property* of the k-NN query: that is, we can partition arbitrarily $X = \biguplus_{l=1}^{P} X_l$ into pairwise disjoint groups, and we always have:

$$\text{NN}_k(x, X) = \text{NN}_k(x, \cup_{l=1}^{P} \text{NN}_k(x, X_l)).$$

On P processors, we partition X into P groups of size $\frac{n}{P}$ (horizontal partitioning[3]), and answer locally the queries $\text{NN}_k(x, X_i)$ on each processor. Finally, a *master processor* receives the kP elements from the slave processes, and perform a k-NN query on that aggregated set. Thus we speed-up the $O(dnk)$-time naive sequential algorithm ($P = 1$), and obtain a parallel query algorithm in time $O(dk\frac{n}{P}) + O(dk(kP))$. When $kP \leq \frac{n}{P}$ (that is, $P \leq \sqrt{\frac{n}{k}}$), we obtain an optimal linear speed-up in $O(P)$.

9.7   Notes and References

For statistical machine learning and more details concerning the k-NN rule, we recommend the textbook [1]. The performance of the k-NN rule has first been studied in [2]. The k-NN queries are well-studied but a difficult problem of *computational geometry* in practice, specially in high-dimensions [3]. In practice, graphics processing units (GPUs) are very well-suited for fast k-NN queries [4] using the built-in inner product facilities. An algorithm is said output-sensitive when its complexity can be analyzed using both the input size and the output size. An output-sensitive

---

[3]For very large dimensions, we may consider *vertical partitioning* that splits blockwise the dimension of data among the distributed memories.

algorithm has been proposed for computing the decision region between two classes of points in the plane, see [5]. One can relax the exact k-NN queries to the problem of finding within a constant multiplicative factor $1 + \epsilon$ the ϵ-NNs. The main advantage of classifying with the k-NN rule is that it is easy to program, can be straightforwardly parallelized, and that it guarantees asymptotically a performance bound with respect to Bayes' minimal misclassification error. In practice, one has to choose the right value of k for the k-NN rule: for large values of k, the decision boundary gets smoother and it yields a more robust non-parametric estimation of conditional probabilities, but it costs more time to answer queries and the non-parametric becomes less local!

In practice, classification using big data-sets exhibits experimentally an empirical *law of diminishing returns*: that is, the larger the size of the training set, the smaller the relative improvement of performance. This observed phenomenon is depicted schematically in Fig. 9.5. This is due to the fact that the identically and independently sampled labeled observations assumption does not hold in practice. Bayes' error provides a lower bound on the performance of any classifier in statistical machine learning. It is often hard to calculate explicitly Bayes' error or the probability of error for statistical models in closed-form formula. Thus one rather seeks to upper bound Bayes' error using closed-form formula [6].

There exists numerous extensions of the k-NN rule. One can adjust for example the voting rule among the k neighbors by taking a weighted average vote [7]. We can prove that in high dimensions the k-NN boundary is piecewise linear by studying bichromatic Voronoi diagrams in high dimensions. However, computing such high-dimensional Voronoi diagrams are intractable in practice as they can have a

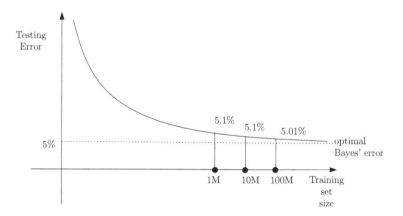

Fig. 9.5 In practice, classification using big data exhibits experimentally a law of diminishing returns: the larger the size of the training set, the smaller the relative improvement of performance. This is due to the fact that the identically and independently sampled labeled observations assumption does not hold. Bayes' error provides a lower bound on the performance of any classifier in statistical machine learning

combinatorial complexity in $O(n^{\lceil \frac{d}{2} \rceil})$ time (already quadratic for $d = 3$), where $\lceil x \rceil$ is the *ceil function* (that returns the smallest integer greater or equal to x).

Let us recall that the k-NN classification rule guarantees asymptotically an error factor of 2 compared to the optimal MAP Bayesian rule but that this classifier needs to store in memory *all* the training set. That can be prohibitive for large data-sets. Another renown classification technique are the *Support Vector Machines* (*SVMs*) that stores only $d + 1$ points in dimension d for linearly separable bichromatic point sets. When classes are not linearly separable, one can use the so-called kernel trick to embed features in a higher-dimensional space so that it becomes separable [1] in that space. It is always possible to find such a kernel to separate classes.

To conclude, let us discuss about model complexity, bias and variance of learning machines, and prediction error. In Chap. 5, we quickly describe the linear regression to motivate the use of linear algebra in data science. Let us compare classification by regression with classification by k-NN as follows:

- Regression model: The model complexity of a linear regression model is $d + 1$, the number of coefficients defining the fitted hyperplane. Regression learning machines have low variance (meaning stable with respect to input perturbation) but high bias (meaning not tight to the true separation of classes).
- k-NN model: The model complexity of a k-NN classifier is $d \times n$, very large since dependent on the input size n of the training set. The properties of the k-NN classifier is to have low bias since it fits well the class separation boundary but it has high variance since a single point perturbation of the training set can significantly affects the decision boundary of the k-NN classifier.

Figure 9.6 illustrates the bias/variance properties of learning machines according to their model complexities. In practice, one has to choose the proper model complexity of a learning machine. The higher the model complexity the lower the

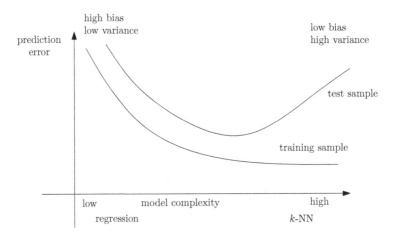

Fig. 9.6 Model complexity, bias and variance of learning machines, and prediction error

prediction error on the training sample. However, at some point, there is an overfitting phenomenon, and the prediction error on the test sample increases instead of continuing to decrease. Since we are interested in minimizing the generalization error (and not on minimizing error on the training sample, which can be optimally reaching zero for the k-NN classifier), the ideal model complexity should be chosen so as to minimize the prediction error on the test sample (see Fig. 9.6).

9.8 Summary

The k-NN classification rule labels a new observation query q from a test set by choosing the dominant class among the k nearest neighbors of q in the training set. One evaluates the performance of a classifier by calculating its F-score that is the harmonic mean of the precision rate and the recall rate. This yields a single quality value that takes into account the four different cases that can occur when classifying observations in one of either two classes (false/true-positive/negative). In statistical machine learning, a classifier can never beat the optimal Bayes' error (or the probability of error), and the 1-NN guarantees asymptotically an error factor of 2. Since the nearest neighbor queries are decomposable queries, meaning that $NN_k(q, X_1 \cup X_2) = NN_k(NN_k(q, X_1), NN_k(q, X_2))$, the k-NN classification rule can be easily parallelized on a distributed memory architecture like a computer cluster. One of the drawback of the k-NN rule is that it needs to store all the training set in order to classify new observations.

Processing Code for Displaying the Nearest Neighbor Classification Rule

Figure 9.7 displays a snapshot of the `processing.org` program.

> WWW source code: NNDecisionBoundary.pde

9.9 Exercises

Exercise 1 (*Pruning the boundary decision of the nearest neighbor classifier*) Prove that when an element of the training set has its neighboring Voronoi cells (called *natural neighbors*) of the same class, then this sample can be safely removed without changing the boundary decision of the NN classification rule. How to prune the training set for the k-NN rule?

Exercise 2 (**Probability of error for conditional Gaussian laws*) Let us consider balanced a priori probabilities $w_1 = w_2 = \frac{1}{2}$ and conditional probabilities following univariate Gaussian distributions $X_1 \sim N(\mu_1, \sigma_1)$ and $X_2 \sim N(\mu_2, \sigma_2)$. Recall that the probability density of a normal distribution is $p(x; \mu, \sigma) = \frac{1}{\sigma\sqrt{2\pi}} \exp(-\frac{(x-\mu)^2}{2\sigma^2})$.

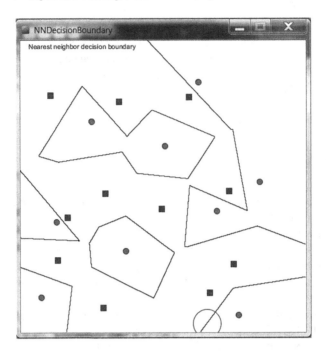

Fig. 9.7 Snapshot of the `processing` code for displaying the nearest neighbor decision border

- Calculate exactly the probability of error when P_e when $\sigma_1 = \sigma_2$,
- Calculate P_e using the standard normal cumulative distribution function $\Phi(\cdot)$ when $\sigma_1 \neq \sigma_2$.
- Since it is difficult to compute P_e in closed-form formula, using the mathematical rewriting $\min(a, b) = \frac{a+b-|b-a|}{2}$ with the following inequality $\min(a, b) \leq a^\alpha b^{1-\alpha}, \forall \alpha \in (0, 1)$ when $a, b > 0$, deduce an upper-bound formula in closed-form bounding P_e for Gaussian distributions.

Exercise 3 (**The k-NN rules and the order-k Voronoi diagrams* [8]) Consider a finite point set $X = \{x_1, \ldots, x_n\}$. Show that the decomposition of the space $\mathbb{R}^d$ induced by the first k nearest neighbors yield convex polyhedral cells. We define the k-order Voronoi diagram as the partition of space induced by all the $\binom{n}{k}$ $X_i \subset 2^X$ subsets of X for the following distance function: $D(X_i, x) = \min_{x' \in X_i} D(x', x)$. That is, the k-order Voronoi diagram is the collection of non-empty cells $V_k(X_i)$ defined by $V_k(X_i) = \{x \mid D(X_i, x) \leq D(X_j, x), \forall i \neq j\}$ (with $|X_l| = k$ for all l). How one can simplify the boundary decision of the k-NN classification rule?

Exercise 4 (**Sensitivity of the k-NN classification rule with respect to the magnitude order of axes*) The performance of a classifier for the nearest neighbor classification rule is quite sensitive to a rescaling of axis since it may change significantly the Euclidean distance. In practice, one has to find a good weighting rule on the attributes (*feature weighting*) to calibrate the "Euclidean distance":

$D_w(p, q) = \sqrt{\sum_{j=1}^{d} w_j (p^j - q^j)^2}$. Study different methods of attribute rewriting and discuss on their performance [1] (refer to Mahalanobis distance with diagonal precision matrix as well).

References

1. Hastie, T., Tibshirani, R., Friedman, R.: Elements of Statistical Learning Theory. Springer, New York (2002)
2. Cover, T.M., Hart, P.E.: Nearest neighbor pattern classification. IEEE Trans. Inf. Theory **13**(1), 21–27 (1967)
3. Arya, S.: An optimal algorithm for approximate nearest neighbor searching fixed dimensions. J. ACM **45**(6), 891–923 (1998)
4. Garcia, V., Debreuve, E., Nielsen, F., Barlaud, M.: k-nearest neighbor search: Fast GPU-based implementations and application to high-dimensional feature matching. In: Proceedings of the International Conference on Image Processing (ICIP), pp. 3757–3760 (2010)
5. Bremner, D., Demaine, E., Erickson, J., Iacono, J., Langerman, S., Morin, P., Toussaint, G.: Output-sensitive algorithms for computing nearest-neighbour decision boundaries. Discret. Comput. Geom. **33**(4), 593–604 (2005)
6. Nielsen, F.: Generalized Bhattacharyya and Chernoff upper bounds on Bayes error using quasi-arithmetic means. Pattern Recognit. Lett. **42**, 25–34 (2014)
7. Piro, P., Nock, R., Nielsen, F., Barlaud, M.: Leveraging k-NN for generic classification boosting. Neurocomputing **80**, 3–9 (2012)
8. Lee, D.-T.: On k-nearest neighbor voronoi diagrams in the plane. IEEE Trans. Comput. **C–31**(6), 478–487 (1982)

Chapter 10
Fast Approximate Optimization in High Dimensions with Core-Sets and Fast Dimension Reduction

10.1 Approximate Optimization for Large-Scale Data-Sets

Often one is interested to solve optimization problems on very large size data-sets. It can be computationally interesting *not* to solve for the exact optimal solution (or one of the optimal solutions when several such optimal solutions exist) but rather seek for a *guaranteed approximation* in faster time. For example, consider the *k-means clustering* problem: we seek to minimize the k-means cost function (i.e., weighted sum of cluster variances, see Chap. 7). It makes sense to think that under some stability hypothesis to point perturbations of the optimal clustering, an approximation of the minimization of the cost function (instead of the regular k-means objective function) will end up with a good (if not an optimal) clustering.

Approximated optimization is even more and more attractive when the dimensions increase since those problems generally tend to become harder and harder then. This phenomenon is called the *curse of dimensionality* (pioneered by Bellman, the founder of the dynamic programming paradigm). Indeed, when the dimension d is to be taken as a parameter of the problem for analysis the resource complexity, we often obtain algorithms that depend exponentially in d, and that can thus unfortunately not scale properly with the dimension in practice.

10.1.1 An Example that Illustrates the Needs for High Dimensions

In practice, one often need to manipulate internally high dimensions, even on low-dimensional input raw data. For example, let us consider the task of finding a *source image patch* of size $s \times s$ in a large size target image. For sake of simplicity, consider intensity images where each pixel stored a single grey value (grey value channel). We can represent the intensity patch as vector of dimension $d = s^2$ by stacking all

© Springer International Publishing Switzerland 2016

F. Nielsen, *Introduction to HPC with MPI for Data Science*, Undergraduate Topics in Computer Science, DOI 10.1007/978-3-319-21903-5_10

the pixel intensity values inside the patch (say, following the scan line order). We say that we *vectorize* (or *linearize*) the patch. It is the same for a patch at a given location in the (large) target image of dimension $n = w \times h$, where w and h denote respectively the image width and image height. We can thus interpret our large image as a cloud of n points in dimension $d = s^2$, the sets of all the $s \times s$ patches of the target image. For pixels located close to the image border, we consider clamping the intensity values. Thus finding the best patch position in the target image (say, the one that minimizes the *sum of squared errors, SSE*) for a given *patch query* amounts to find the nearest neighbor in the high-dimensional space of dimension $d = s^2$.

10.1.2   Some Distance Phenomena in High Dimensions

In large dimensions, we have phenomena that may first seem to be counter-intuitive (fortunately, they are very well explained mathematically). For example, the volume $V_d(r)$ of a ball of radius r in dimension d is given by the following formula:

$$V_d(r) = \frac{\pi^{d/2}}{\Gamma\left(\frac{d}{2}+1\right)} r^d,$$

with Γ the Euler function that generalizes the factorial function: $\Gamma(t) = \int_0^\infty x^{t-1} e^{-x} dx$ (with $\Gamma(k) = (k-1)!$ for $k \geq 2$, $k \in \mathbb{N}$). Thus the volume of a unit radius ball tends to zero as the dimension d increases ($d \to \infty$). But this unit ball centered at the origin touches the $2d$ facets of a cube of side length 2 centered at the origin. Therefore, as the dimension increases, the ball covers less and less proportion of the volume of the cube[1] that contains it. This has a strong impact for Monte-Carlo rejection sampling methods (say, to estimate the volume of the unit ball as we did in Part I for estimating π) that provably will require exponentially more samples with the dimension.

10.1.3   Core-Sets: From Big Data-Sets to Tiny Data-Sets!

We shall see that sometimes there exist for optimization problems some small size sub-sets (sometimes even independent of the extrinsic dimension d and the input size n), called *core-sets*, for which the optimal optimization solutions on them provide a guaranteed approximation for the full set. Interestingly, it is also the case for k-means. Thus core-sets allows one to transform potentially large-scale data-sets into tiny data-sets [1]. It is therefore an important technique for processing *big data*!

---

[1]Commonly called *hypercube* when $d > 3$.

10.2 Core-Sets (Coresets, Core sets): Definition

Let us now precisely define the core-sets for fast approximated optimization. Consider an optimization problem on a data-set $X = \{x_1, \ldots, x_n\}$. Let us mathematically write the optimization as follows:

$$\min_{\theta \in \Theta} f(\theta | x_1, \ldots, x_n),$$

with θ the model parameters to optimize (for example, the k prototypes in the k-means), and Θ the space of admissible parameters. The optimal solution θ^* (or an optimal solution when there exist several optimal such solutions) of minimal cost c^* is obtained by:

$$\theta^* = \mathrm{sol}(\theta | X) = \mathrm{argmin}_{\theta \in \Theta} f(\theta | x_1, \ldots, x_n),$$
$$c^* = \mathrm{cost}(\theta | X) = \min_{\theta \in \Theta} f(\theta | x_1, \ldots, x_n).$$

Instead of solving this optimization on the full data-set X, we rather seek a core-set subset $C \subseteq X$ such that we have the following inequality:

$$\mathrm{cost}(\theta | X) \leq \mathrm{cost}(\theta | C) \leq (1 + \epsilon) \mathrm{cost}(\theta | X).$$

Moreover, we wish to have $|C| \ll |X|$ (that is the size of C neglectable compared with the size of X, *i.e.*, $|C| = o(|X|)$). That is, the cardinality of C should be very small compared to the one in X, with $|C|$ depending ideally only on $\epsilon > 0$ (and not on $n = |X|$, nor on the dimension d of the ambient space of the x_i's).

10.3 Core-Sets for the Smallest Enclosing Balls

The *smallest enclosing ball*[2] (*SEB*) asks to find a ball $B = \mathrm{Ball}(c, r)$ of minimal radius that fully covers X. We can model this optimization problem as follows:

$$\boxed{c^* = \arg\min_{c \in \mathbb{R}^d} \max_{i=1}^{n} \|c - x_i\|}$$

The smallest enclosing ball is provably always *unique* and its center (called *circumcenter*) shall be denoted by c^*. Notice that instead of minimizing the radius, we could have equivalently taken the volume (a power function of the radius), or define "minimality" with respect to the inclusion $\subset$ operator. Figure 10.1 displays an example of the smallest enclosing ball for a planar point set.

---

[2] Also called in the literature the *minimum enclosing ball*, or *minimum covering ball*.

Fig. 10.1 An example of the smallest enclosing ball for a planar point set. For point sets in general position, at most 3 points are lying on the boundary *circle* (at most $d + 1$ in dimension d)

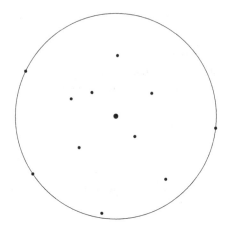

Let $c(X)$ denote the center of the smallest enclosing ball of X, $\text{SEB}(X) = \text{Ball}(c(X), r(X))$, and $r(X)$ its radius. For any $\epsilon > 0$, an *ϵ-coreset* is a sub-set $C \subseteq X$ such that:

$$X \subseteq \text{Ball}(c(C), (1 + \epsilon)r(C)).$$

That is, by enlarging the smallest enclosing ball by a homothetic factor $1 + \epsilon$ while keeping the center unchanged, we shall fully cover X. Figure 10.2 illustrates such a core-set example for the smallest enclosing ball. It has been shown [2, 3] that there exist core-sets of optimal size $\lceil \frac{1}{\epsilon} \rceil$ for the smallest enclosing ball, that are both independent of the dimension d and of the original input size n!

In practice, core-sets find many applications in large dimensions, even when $d \gg n$. That is, when the number of data elements is far less than the dimension of these data with those data contained on a proper subspace of the full space (with *extrinsic dimension* the dimension of the ambient space $\mathbb{R}^d$). The *intrinsic*

Fig. 10.2 Illustrating a core-set: the core-set C is graphically represented by the points enclosed with *squares*. By enlarging the smallest enclosing ball $\text{SEB}(C)$ by a factor $1 + \epsilon$, we fully cover X: $X \subseteq \text{Ball}(c(C), (1 + \epsilon)r(C))$

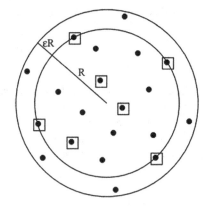

dimension is the minimum dimension of the subspace that contains all the data. For example, consider 3 points in $\mathbb{R}^5$: then the extrinsic dimension is 5 while the intrinsic dimension is 2 (plane) when the three points form the vertices of a non-degenerate triangle, and intrinsic dimension 1 (line) when the three points are collinear (degenerate position).

Let us observe that in the case $d \gg n$, one could mathematically consider without loss of generality an affine subspace of dimension $d' = n - 1$ for points in general position (that is, reduce the extrinsic dimension to the intrinsic dimension). A set of n points are said to be in *general position* if and only if there does not exist $k + 1$ points in an affine sub-space of dimension k (for example, 3 collinear points are not in general position). However, computing explicitly this affine sub-space requires to compute determinants, that are not only time consuming, but also numerically very unstable in practice since we loose numerical precision when we perform a multiplication.[3]

10.4 A Simple Iterative Heuristic for Approximating the Smallest Enclosing Ball

We describe below a $(1 + \epsilon)$-approximation heuristic for computing a guaranteed approximation of the smallest enclosing ball using $\lceil \frac{1}{\epsilon^2} \rceil$ iterations. For example, to get a 1 % approximation we need to perform 10000 iterations. The pseudo-code is given below:

APPROXMINIBALL($X, \epsilon > 0$):

- Initialize center $c_1 \in X = \{x_1, \dots, x_n\}$ (we can also choose any other arbitrary point for c_1, or the center of mass, in fact we need this initial point to lie inside the convex hull of X),
- Update iteratively for $i = 2, \dots, \lceil \frac{1}{\epsilon^2} \rceil$ the center as follows:

$$\boxed{c_i \leftarrow c_{i-1} + \frac{f_{i-1} - c_{i-1}}{i}}$$

where f_i denotes the farthest point of X with respect to the current circumcenter c_i:

$$f_i = p_s, \quad s = \operatorname{argmax}_{j=1}^n \|c_i - x_j\|.$$

- Return Ball($c_{\lceil \frac{1}{\epsilon^2} \rceil}$, $\max_i \|x_i - c_{\lceil \frac{1}{\epsilon^2} \rceil}\|$).

---

[3]To bypass this numerical precision, we could not use the usual IEEE 754 floating-point standard, but rather use a multi-precision library like the GNU mpf package, multi-precision floating point package.

Fig. 10.3 Visualizing the core-set heuristic for approximating the smallest enclosing ball of a point set: the *circle* point displays the current circumcenter, the *square* point the farthest point with respect to the current circumcenter, and the filled disk points the set of points that define the core-set

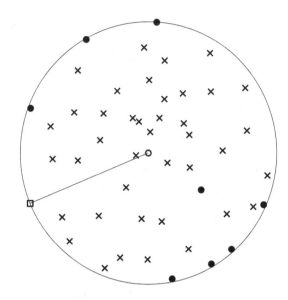

This algorithm[4] looks like a gradient descent method and has an overall cost of $O(\frac{dn}{\epsilon^2})$ time. As a byproduct, this (greedy) heuristic also constructs a core-set: $f_1, \ldots, f_l$ with $l = \lceil \frac{1}{\epsilon^2} \rceil$. Figure 10.3 displays the configuration after a few iterations of the algorithm, and visualize the corresponding core-set. Let us emphasize on the fact that the core-set produced by this algorithm is of size $\lceil \frac{1}{\epsilon^2} \rceil$, and is not optimal since we know that there exist optimal core-sets of optimal size $\lceil \frac{1}{\epsilon} \rceil$ for the smallest enclosing balls.

10.4.1 Convergence Proof

Theorem 12 *The circumcenter c^* of the smallest enclosing ball $\mathrm{Ball}(c^*, r^*)$ is approximated by the algorithm* APPROXMINIBALL *that yields after the ith iteration, the following guarantee:* $\|c_i - c^*\| \leq \frac{r^*}{\sqrt{i}}$.

This theorem ensures that we obtain a $(1 + \frac{1}{\sqrt{i}})$-approximation. Indeed, for all $x \in X$, using the triangular inequality of the Euclidean distance, we have:

$$\|x - c_i\| \leq \|x - c^*\| + \|c^* - c_i\| \leq r^* + \frac{r^*}{\sqrt{i}} = \left(1 + \frac{1}{\sqrt{i}}\right) r^*.$$

---

[4]See the online demo at http://kenclarkson.org/sga/t/t.xml.

Fig. 10.4 Notations used in the proof

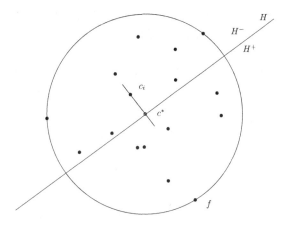

The technical proof of this theorem is concisely reported below. We proceed by induction: for $i = 1$, we have $\|c_1 - c^*\| \leq r^*$. At stage i, we distinguish between these two cases:

- either $c_i = c^*$ and then we move at most by $\frac{r^*}{i+1} \leq \frac{r^*}{\sqrt{i+1}}$, and finally we have $\|c^* - c_{i+1}\| \leq \frac{r^*}{\sqrt{i+1}}$,
- or $c_i \neq c^*$, and we consider the orthogonal hyperplane at line segment $[c^*c_i]$ that contains c^*. We denote by H^+ the half-space delimited by H that does not contain c_i, and by H^- the other complementary half-space (see Fig. 10.4). One can show that the farthest point f is necessarily contained in $X \cap H^+$. There are two new cases:

  - case $c_{i+1} \in H^+$: distance $\|c_{i+1} - c^*|$ is maximal when $c_i = c^*$, and therefore $\|c_{i+1} - c^*\| \leq \frac{r^*}{i+1} \leq \frac{r^*}{\sqrt{i+1}}$,
  - case where $c_{i+1} \in H^-$: by moving c_i the farthest from c^* and by taking f on the sphere the closest to H^-, we necessarily increase the distance $\|c_{i+1} - c^*\|$. In that case, line segment $[c^*c_{i+1}]$ is orthogonal to line segment $[c_i f]$, and by using the *Pythagorean identity*,[5] we have:

$$\|c_{i+1} - c^*\| = \frac{\frac{(r^*)^2}{\sqrt{i}}}{\frac{r^*}{\sqrt{1+\frac{1}{i}}}} = \frac{r^*}{\sqrt{i+1}}.$$

In order to guarantee 1 % of precision, heuristic APPROXMINIBALL needs therefore to perform 10000 iterations. This is thus time consuming but has the merit to work in any dimension.

---

[5]Pythagoras' theorem is a corner stone in Euclidean geometry. It states that for a right triangle the square of the hypotenuse (that is, the side opposite the right angle) is equal to the sum of the squares of the other two sides.

10.4.2   Small Enclosing Balls and Good Margin Linear Separators for SVMs

Computing the smallest enclosing ball can mathematically be rewritten as an example of *quadratic programming* (*QP*) where we seek to minimize the squared radius given a set of linear constraints (one constraint per point), see [4]. We have described in Chap. 9, the k-nearest neighbor rules for classification (under supervised training). Another popular technique in supervised learning are *support vector machines*, or *SVMs* for short. A SVM distinguishes two population of points (say, those labeled $+1$ from those labeled -1) using a *separating hyperplane* that maximizes the *margin*, defined as the minimum distance of a point to the SVM separating hyperplane. One can prove that finding the best margin separating hyperplane is dually equivalent to computing a smallest enclosing ball [4]. Thus core-sets for balls can be used "as is" to define a good separating hyperplane in SVMs. This latter technique gave rise to the so-called *Core Vector Machines* (*CVMs*) [4] that are a popular technique in machine learning.

10.5   Core-Sets for k-Means

We explained in Chap. 7 that clustering data by minimizing the k-means objective function is a NP-hard problem when both $d > 1$ and $k > 1$. We can write the k-means with respect to the k prototype centers in set C by $l_C(X) = \sum_{x \in X} D^2(x, C)$ where $D^2(x, C)$ denote the minimal squared Euclidean distance between x and one of its k centers of C.

We say that S is a (k, ϵ)-*core-set* for X iff.

$$\forall C = (c_1, \ldots, c_k), \quad (1 - \epsilon)l_C(P) \leq l_C(S) \leq (1 + \epsilon)l_C(P).$$

In 1D, there exist (k, ϵ)-coresets of size $O(\frac{k^2}{\epsilon^2})$, and in high dimension, one has proved [5] that there exist core-sets of size $O(k^3/\epsilon^{d+1})$. We can thus perform k-means clustering on very large data-sets since the size of core-set are independent of the input size, n.

10.6   Fast Dimension Reduction via Random Projection Matrices

10.6.1   The Curse of Dimensionality

The *curse of dimensionality* was first emphasized by Bellman (the inventor of the celebrated dynamic programming technique). Bellman noticed that the efficiency of the algorithms depends on the dimension of the data, that is the number of attributes in vector elements. For example, computing distances (dissimilarities) or similarities between two d-dimensional vectors require $\Omega(d)$ time. Often the algorithms relying on partition data-structures have a time complexity exponential in the dimension d, that is hidden in the big-Oh notation, $O_d(1)$. Moreover, it is extremely difficult to visualize data-set structures in high-dimensions. Nowadays, it is common to work with high-dimensional data-sets (say, $d = 1000$ like gene expressions), and sometimes the extrinsic dimension is far more than the number of data, n: $d \gg n$.

There are many counter-intuitive facts in high dimensions:

- For example, the volume of the unit-diameter ball inscribed in the unit cube tend to zero as the dimension increase. Indeed, the volume V_d of a ball of radius $r = \frac{1}{2}$ is given by the following formula:

$$V_d = \frac{\pi^{\frac{d}{2}}}{\Gamma\left(\frac{d}{2} + 1\right)} r^d, \quad r = \frac{1}{2},$$

where $\Gamma(t) = \int_0^\infty x^{t-1} e^{-x} dx$ is the extension of the factorial function, with $\Gamma(n) = (n-1)!$ for $n \in \mathbb{N}$.

- The *regular grid* of side length l in $\mathbb{R}^d$ has l^d elementary hypercubes, growing exponentially with the dimension d (we have $l^d = e^{d \log l}$), and an adaptive subdivision does not scale either in very large dimensions.

- Monte-Carlo stochastic integration ($\int \approx \sum$) become useless in high dimensions (too much rejection samples when computing high-dimensional integrals).

- As underlined by Beyer et al. [6], "... the distance to the nearest data point approaches the distance to the farthest data point ...".

10.6.2 Two Illustrating Examples of High-Dimensional Tasks

Consider the task of finding *near duplicate images* in a large collection of n images. A RGB color image $I[y][x]$ of dimension $w \times h$ is converted into a vector $v(I)$ of dimension $\mathbb{R}^{3wh}$ by stacking in the scanline order all triples of pixel colors. This process is called *image vectorization*. Then the distance between two images I_1 and I_2 can be chosen to be the *sum of squared differences (SSD)*:

$$\mathrm{SSD}(I_1, I_2) = \sum_{i=1}^{h} \sum_{j=1}^{w} (I_1[i][j] - I_2[i][j])^2$$
$$= \|v(I_1) - v(I_2)\|^2$$

There is a near duplicate image in a database if its closest image (a nearest neighbor query, NN) is at a close distance. That is, image I has a near duplicate image whenever

$\mathrm{SSD}(I, \mathrm{NN}(I)) \leq \epsilon$ for a prescribed value of ϵ. A naive algorithm to solve NN queries requires $O(dn)$ time. This is too prohibitive. Thus this near duplicate image problem rises the question of computing efficiently nearest neighbors in high dimensions, in sub-linear time, $o(d)$.

For our second illustrative example, consider the problem of clustering a large collection of images. For example, consider the *MNIST data-set*[6] that consists in $n = 60000$ handwritten digits (from '0' digit to '9' digit) of US postal codes, with each digit being stored as a 28×28 gray image. The image vectorization of this MNIST data-base yields a point cloud in moderate dimension $d = 28^2 = 784$. Ideally, we expect to find the ten clusters with each cluster regrouping all the same digits. But using the k-means clustering technique is too slow. This asks for a different approach: how to reduce effectively dimension while preserving the pairwise distance between elements of the data-base?

10.6.3   Linear Dimension Reduction

Consider a data-set X of n vectors of $\mathbb{R}^d$. X is interpreted as a matrix of dimension $n \times d$ with a point stored per matrix row (row vector convention). At first, we may think of two techniques for reducing the dimension

- select dimensions to keep and drop the other less important dimensions: that is, perform *feature selection*,
- recompose dimensions into new dimensions while preserving as much as possible the distance information.

The *linear dimension reduction* associates to each input vector x another vector $y = y(x) \in \mathbb{R}^k$ (with $k < d$) via a *linear mapping* $A : \mathbb{R}^d \to \mathbb{R}^k$ that can be written using matrix formalism as:

$$y = x \times A, \qquad Y = X \times A.$$

A is a matrix of size $d \times k$ (and both x and y are row vectors). We seek a matrix A that should be well suited to preserve the pairwise distances of elements stored in the data-set matrix X (quasi-isometric embedding):

$$\forall x, x' \in X, \quad \|y - y'\|^2 = \|xA - x'A\|^2 \approx \|x - x'\|^2$$

Once A has been found, we have a more compact representation of X as $X \times A$. How can we efficiently find such a matrix transform A?

---

[6] Available freely online, see https://en.wikipedia.org/wiki/MNIST_database.

10.6.4 The Johnson–Lindenstrauss' Theorem

The Johnson–Lindenstrauss' theorem [7] opened a breakthrough in dimension reduction:

Theorem 10.1 (Johnson–Lindenstrauss' theorem [7]) *Let X be a set of n points of $\mathbb{R}^d$ and fix a $\epsilon \in (0, 1)$. Then there exists a linear transformation $A : \mathbb{R}^d \to \mathbb{R}^k$ with $k = O(\frac{1}{\epsilon^2} \log n)$ such that:*

$$\boxed{\forall x, x' \in X, \quad (1 - \epsilon)\|x - x'\|^2 \leq \|xA - x'A\|^2 \leq (1 + \epsilon)\|x - x'\|^2}$$

The Johnson–Lindenstrauss' theorem states that there exists mathematically a *low distortion embedding*, and allows one to consider a quasi-equivalent point set in dimension $k = O(\frac{1}{\epsilon^2} \log n)$, that is independent of the extrinsic dimension d.

10.6.5 Random Projection Matrices

There is a simple recipe for finding such a good linear transformation A: draw its coefficients randomly as follows:

- Draw at random identically and independently (iid) the coefficients of a matrix A' where each coefficient follows a standard normal distribution:

$$A' = [a_{i,j}], \quad a_{i,j} \sim N(0, 1)$$

A standard normal variate $x \sim N(0, 1)$ is obtained from two iid uniform laws U_1 and U_2 by the Box-Muller transformation:

$$x = \sqrt{-2 \log U_1} \cos(2\pi U_2)$$

- Then adjust the scale of the random matrix:

$$A = \frac{k}{d} A'$$

Let us put this approach in practice by considering again the image clustering problem in high dimension: with the simple-to-implement dimension reduction technique that we shall describe next, it becomes easy cluster a data-base of n color images of dimension 300×300 ($\mathbb{R}^{300 \times 300 \times 3} = \mathbb{R}^{270000}$) by reducing it to dimension $k = 532$ ($\mathbb{R}^{532}$) while finding similar clustering. Thus we obtain a major speed-up since the Lloyd's k-means heuristic requires originally $O(sdkn)$ time (where s denotes the number of iterations) in dimension d but only $O_\epsilon(skn \log n)$ once the embedded as been computed. Notice that it costs $O_\epsilon(nd \log n)$ time to compute the data projections before calling a k-means on the quasi-similar reduced dimension data-set.

We skip the theoretical background that explains why such a construction is valid with high probability, and mention some recent results on the Johnson–Lindenstrauss' theorem: first, the dimension $k = \Omega(\epsilon^{-2} \log n)$ is optimal when considering linear transformation [8]. Second, it is better to consider random projection matrices with random rational weights [9] obtained by tossing a dice. For example, choose

$$a_{i,j} = \begin{cases} 1 & \text{with probability } \frac{1}{6} \\ 0 & \text{with probability } \frac{2}{3} \\ -1 & \text{with probability } \frac{1}{6} \end{cases}$$

Third, consider sparse random matrices: it is enough to have $O(\frac{1}{\epsilon})$ non-zero coefficients [10].

10.7 Notes and References

It has been quite an astonishing result to discover that there exist core-sets [2] of size $\lceil \frac{1}{\epsilon} \rceil$ for the minimum enclosing ball, that depends only on ϵ, and *not* on the input data size n, nor on the ambient space dimension d. This discovery has allowed to revisit many classic optimization problems under this novel framework of core-sets. Computing the smallest enclosing ball is also interesting to find the best separating hyperplanes that maximize margins for support vector machines (technically speaking, the smallest enclosing ball is the dual problem in core vector machines [4]). Core-sets have been investigated for clustering problems [5] like k-means and other objective function clustering. This has open the door to cluster efficiently big data-sets. Indeed, the rationale of core-sets [1] is to allow to transform large-scale data sizes into core-sets of tiny sizes provided that we allow some approximation factor ϵ. We recommend the following article [11] for an overview of the challenges in data mining and *big data* that includes a discussion on core-sets. There are many techniques for linear dimension reduction and non-linear dimension reduction (also called *manifold learning* although it is a special case of non-linear dimension reduction).

10.8 Summary

A large class of optimization problems to solve consists in optimizing a parametric function on data-sets. A core-set is a subset of the data on which the exact optimization result yields a guaranteed approximation of the optimization on the complete data-set. There exist core-sets of size $\lceil \frac{1}{\epsilon} \rceil$ for computing the smallest enclosing ball (independent of the input size n, and the extrinsic dimension d), and core-sets of size $O(k^3/\epsilon^{d+1})$ for computing an approximation of the k-means cost function that guarantees a $(1+\epsilon)$-approximation. These core-set sizes are independent of the input size n, and only depend on the approximation factor $1+\epsilon$. Thus core-sets allow one to transform problems on gigantic data-sets to problems on tiny data-sets, and therefore yield an efficient paradigm to process big data or data flows.

10.9 Exercises

Exercise 1 (*Smallest enclosing ball and farthest Voronoi diagram*) Prove that the circumcenter c^* of the smallest enclosing ball of point set $X = \{x_1, \ldots, x_n\}$ is necessarily located on the *farthest Voronoi diagram*. We define the Voronoi cells of the farthest Voronoi diagram by reversing the inequality:

$$V_F(x_i) = \{x \mid \|x - x_j\| \le \|x - x_i\|, \forall j \ne i\}.$$

Cell $V_F(x_i)$ is thus the set of points for which generator x_i is the farthest point of X.

Exercise 2 (*A parallel heuristic for* APPROXMINIBALL) Show how to implement in parallel using MPI the heuristic APPROXMINIBALL on a cluster of P machines with distributed memory. What is the complexity of your algorithm?

References

1. Feldman, D., Schmidt, M., Sohler, C.: Turning big data into tiny data: Constant-size coresets for k-means, PCA and projective clustering. In: Proceedings of the Twenty-Fourth Annual ACM-SIAM Symposium on Discrete Algorithms, pp. 1434–1453. SIAM (2013)
2. Badoiu, M., Clarkson, K.L.: Optimal core-sets for balls. Comput. Geom. **40**(1), 14–22 (2008)
3. Martinetz, T., Mamlouk, A.M., Mota, C.: Fast and easy computation of approximate smallest enclosing balls. In: 19th Brazilian Symposium on Computer Graphics and Image Processing (SIBGRAPI), pp. 163–170, Oct 2006
4. Tsang, IW., Kocsor, A., Kwok, JT.: Simpler core vector machines with enclosing balls. In Proceedings of the 24th International Conference on Machine Learning, pp. 911–918. ACM (2007)
5. Har-Peled, S., Kushal, A.: Smaller coresets for k-median and k-means clustering. Discret. Comput. Geom. **37**(1), 3–19 (2007)
6. Beyer, K., Goldstein, J., Ramakrishnan, R., Shaft, U.: When is "Nearest Neighbor" Meaningful? In: Database Theory (ICDT). Springer, Berlin (1999)
7. Johnson, W., Lindenstrauss, J.: Extensions of Lipschitz mappings into a Hilbert space. In: Conference in modern analysis and probability. Contemporary Mathematics, pp. 189–206. American Mathematical Society, New Haven (1984)
8. Larsen, KG., Nelson, J.: The Johnson–Lindenstrauss lemma is optimal for linear dimensionality reduction. arXiv preprint arXiv:1411.2404, 2014

9. Achlioptas, D.: Database-friendly random projections: Johnson–Lindenstrauss with binary coins. J. comput. Syst. Sci. **66**(4), 671–687 (2003)
10. Kane, D.M., Nelson, J.: Sparser Johnson–Lindenstrauss transforms. J. ACM (JACM) **61**(1), 4 (2014)
11. Fan, W., Bifet, A.: Mining big data: current status, and forecast to the future. ACM SIGKDD Explor. Newsl. **14**(2), 1–5 (2013)

Chapter 11
Parallel Algorithms for Graphs

11.1 Finding Dense(st) Sub-graphs in Large Graphs

11.1.1 Problem Statement

Let $G = (V, E)$ be a *graph* with $|V| = n$ *nodes* (or *vertices*) and $|E| = m$ *edges*. We seek the sub-graph $V' \subseteq V$ that maximizes the following *graph density function*:

$$\rho(V') = \frac{|E(V')|}{|V'|}$$

where $E(V') = \{(u, v) \in E \mid (u, v) \in V' \times V'\}$ (*i.e.*, both nodes should belong to the vertex subset). Let us denote by $G_{|V'} = (V', E(V'))$ this *restricted sub-graph*. In other words, the density of a sub-graph is the mean or average degree of that sub-graph. For the complete graph, the clique $G = K_n$, we thus have $\rho_{\max} = \rho(V) = \frac{n(n-1)}{2n} = \frac{n-1}{2}$, the maximal density of any graph.

Therefore finding the Densest Sub-Graph $G_{|V^*}$ (the DSG problem for short), of density ρ^*, amounts to the following optimization problem:

$$\rho^* = \max_{V' \subseteq V} \rho(V').$$

Let us notice that there can exist several such densest sub-graphs V^* having the same optimal density value (i.e., think of several disconnected maximal cliques): $\rho^* = \rho(V^*)$. Figure 11.1 depicts a graph with its densest sub-graph.

Computing the densest sub-graph is very useful when analyzing graphs. For example, on large graphs when modeling connections in social networks! This primitive is also related to the problem of detecting *graph communities*, or to compress efficiently graphs. Nowadays, data-sets modeling networks are available ubiquitously:

© Springer International Publishing Switzerland 2016
F. Nielsen, *Introduction to HPC with MPI for Data Science*, Undergraduate
Topics in Computer Science, DOI 10.1007/978-3-319-21903-5_11

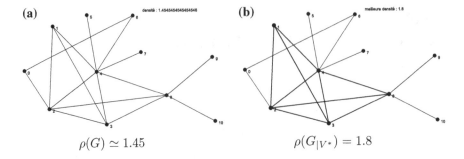

Fig. 11.1 Example of a densest sub-graph (**b**, sub-graph $G_{|V*}$ drawn in *thick lines*) of an input graph (**a**) with 11 nodes

for example, let us cite the telecommunication networks, the scientific citation networks, the collaborative networks, the networks of protein interactions, the networks of mass media information, the financial networks, and so on.

11.1.2 Densest Sub-graph Complexity and a Simple Greedy Heuristic

In theory, one can solve the densest sub-graph problem in *polynomial time* using the mathematical technique of *linear programming* [1] (*LP*). However, this problem becomes (surprisingly?) *NP-hard* when we enforce the constraint $|V'| = k$: that is, when we constrain the cardinality of the sub-graph to have exactly k vertices.

We describe a guaranteed heuristic that yields a 2-approximation factor: that is, we provide a method that returns a sub-set of vertices $V'' \subseteq V$ such that $\rho(G_{|V''}) \geq \frac{1}{2}\rho^*$. In plain words, the sub-graph $G_{|V''}$ has an average degree at most 50 % worse than the average degree of the best densest sub-graph $G_{|V*}$. This quite recent heuristic has been proposed by Professor Charikar[1] of Princeton University (USA) in 2000, and proceeds iteratively as follows:

- Remove the node with the *smallest degree* and all its incoming edges (in case of ties, choose arbitrarily one node having the smallest degree valency), and reiterate until all nodes are removed (so that in the end we obtain the empty graph).
- Keep the intermediate sub-graph that was found with the densest ρ value in this sequence of n iterations.

Figures 11.2 and 11.3 illustrate the different iterations of this heuristic on a simple toy graph.

In general, an α-*approximation* of the densest sub-graph is a sub-graph $G_{|V'}$ so that we have: $\rho(V') \geq \frac{1}{\alpha}\rho(V^*)$. Let us prove that this simple "select smallest degree vertex, remove, and reiterate until obtaining the empty graph" heuristic guarantees a 2-approximation. Let us denote by $\rho^* = \rho(V^*) = \frac{|E(V^*)|}{|V^*|}$ the optimal density obtained for a vertex set V^*.

---

[1] http://www.cs.princeton.edu/~moses/.

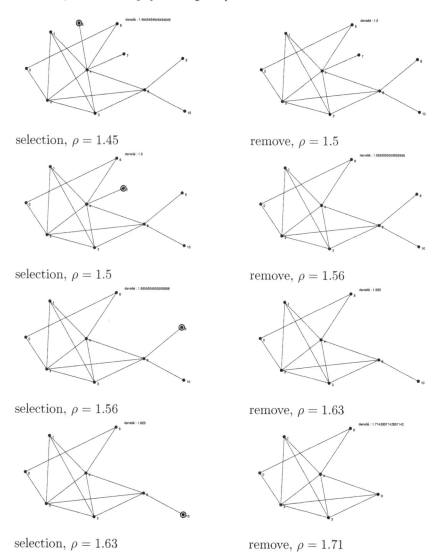

selection, $\rho = 1.45$ remove, $\rho = 1.5$

selection, $\rho = 1.5$ remove, $\rho = 1.56$

selection, $\rho = 1.56$ remove, $\rho = 1.63$

selection, $\rho = 1.63$ remove, $\rho = 1.71$

Fig. 11.2 Illustrating Charikar's heuristic to find a 2-approximation of the densest sub-graph: the different steps are displayed from *left* to *right*, and from *top* to *bottom*. The vertices surrounded by *circles* indicates the vertices that shall be removed at the next stage. To be continued on Fig. 11.3

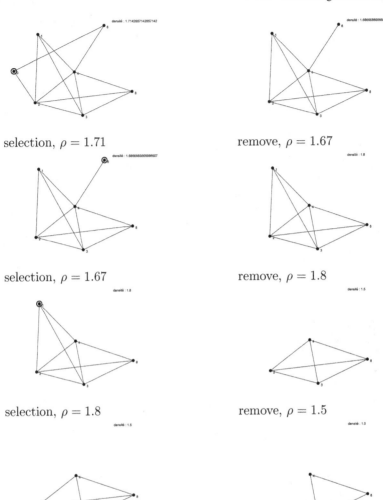

selection, $\rho = 1.71$ remove, $\rho = 1.67$

selection, $\rho = 1.67$ remove, $\rho = 1.8$

selection, $\rho = 1.8$ remove, $\rho = 1.5$

selection, $\rho = 1.5$ remove, $\rho = 1.0$

Fig. 11.3 Illustrating Charikar's heuristic to find a 2-approximation of the densest sub-graph: the different steps are displayed from *left* to *right*, and from *top* to *bottom*. The best density obtained in that sequence of graph yields $\rho^* = \frac{9}{5} = 1.8$. At each step, the vertex surrounded by a *circle* shows the vertex that shall be removed at the next iteration (of smallest degree)

Charikar's heuristic is described in pseudo-code below:

Data: A non-oriented graph $G = (V, E)$
$\tilde{S} \leftarrow V$;
$S \leftarrow V$;
while $S \neq \emptyset$ **do**
    $s \leftarrow \arg\min_{s \in S} \deg_S(s)$;
    $S \leftarrow S \backslash \{s\}$;
    if $\rho(S) > \rho(\tilde{S})$ **then**
        $\tilde{S} \leftarrow S$
    end
end
return $\tilde{S}$

Algorithm 6: The greedy heuristic of Charikar returns a 2-approximation $\tilde{S}$ of the densest sub-graph of $G = (V, E)$.

It is a so-called *greedy algorithm* because it iteratively makes local choices in order to build an approximate solution.

First, let us notice that $\sum_{s \in S} \deg_S(s) = 2|E(S)| = 2|S|\rho(S)$. Let us prove that the maximal density $\rho^* \leq d_{\max}$, with $d_{\max}$ the maximum degree of a node of graph G. Indeed, there are at most $|V^*|d_{\max}$ edges in $E(V^*)$ (otherwise, it would contradict that the maximal degree is $d_{\max}$!). Therefore we deduce that $E(V^*) \leq |V^*|d_{\max}$. It follows that:

$$\rho^* = \frac{E(V^*)}{|V^*|} \leq d_{\max}.$$

Let us consider the sequence of iterations that removes the vertices one by one, and consider the the first time we remove a node of V^* (that we do not know explicitly). Then each node of V^* has necessarily a degree at least equal to ρ^*. Otherwise, we could increase the density $\rho^* = \frac{|E^*|}{|V^*|}$. Therefore we deduce that $E(S) \geq \frac{1}{2}\rho^*|V^*|$, and the density of this sub-graph with the vertices S is:

$$\rho(S) = \frac{|E(S)|}{|V(S)|} \geq \frac{\rho^*|V^*|}{2|V^*|} = \frac{\rho^*}{2}.$$

Since we choose, the maximum of the densities of the intermediate sub-graphs in the iteration sequence, we conclude that the heuristic guarantees a 2-approximation.

On the real-RAM model of computation, we can implement this heuristic in several ways. A straightforward implementation would bear a quadratic cost, in $O(n^2)$. This is prohibitive running time for large graphs. We can also use a *heap data-structure* to select in a stepwise fashion the vertices. We recall that a heap is an abstract data-type that is usually implemented using a *perfect binary tree* (that is, with all levels full except eventually the last one) that satisfies the property that the key stored at an internal node is greater or equal to the keys stored at its children (see [2]). By updating the keys when we remove edges, we obtain an overall running time of

$O((n+m)\log n)$. We can also implement this heuristic in linear time $O(|V|+|E|) = O(n + m)$ as follows: we maintain the vertices in at most $n + 1$ lists, the L_i's, so that each list L_i contains all vertices of degree exactly i, for $i \in \{0, \ldots, n\}$. At each iteration, we choose the vertex s of the smallest non-empty list, and remove that vertex from that list. Then we update the adjacent nodes.

Theorem 13 (Sequential greedy heuristic for the DSG) *In linear time $O(n + m)$, we can compute a 2-approximation of the densest sub-graph of a non-oriented graph $G = (V, E)$ with $n = |V|$ nodes and $m = |E|$ edges.*

At first glance, Charikar's heuristic seems difficult to parallelize as it is, since it requires to operate the n sequential iterations. Next, we shall present a slight modification of this heuristic that yields a straightforward parallel efficient solution.

11.1.3   A Parallel Heuristic for the Densest Sub-graph

Let $\epsilon > 0$ be a prescribed real value. We adapt the former sequential greedy heuristic as follows: we replace the select-and-remove the smallest vertex degree step by removing *all vertices* with incoming edges of degree less than $2(1+\epsilon)$ times the average/mean degree of the graph $\bar{d} = \rho(V)$. We calculate the density of the remaining graph, and reiterate until we obtain the empty graph.

We parallelize by blocks these two stages as follows:

- Stage 1: Count the remaining edges, vertices, and node degrees, in order to compute the average degree $\bar{d}$,
- Stage 2: Remove all nodes with degree less than $2(1 + \epsilon)\bar{d}$ from the current graph, and go to 1 until we reach the empty graph.

Data: A graph $G = (V, E)$ and $\epsilon > 0$
$\tilde{S} \leftarrow V$;
$S \leftarrow V$;
while $S \neq \emptyset$ **do**
  $\quad A(S) \leftarrow \{s \in S \mid \deg_S(s) \leq 2(1 + \epsilon)\rho(S)\}$;
  $\quad S \leftarrow S \backslash A(S)$;
  $\quad$ **if** $\rho(S) > \rho(\tilde{S})$ **then**
  $\quad\quad \mid \tilde{S} \leftarrow S$
  $\quad$ **end**
end
return $\tilde{S}$

Algorithm 7: Parallel greedy heuristic to find an approximation $\tilde{S}$ of the densest sub-graph.

Figure 11.4 illustrates the various stages of this new parallel greedy heuristic executed on our toy sample graph. What is the performance of this parallel heuristic?

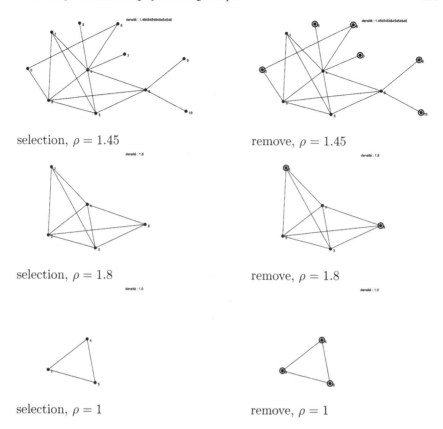

selection, $\rho = 1.45$ remove, $\rho = 1.45$

selection, $\rho = 1.8$ remove, $\rho = 1.8$

selection, $\rho = 1$ remove, $\rho = 1$

Fig. 11.4 Illustration of the parallel (greedy) heuristic: we simultaneously remove all vertices of degree less than $(1 + \epsilon)\bar{d}$, where $\epsilon > 0$ is a prescribed value and $\bar{d} = \rho(G)$ denotes the average degree of the current graph G. The vertices surrounded by *circles* indicates the vertices that shall be removed at the next stage

One can show that we obtain a *guaranteed* $2(1 + \epsilon)$-approximation as follows: let S denote the vertex set of the remaining graph when we first select a vertex of V^* in $A(S)$. Let $s = V^* \cap A(S)$ denote a vertex of the optimal solution. Then we have $\rho(V^*) \leq \deg_{V^*}(s)$ and since $V^* \subseteq S$, we have $\deg_{V^*}(s) \leq \deg_S(s)$. But s belongs to $A(S)$, therefore we have $\deg_S(s) \leq (2 + 2\epsilon)\rho(S)$. Therefore we can deduce using transitivity that:

$$\rho(S) \geq \frac{\rho(V^*)}{2 + 2\epsilon}.$$

Now, since we have chosen the best density obtained during all the iterations, we have $\rho(\tilde{S}) = \max_S \rho(S) \geq \frac{\rho(V^*)}{2+2\epsilon}$. We can choose $\gamma = 2\epsilon$, and get $\forall \gamma > 0$ a $(2 + \gamma)$-approximation.

Let us now analyze the complexity in terms of the number of iterations of this algorithm. We have:

$$2|E(S)| = \sum_{s \in A(S)} \deg_S(s) + \sum_{s \in S \setminus \{A(S)\}} \deg_S(s),$$

$$> 2(1 + \epsilon)(|S| - |A(S)|)\rho(S),$$

by taking account only of the terms of the second sum.

Since $\rho(S) = |E(S)|/|S|$, we deduce that

$$|A(S)| \geq \frac{\epsilon}{1 + \epsilon}|S|,$$

$$|S \setminus \{A(S)\}| < \frac{1}{1 + \epsilon}|S|.$$

Thus we remove a fraction of the vertices at each iteration, and we conclude that we have at most $O(\log_{1+\epsilon} n)$ iterations (that is, parallel steps).

Theorem 14 (Greedy parallel heuristic for the DSG) *For any $\epsilon > 0$, the greedy parallel heuristic guarantees a $2 + \epsilon$ approximation after $O(\log_{1+\epsilon} n)$ iterations.*

We describe below a parallel implementation of this heuristic using the MapReduce framework. We need to implement these three primitives as follows:

1. Compute the density ρ: it is a trivial operation since we only need to compute the total number of edges, and the total number of nodes at a given stage. We recall that data are stored in (key;value) pairs in MapReduce. We emit ("node";"1") for each pair (key;value) that encode a node with the node id as the key, and also emit ("edge";"1") for each pair (key;value) that encodes an edge with edge id as the key. Then we reduce after grouping intermediate keys by distinct values (either "nodes" or "edges") by calculating the cumulative sums for these intermediate keys.

2. Computing the degree of each node: we duplicate each edge (u, v) into two pairs (key;value): $(u; v)$ and $(v; u)$. We perform a reduction by computing the cumulative sum on the pairs $(u; v_1, v_2, ..., v_d)$ and by producing the result pair $(u, \deg(u))$.

3. Removing nodes with degrees smaller than a given threshold and their incoming edges: we shall use two stages of MapReduce. In the first stage, we start by marking nodes v that need to be eliminated by emitting a pair $(v; \$)$. We associate to each edge (u, v) a pair $(u; v)$. The reduce operation to u collects all edges that have one extremity being u with the potential dollar symbol $\$$. When the node is marked, the reducer process returns nothing, otherwise it copies its entry. Then in the second stage, we associate to each edge (u, v) the pair $(v; u)$ and we reiterate the process. Thus only the edges that have not been marked will survive these two stages of MapReduce.

In practice, it has been observed experimentally that we can compute an approximation $G_{|V''}$ of the densest sub-graph in a dozen of iterations, even for big graphs with a billion of nodes. This algorithm is useful because it allows one to decompose the graph into dense sub-graphs by recursively applying the heuristic on the remaining graph $G' = G \backslash G_{|V''}$, etc. Thus this heuristic can serve to discover communities in large data graphs.

11.2 Testing (Sub)graph Isomorphisms

Let $G_1 = (V_1, E_1)$ and $G_2 = (V_2, E_2)$ be two graphs with $n_i = |V_i|$ nodes and $m_i = |E_i|$ edges. We consider the problem to detect whether two graphs are identical up to some permutation σ of their labels: this problem is know as the *Graph Isomorphism* (GI) test problem. Of course, a necessary condition is that $n_1 = n_2 = n$ and $m_1 = m_2 = m$. Let us denote by $v_1^{(i)}$ and $v_2^{(i)}$ the vertices of V_1 and V_2, respectively. Figure 11.5 displays some isomorphic graphs. Those graphs are drawn in the plane, that is their combinatorial structures are embedded in the plane: that is the art of the field of graph drawing: draw pretty graphs!

This graph isomorphism problem belongs to the NP class but its complexity has not been yet (fully) settled. A breakthrough in November 2015 was obtained by Professor László Babai (a world renown expert on complexity theory) that claims a *quasi-polynomial algorithm* in time complexity $2O(\log n)^c$ for some constant c.

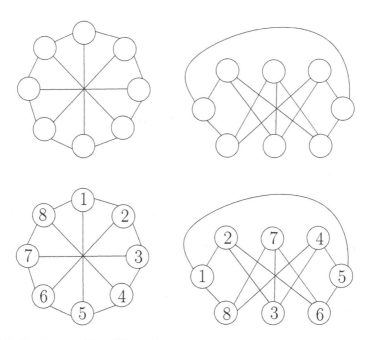

Fig. 11.5 Graph isomorphism (GI): graphs drawn without labels (*top*) and with corresponding labels (*bottom*)

Indeed, when wee are given a permutation σ, we can easily check in $O(m)$ time if those graphs are isomorphic, or not. We denote by $G_1 \cong G_2$ the fact that those graphs are congruent to each other. Permutation σ associate to nodes $v_1^{(i)}$ nodes $v_2^{(\sigma(i))}$, for all $i \in \{1, \ldots, n\}$. Let us observe that the permutation σ is defined up to some sub-permutations that depend on the sub-graph symmetries of the graph. For example, for complete sub-graphs (cliques), we can choose any permutation equivalently. Indeed, we can check that the complete graph K_n with n nodes is equivalent to any of its node permutation: $K_n \cong K_n^{(\sigma)} \forall \sigma$.

The main difficulty of the problem comes from the fact that there exits $n!$ potential permutations (see Fig. 11.5). This problem has been well-studied since the 1950s in chemistry to find whether a molecule given by its graph representation was already entered inside a data-base or not. In other word, if the graph of that molecule is isomorphic to one of the graph of the graph data-base of molecules.

On the other hand, testing whether there exists a sub-graph G_1' of G such that G_1' is isomorphic to a graph G_2 is known to be NP-complete. A sub-graph $G_1' \subseteq G_1$ is a graph defined for a subset V_1' of the vertices of V_1 so that edges of G_1 are defined by $E_1 = E_1 \cap (V_1' \times V_1')$ (we keep edge (u, v) if and only if both u and v belong to V_1').

Given a graph $G = (V, E)$ with $|V| = n$ and $|E| = m$, we can represent combinatorially this graph with a binary matrix, called the adjacency matrix, so that each edge $(v_i, v_j) \in E$ if and only if $M_{i,j} = 1$, and 0 otherwise. Matrix M is symmetric for non-oriented graphs and has exactly $2m$ entries set to 1. When we consider the adjacency matrix M_1 and M_2 of graphs G_1 and G_2, we can test the isomorphism of the corresponding graphs by testing whether there exists a permutation σ on the indexes so that $G_1 = G_2^{(\sigma)}$ with $G_2^{(\sigma)} = (\sigma(V_2), \sigma(E_2))$.

11.2.1 General Principles of Enumerating Algorithms

Most of the algorithms that have been conceived for testing the graph isomorphisms proceed as follows:

- We iteratively increase the partial matching of vertices,
- Pairs of associated vertices are chosen in order to satisfy some conditions (like having the same degree),
- We eliminate search paths that do not yield to a perfect complete vertex matching (pruning)
- When we reach a dead street, we remove the last hypothesis, and backtrack,
- The exploration algorithm stops when it has found a solution (providing a permutation certificate σ), or when all possible paths have been explored without yielding to a permutation solution.

The complexity of this generic but naive algorithm is in the worst case in $O(n!)$ time, a super-exponential[2] complexity! This algorithm also allows to test the sub-graph isomorphism.

Note that some problems intrinsically require exponential time like the Hanoi towers. However, the graph isomorphism is not yet know to be polynomially solvable for general graphs (Fig. 11.6).

11.2.2 Ullman's Algorithm to Test the Sub-graph Isomorphism

Ullman's algorithm is one of the oldest algorithm (1976) to test the sub-graph isomorphism. It relies on the adjacency matrices. We introduce the notion of *permutation matrices* that are square matrices with binary entries so that on each row and on each column, we have exactly one entry set to 1. For example, this matrix:

$$P = \begin{bmatrix} 1\ 0\ 0\ 0 \\ 0\ 0\ 1\ 0 \\ 0\ 0\ 0\ 1 \\ 0\ 1\ 0\ 0 \end{bmatrix},$$

is a permutation matrix. Those matrices are in one-to-one mapping with permutations σ of $(1, ..., n)$. The permutation matrix P_σ corresponding to σ is:

$$[P_\sigma]_{i,j} = \begin{cases} 1 & \text{si } i = \sigma(j), \\ 0 & \text{otherwise.} \end{cases}$$

Moreover, the permutation matrices form a group since we have $P_{\sigma_1} P_{\sigma_2} = P_{\sigma_1 \circ \sigma_2}$, with $\sigma_1 \circ \sigma_2$ the composition of permutations σ_1 and σ_2. An essential property is that two graphs G_1 and G_2 are isomorphic if and only if their adjacency matrices M_1 and M_2 are related by the following identity:

$$M_2 = P \times M_1 \times P^\top, \tag{11.1}$$

with $P^\top$ the transposed matrix of P, for a given permutation matrix P. This identity is equivalent to $M_2 P = P M_1$.

Thus we can enumerate all permutation matrices[3] and test whether the matrix identity of Eq. 11.1 holds for at least one of these matrices.

---

[2]Indeed, we have $\log n! = O(n \log n)$.

[3]This problem is in spirit similar to the problem of setting n queens in safe positions on a checkerboard of size $n \times n$. See [2].

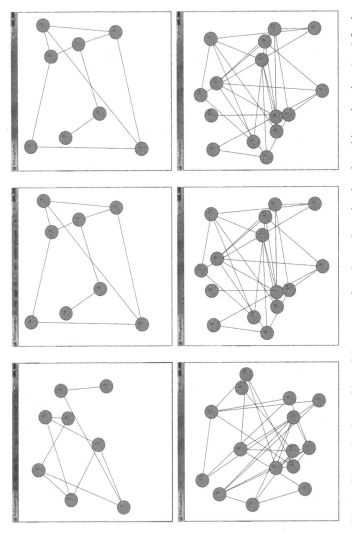

Fig. 11.6 Example of isomorphic graphs: the combinatorial structures of graphs are drawn by choosing arbitrary locations (x, y) for the nodes. *Top* (for $n = 8$ nodes): **a** original graph, **b** same graph drawn from other (x, y) locations of the vertices, and **c** after applying a permutation on the labels. It is more difficult to compare directly (**a**)–(**c**). *Bottom* Another example for $n = 15$ nodes. The permutation is $\sigma = (1, 4, 6, 0, 3, 7, 5, 2)$: it proves that graphs (**a**) and (**c**) are isomorphic.

Ullman's algorithm [3] relies on this principle by performing a depth first search (DFS) exploration. The complexity of Ullman's algorithm to test the isomorphism of graphs of size n is in $O(n^n n^2)$. In practice, we can test the isomorphism of graphs with a few hundreds nodes thanks to the pruning and backtracking technique.

11.2.3 Parallelizing Enumerating Algorithms

When using P processors in parallel, we can reduce the sequential running time by an optimal factor of P. Parallelizing the algorithm is straightforward by considering the vertex $v_1^{(1)}$ and all its vertices $v_2^{(j)}$ with $j \in \{1, \ldots, P = n\}$ allocated to processor P_j. Thus the parallel complexity is in $O(n^n n^2/P)$. That is, in $O(n^n n)$ when $P = n$. Of course, in practice, we associate $v_1^{(1)}$ to $v_2^{(j)}$ only if those vertices have the same degree. Thus, some processors will have no workload (when we consider graphs different from the self-symmetric complete graph). We choose a master-slave architecture with one dedicated processor being the master and the $P - 1$ remaining others being the slaves. The master processor gives research instructions to other slave processors by sending messages. When a slave processor has completed its computation either by reaching an incomplete permutation, or by finding a complete permutation (matching the graphs), it sends back its result in a message to the master processor. The master process needs to implement a routine to perform load-balancing for the $P - 1$ slave processors.

Generally speaking, many of the graph isomorphism algorithms are similar: it requires to balance the workload efficiently between the processors in order to achieve to good speed-up in practice. This is the problem of task scheduling.

11.3 Notes and Discussions

The greedy heuristic to approximate the densest subgraph has been proposed by Moses Charikar [1]. The parallel algorithm described can be implemented using the MapReduce framework. Testing the isomorphism of a n-node graph can be performed in $2^{O(\sqrt{n \log n})}$ time (exponential time), see [4]. Very recently, at the time of this book writing, Professor László Babai[4] (a world renown expert on complexity theory) claims a *quasi-polynomial algorithm* based on sophisticated group theory in time complexity $2O(\log n)^c$ for some constant c (note that when $c = 1$, the notation yields polynomial complexity). This is one big achievement in Theoretical Computer Science (TCS) after 30+ years. For planar graphs (graphs for which an embedding on the plane ensures that edges are pairwise non-intersecting), one can test the graph isomorphism in linear time. The class of trees belong to the planar graphs. Ullman's algorithm [3] is an efficient technique that relies on the adjacency matrix (1976).

---

[4]http://people.cs.uchicago.edu/~laci/.

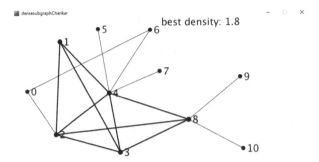

Fig. 11.7 Snapshot of the `processing` code for approximating greedily the densest sub-graph

A more efficient algorithm is the so-called VF2 algorithm (that improves over the VF algorithm [5]) and this algorithm is implemented in the `Boost`[5] C++ library. An experimental comparison of five algorithms for testing the graph isomorphism is reported in [6]. An implementation of both the sequential and parallel greedy heuristics are provided in http://processing.org on the accompanying book web page.

11.4   Summary

Graphs are convenient to model structures in data by taking into account relationships between them (edges). Nowadays, large graph data-sets are available and commonly use when we perform social network analytics (facebook, twitter, etc.). We attest a trend of analyzing efficiently voluminous graphs in data science. In this chapter, we described a greedy heuristic that finds an approximation of the densest sub-graph. Densest sub-graphs can represent communities. We showed how to efficiently parallelize this Charikar's heuristic. Then we have introduced the fundamental problem of testing whether two graphs are identical or not, up to relabeling of their nodes. This is the graph isomorphism problem. Although it is very easy to check whether a given permutation yields graph isomorphism or not, the complexity of this fundamental problem is not yet known. We presented a simple enumeration algorithm that uses pruning techniques and backtracking mechanism, and show how to parallelize this algorithm. This algorithm highlights the problem of load-balancing. That is, to split the configuration space between the processors to get good parallel times.

Processing Code for Approximating the Densest Sub-graph

Figure 11.7 displays a snapshot of the `processing.org` program.

WWW source code: `SequentialDenseSubgraph.pde`

WWW source code: `ParallelDenseSubgraph.pde`

---

[5]http://www.boost.org/.

11.5 Exercises

Exercise 1 (*Densest sub-graph for a weighted graph*) Let $G = (V, E, w)$ be a graph with edges weighted by a positive function $w(\cdot)$. Show how to generalize the Charikar's heuristic [1] to find an approximation of the densest sub-graph.

Exercise 2 *(Fast implementation of the densest sub-graph)* Show how to implement Charikar' heuristic [1] in linear time $O(n + m)$ by maintaining lists of vertices sorted by vertex degrees. Describe an efficient way to determine the minimum degree of vertices at each iteration of Charikar's heuristic using a Fibonacci heap.

Exercise 3 (*Parallelizing the approximation of the densest sub-graph*) Design a parallel algorithm in MPI that removes at each stage a sub-set of vertices. Implement in parallel Charikar's heuristic [1] and distributed memory architectures using MPI. What is the speed-up of your implementation?

References

1. Charikar, M.: Greedy approximation algorithms for finding dense components in a graph. In: Proceedings of the Third International Workshop on Approximation Algorithms for Combinatorial Optimization, APPROX '00, pp. 84–95. Springer, London (2000)
2. Nielsen, F.: A Concise and Practical Introduction to Programming Algorithms in Java. Undergraduate Topics in Computer Science (UTiCS). Springer, London (2009). http://www.springer.com/computer/programming/book/978-1-84882-338-9
3. Ullmann, J.R.: An algorithm for subgraph isomorphism. J. ACM **23**(1), 31–42 (1976). January
4. Babai, L., Luks, E.M.: Canonical labeling of graphs. In: Proceedings of the Fifteenth Annual ACM Symposium on Theory of Computing, STOC '83, pp. 171–183. ACM, New York (1983)
5. Cordella, L.P., Foggia, P., Sansone, C., Vento, M.: Performance evaluation of the VF graph matching algorithm. In: Proceedings International Conference on Image Analysis and Processing, pp. 1172–1177. IEEE (1999)
6. Foggia, P., Sansone, C., Vento, M.: A performance comparison of five algorithms for graph isomorphism. In: Proceedings of the 3rd IAPR TC-15 Workshop on Graph-based Representations in Pattern Recognition, pp. 188–199 (2001)

Appendix A
Written Exam (3 h)

The following four exercises are independent of each other. They are marked with estimated time to complete as follows:

Exercise	%	Difficulty level	Estimated time (min)
1	10	Low	30
2	20	Average	30
3	30	Average	45
4	40	High	60

Exercise 1 (*Speed-up and Amdahl's law*) Let $\mathcal{P}$ be a sequential program that can be parallelized at 75 %:

1. Give the numerical speed-up for $P = 3$ and $P = 4$ processors.
2. Explain the asymptotic speed-up and efficiency when $P \rightarrow +\infty$.

Consider now the following sequential program $\mathcal{P} = \mathcal{P}_1; \mathcal{P}_2$ that consists of two procedures $\mathcal{P}_1$ and $\mathcal{P}_2$ consecutively executed (serial code). Assume that the first procedure can be parallelized at 50 % and requires a sequential time t_1, while the second procedure can be parallelized at 75 % and require a time t_2. Moreover, consider that for the sequential code the second procedure always spend twice as much time as the first procedure: That is, $t_2 = 2t_1$.

3. Report the speed-up obtained when using P processors.
4. Deduce the asymptotic speed-up when $P \rightarrow \infty$.

Let us now consider a parallel algorithm on a data set of size n that has parallel time complexity $O_{\parallel}\left(\frac{n^2}{\sqrt{P}}\right)$ when using P processors. Assume in the remainder that the data-set holds in local memory of all processors. In practice, one has only a cluster of $P_0 \ll P$ physical machines to execute the parallel program with P processors (`mpirun -np P program`) (with P a multiple factor of P_0: $P \bmod P_0 = 0$).

© Springer International Publishing Switzerland 2016   261
F. Nielsen, *Introduction to HPC with MPI for Data Science*, Undergraduate
Topics in Computer Science, DOI 10.1007/978-3-319-21903-5

5. By emulating a virtual cluster of P machines on a physical cluster of P_0 machines (that is, by mapping several processes on a same processor with time sharing), report the parallel time complexity of the algorithm launched with P processes on the physical cluster of P_0 machines.

Solution 1 (*Speed-up and Amdahl's law*)

1. Let us apply Amdahl's law $S(P) = \dfrac{1}{\alpha_{\text{seq}} + \frac{1-\alpha_{\text{seq}}}{P}}$ with $\alpha_{\text{seq}} = 1 - \alpha_{\|} = \frac{1}{4}$. We get
   $S(3) = 2$ and $S(4) = \frac{16}{7} \simeq 2.29$.
2. The asymptotic speed-up is $S = \dfrac{1}{\alpha_{\text{seq}}} = 4$, and the asymptotic efficiency is 0.
3. Let us calculate the overall global fraction of parallelizable code as follows (see picture for an illustration): $\alpha_{\|} = \dfrac{\alpha_{\|}^{(1)} t_1 + 2\alpha_{\|}^{(2)} t_1}{3t_1} = \frac{2}{3}$. Thus we have $\alpha_{\text{seq}} = 1 - \alpha_{\|} = \frac{1}{3}$, and we conclude by applying Amdahl's law that $S(P) = \dfrac{1}{\frac{1}{3} + \frac{2}{3P}} = \dfrac{3}{1 + 2/P}$.

4. Asymptotic speed-up is 3 when $P \to \infty$.
5. Let us map on each physical processor $\frac{P}{P_0}$ logical processes in *time sharing* mode. The parallel complexity is thus $O_{\|}\left(\frac{n^2}{\sqrt{P}} \frac{P}{P_0}\right) = O_{\|}\left(n^2 \frac{\sqrt{P}}{P_0}\right)$.

Exercise 2 (*Parallel statistical inference of a normal distribution with MPI*) Let $X = \{x_1, \ldots, x_n\} \subset \mathbb{R}$ be a large random variate data set assumed to be independently and identically distributed from a Gaussian law

$$N(\mu, \sigma^2) : x_1, \ldots, x_n \sim N(\mu, \sigma^2).$$

We recall that the unbiased *maximum likelihood estimator* (MLEs) for the mean and variance are respectively:

$$\hat{\mu}_n = \frac{1}{n} \sum_{i=1}^{n} x_i \tag{A.1}$$

$$\hat{\sigma}_n^2 = \frac{1}{n-1} \sum_{i=1}^{n} (x_i - \hat{\mu}_n)^2. \tag{A.2}$$

1. Prove that $\hat{\mu}_n$ and $\hat{\sigma}_n^2$ can be calculated uniquely using the following three quantities: n, $S_1 = \sum_{x \in X} x$ and $S_2 = \sum_{x \in X} x^2$. Report explicitly the formula for $\hat{\mu}_n$ and $\hat{\sigma}_n^2$ as functions of n, S_1 and S_2 (without using any other variable).
2. Let us assume that data set X is fully stored in the local memory of one of the computer (the root machine) of a distributed cluster of p machines. By using

the following idealized MPI primitives `scatter()` and `reduce()`, write in *pseudo-code* a parallel algorithm that performs the following tasks:

- Share fairly data on all processors,
- Compute in a distributed fashion $\hat{\mu}_n$ and $\hat{\sigma}_n^2$ for the full data set X.

Solution 2 (*Parallel statistical inference of a normal distribution with MPI*)

1. Let $S_1 = \sum_{i \leq n} x_i$ and $S_2 = \sum_{i \leq n} x_i^2$. We have:

$$\hat{\mu}_n = \frac{S_1}{n}$$

$$\hat{\sigma}_n^2 = \frac{1}{n-1} \sum_{i \leq n} (x_i - \hat{\mu}_n)^2 = \frac{1}{n-1} \left(S_2 + n\hat{\mu}_n^2 - 2\hat{\mu}_n \sum_{i \leq n} x_i \right)$$

$$= \frac{S_2 + \frac{S_1^2}{n} - 2\frac{S_1}{n}S_1}{n-1} = \frac{S_2 + \frac{1}{n}(S_1^2 - 2S_1^2)}{n-1} = \frac{1}{n-1} \left(S_2 - \frac{S_1^2}{n} \right)$$

2. The following pseudo-code is an example of a correct solution for parallel statistical inference:

```
p = number of processes;
r = rank of the current process;
master = rank of the root process;
chunksize = n/p;
lastchunksize = n mod p;
if lastchunksize = 0 then
|  chunksize ← chunksize + 1;
end
m = p × chunksize;
resize X to have m vectors;
pad with zero vectors the last m − n vectors of X;
let Y_r be an array of chunksize vectors;
scatter(X, Y, master);
if r = p − 1 then
|  chunksize = lastchunksize;
end
slaveS1 = 0;
slaveS2 = 0;
for i ≤ chunksize do
|  slaveS1 ← slaveS1 + Y_r[i];
|  slaveS2 ← slaveS2 + Y_r^2[i];
end
reduce(slaveS1, S_1, master, MPI_SUM);
reduce(slaveS2, S_2, master, MPI_SUM);
if r = master then
|  μ̂_n = S_1/n;
|  σ̂_n = (S_2 − S_1^2/n)/(n − 1);
end
```

Exercise 3 (*Topology and communication on the hypercube*) In this exercise, you can refer to the following functions:

- the boolean operators AND, OR, XOR, NOT;
- bin: maps an integer into its binary code,
- Gray: maps an integer into its associated Gray code,
- 2^i, the ith power of 2,
- dec: maps a binary vector into the corresponding integer,
- leftmost: give the leftmost component of a vector: For example, leftmost(x_4, x_5, x_6, x_7) $= x_4$,
- significant(g), defined for any argument $g \neq 0$: Give the index i of the leftmost non-zero component in the binary vector $g = (g_{d-1}, \ldots, g_0)$. For example, by taking $g = (0, 1, 0, 1)$ and $d = 4$, we have significant($(0, 1, 0, 1)) = d - 2 = 2$,
- rightfill: report a binary vector obtained by exchanging all zeros into ones on the "right" (defined according to the first bit at one encountered from the right) of a binary vector. For example, rightfill($(0, 1, 0, 0)) = (0, 1, 1, 1)$.

1. Give an example of an irregular topology, and an example of a regular topology of degree 3 with 4 vertices. Is the topology of the hypercube regular? How many neighbor nodes is there in a hypercube?
2. Give two examples of a regular topology of degree 3: One with 12 vertices and the other with 16 vertices. Generalize your results to a family of regular topologies of degree 3 with $4k$ vertices for all $k \geq 3$.
3. Compute the Hamming distance between node $(0, 1, 0, 1)_2$ and node $(1, 1, 1, 0)_2$.
4. What are the neighbors of node $(0, 1, 1, 0)_2$ in the hypercube topology labeled with the Gray code? In general, given a node $g = (g_{d-1}, \ldots, g_0)$ labeled using the Gray code, report a formula for the function neighbor$_i$: $\{0, 1\}^d \rightarrow \{0, 1\}^d$ that labels its ith neighbor, for $i \in \{0, \ldots, d - 1\}$.
5. Draw a square in 2D, and label the nodes with their Gray code. Consider now a function f that associates a binary vector to an interval with integer bounds, as follows:

$$(0, 0) \rightarrow [0, 3]$$
$$(0, 1) \rightarrow [1, 1]$$
$$(1, 0) \rightarrow [2, 3]$$
$$(1, 1) \rightarrow [3, 3]$$

Now, consider a 3D cube ($d = 3$), and label the nodes with their Gray code. Consider the following extension of the function f when $d = 3$:

$$(0, 0, 0) \rightarrow [0, 7]$$
$$(0, 0, 1) \rightarrow [1, 1]$$
$$(0, 1, 0) \rightarrow [2, 3]$$
$$(0, 1, 1) \rightarrow [3, 3]$$

$$(1, 0, 0) \rightarrow [4, 7]$$
$$(1, 0, 1) \rightarrow [5, 5]$$
$$(1, 1, 0) \rightarrow [6, 7]$$
$$(1, 1, 1) \rightarrow [7, 7]$$

Generalize function f to an arbitrary hypercube in d dimensions. That is, report a formula for each d, to associate the binary vectors of $\{0, 1\}^d$ to appropriate intervals, matching the example intervals given for the 2D and 3D cases. Note that there are several solutions to this question.

6. Assume that the root process (master) of a d-dimensional hypercube with 2^d nodes fully contains the array $x = (x_0, \ldots, x_{p-1})$, where $p = 2^d$. Design a `scatter` algorithm (also known as personalized diffusion) on the hypercube (with root node labeled 0) so that the ith process receives element x_i. You can use function f defined previously above.

Solution 3

1. A complete graph with 4 vertices (clique) is a regular graph with nodes of degree 3. A complete binary tree has an irregular topology: Its root and inner nodes have degree 2 while leaves have degree 1. The hypercube in d dimensions has a regular topology with nodes of degree d (d neighbors/node).

2. Consider the graph *flower snark* J_k that is built from k stars[1]:

$$(\{O_i, A_i, B_i, C_i\}, \{\{O_i, A_i\}, \{O_i, B_i\}, \{O_i, C_i\}\})$$

for all $i \leq k$, by connecting $O_1, \ldots, O_k$ with a simple cycle, $A_1, \ldots, A_k$ with another simple cycle, and $B_1, \ldots, B_k, C_1, \ldots, C_k$ with a third simple cycle (that is of double length with respect to the others). The family of graphs J_k are all regular of degree 3. J_3 has 12 vertices (3 stars of 4 vertices each), and J_4 has 16 (4 stars of 4 vertices each). J_n has $4n$ vertices of degree 3 with $6n$ edges.

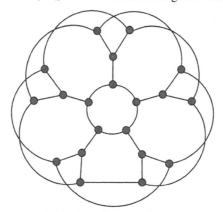

Flower snark J_5 (regular topology with degree 3).

---

[1] https://en.wikipedia.org/wiki/Flower_snark.

3. The Hamming distance is the number of different components between two binary vectors. In particular, we have: $\text{dist}_H((0, 1, 0, 1), (1, 1, 1, 0)) = 3$.

4. When the vertices of a hypercube are labeled using the Gray code, all pairs of neighboring nodes (that is, edges) are at Hamming distance one of each other. The four neighbors of $(0, 1, 1, 0)$ are therefore $(0, 1, 1, 1), (0, 1, 0, 0), (0, 0, 1, 0), (1, 1, 1, 0)$. When $g = (g_{d-1}, \ldots, g_0)$ is a node labeled using the Gray code, the formula is:

$$\forall i \in \{0, \ldots, d-1\} \quad \text{neighbor}_i(g) = g \text{ XOR } \text{bin}(2^i).$$

5. For all binary vector τ, the formula is:

$$[\text{dec}(\tau), \text{dec}(\text{rightfill}(\tau))].$$

Another correct formula consists in using the least significant bit at 1 provided by the function insignificant():

$$[\text{dec}(\tau), \text{dec}(\tau) + 2^{\text{insignificant}(\tau)} - 1].$$

6. Here is an implementation in pseudo-code of the `scatter` communication procedure on the hypercube. Data element x_p will be stored in the local variable v on the process ranked p.

```
Data: The master node is 0
Result: scatter(d, x, v)
p ← world.rank();
g ← Gray(p);
if p ≠ 0 then
    // g receives data y from neighbor
    i ← significant(g);
    receive(neighbor_i(g), y);
    // v contains a local copy of x_p
    v ← leftmost(y);
else
    i ← d;
end
for τ ∈ (neighbor_{i-j}(g) | 1 ≤ j < i) do
    // send correct chunk of data to neighbor
    send( τ, (x_j | dec(τ) ≤ j ≤ dec(rightfill(τ)) ) );
end
```

Another implementation is:

```
Data: the master node is 0
Result: scatter(d, x, v)
for i ∈ (d, d − 1, ..., 1) do
    if p mod 2^i = 0 then
        τ ← p + 2^{i−1};
        send( τ, (x_j | dec(τ) ≤ j ≤ dec(rightfill(τ))) );
    else if p mod 2^i = 2^{i−1} then
        φ ← p − 2^{i−1};
        receive( φ, (x_j | dec(φ) ≤ j ≤ dec(rightfill(φ))) );
        v ← x_dec(φ);
    end
end
```

Exercise 4 (*Centroid, variance, and k-medoid clustering*) For a finite point set $Z \subseteq \mathbb{R}^d$, we denote by $c(Z) \overset{\text{def}}{=} \frac{1}{|Z|} \sum_{z \in Z} z$ the center of mass (or centroid) of Z, with $|Z|$ the cardinal of set Z. For any two vectors $x = (x^{(1)}, \ldots, x^{(d)})$ and $y = (y^{(1)}, \ldots, y^{(d)})$ of $\mathbb{R}^d$, we define the scalar product as $x \cdot y = \sum_{i=1}^{d} x^{(i)} y^{(i)}$, the squared euclidean norm $\|x\|^2 = x \cdot x$, and the induced *squared Euclidean distance* by

$$\|x - y\|^2 \overset{\text{def}}{=} (x - y) \cdot (x - y) = \|x\|^2 - 2x \cdot y + \|y\|^2. \tag{A.3}$$

Let $X, Y \subseteq \mathbb{R}^d$ two non-empty subsets.

1. Prove the following centroid decomposition:

$$c(X \cup Y) = \frac{|X|}{|X| + |Y|} c(X) + \frac{|Y|}{|X| + |Y|} c(Y).$$

2. Let $v(Z) \overset{\text{def}}{=} \sum_{z \in Z} \|z - c(Z)\|^2$. Show the following identity:

$$v(Z) = \sum_{z \in Z} \|z\|^2 - |Z| \times \|c(Z)\|^2. \tag{A.4}$$

3. Let $\Delta(X, Y) \overset{\text{def}}{=} v(X \cup Y) - v(X) - v(Y)$. Prove that

$$\Delta(X, Y) = \frac{|X| |Y|}{|X| + |Y|} \|c(X) - c(Y)\|^2.$$

4. Let us extend the notion of unnormalized variance for any given point $x \in \mathbb{R}^d$ as follows:

$$v(Z, x) \overset{\text{def}}{=} \sum_{z \in Z} \|z - x\|^2.$$

Notice that this definition yields for the particular case $x = c(Z)$, the variance: $v(Z) = v(Z, c(Z))$.

(a) First, prove that:

$$v(Z, x) = v(Z) + |Z| \, \|c(Z) - x\|^2. \qquad (A.5)$$

(b) Second, by using Eq. (A.5), show that:

$$v(Z) \leq \min_{x \in Z} v(Z, x) \leq 2v(Z).$$

5. The *medoid* of a cluster $C \subseteq \mathbb{R}^d$ is defined as $\arg\min_{x \in C} \sum_{z \in C} \|z - x\|^2$. For sake of simplicity and without loss of generality, we shall assume in the remainder that all medoids are uniquely calculated. This is not true in general. For example, consider three vertices of an equilateral triangle. Then the medoid is not unique. Notice that we can order the points lexicographically to define uniquely the arg min, or we can add some random noise to every point.

Consider Lloyd 's batched k-means heuristic, and replace the prototypes of clusters by medoids instead of centroids, with the same k-means objective function to minimize: That is, the sum on all clusters of the squared distances of the cluster points to their prototype.

(a) Prove that the k-medoid algorithm initialized from any arbitrary k prototype configuration minimizes monotonically the objective function.
(b) Upper bound asymptotically the maximum number of iterations before convergence as a function of the data size n, and the number of clusters k.
(c) Prove that the optimal value of the objective function for the k-medoids is at most twice the optimal value of the objective function of the k-means.

Solution 4 Centroid, variance, and k-medoid clustering:

1. We have:

$$\sum_{z \in X \cup Y} \|z\|^2 = \sum_{z \in X} \|z\|^2 + \sum_{z \in Y} \|z\|^2, \qquad (A.6)$$

and therefore

$$c(X \cup Y) = \frac{1}{|X \cup Y|} \sum_{z \in X \cup Y} z$$

$$(\text{using } X \cap Y = \emptyset) = \frac{1}{|X| + |Y|} \left(\sum_{z \in X} z + \sum_{z \in Y} y \right)$$

$$(\text{from the definition of}) \, c(\cdot) = \frac{|X|}{|X| + |Y|} c(X) + \frac{|Y|}{|X| + |Y|} c(Y).$$

2. We have:

$$v(Z) = \sum_{z \in Z} \|z - c(Z)\|^2$$

$$\text{(from Eq. (A.3), 2nd part)} = \sum_{z \in Z} \|z\|^2 - 2\sum_{z \in Z}(z \cdot c(Z)) + \sum_{z \in Z} \|c(Z)\|^2$$

$$\text{(pulling out indep. terms of } z) = \sum_{z \in Z} \|z\|^2 - 2\left(\sum_{z \in Z} z\right) \cdot c(Z) + |Z|\,\|c(Z)\|^2$$

$$\text{(following the def. of } c(\cdot)) = \sum_{z \in Z} \|z\|^2 - 2|Z|(c(Z) \cdot c(Z)) + |Z|\,\|c(Z)\|^2$$

$$\text{(from Eq. (A.3), 1st part)} = \sum_{z \in Z} \|z\|^2 - 2|Z|\,\|c(Z)\|^2 + |Z|\,\|c(Z)\|^2$$

$$= \sum_{z \in Z} \|z\|^2 - |Z|\,\|c(Z)\|^2.$$

3. Following question 2, we have:

$$v(X) = \sum_{z \in X} \|z\|^2 - |X|\,\|c(X)\|^2 \tag{A.7}$$

$$v(Y) = \sum_{z \in Y} \|z\|^2 - |Y|\,\|c(Y)\|^2 \tag{A.8}$$

$$v(X \cup Y) = \sum_{z \in X \cup Y} \|z\|^2 - |X \cup Y|\,\|c(X \cup Y)\|^2. \tag{A.9}$$

By definition of $\Delta(X, Y)$, we have:

$$\Delta(X, Y) = v(X \cup Y) - v(X) - v(Y)$$

$$\text{(from Eqs. (A.7)–(A.9))} = \sum_{z \in X \cup Y} \|z\|^2 - |X \cup Y|\,\|c(X \cup Y)\|^2 +$$

$$- \sum_{z \in X} \|z\|^2 + |X|\,\|c(X)\|^2 - \sum_{z \in Y} \|z\|^2 + |Y|\,\|c(Y)\|^2$$

$$\text{(Eq. (A.6))} = |X|\,\|c(X)\|^2 + |Y|\,\|c(Y)\|^2 - |X \cup Y|\,\|c(X \cup Y)\|^2 (\star)$$

From Eq. (A.3), 1st part, we have $\|c(X \cup Y)\|^2 = c(X \cup Y) \cdot c(X \cup Y)$, and we can rewrite the result of question 1 as:

$$(|X| + |Y|)c(X \cup Y) = |X|c(X) + |Y|c(Y). \tag{A.10}$$

It follows that we have:

$$|X \cup Y| \|c(X \cup Y)\|^2 = (|X| + |Y|)c(X \cup Y) \cdot c(X \cup Y)$$
$$(\text{Eq. (A.10)}) = c(X \cup Y) \cdot (|X|c(X) + |Y|c(Y))$$
$$(\text{again Eq. (A.10)}) = \frac{1}{|X| + |Y|}(|X|c(X) + |Y|c(Y)) \cdot (|X|c(X) + |Y|c(Y)).$$
$$= \frac{|X|^2}{|X| + |Y|}\|c(X)\|^2 + \frac{|Y|^2}{|X| + |Y|}\|c(Y)\|^2$$
$$+ \frac{2|X||Y|}{|X| + |Y|}c(X) \cdot c(Y). \tag{A.11}$$

Now we apply (A.11) at the third term of the right hand side of Eq. $(\star)$, to get:

$$\Delta(X, Y) = (\star) = \left(|X| - \frac{|X|^2}{|X| + |Y|}\right)\|c(X)\|^2 + \left(|Y| - \frac{|Y|^2}{|X| + |Y|}\right)\|c(Y)\|^2$$
$$- \frac{2|X||Y|}{|X| + |Y|}c(X) \cdot c(Y)$$
$$= \frac{|X||Y|}{|X| + |Y|}(\|c(X)\|^2 + \|c(Y)\|^2 - 2c(X) \cdot c(Y))$$
$$(\text{from Eq. (A.3)}) = \frac{|X||Y|}{|X| + |Y|}\|c(X) - c(Y)\|^2.$$

4. (a) Notice that the structure of Eq. (A.5) is very similar to that of Eq. (A.4). Thus it is enough to adapt the proof given in question 2:

$$v(Z) = \sum_{z \in Z} \|z - c(Z)\|^2$$
$$(\text{for all } x) = \sum_{z \in Z} \|(z - x) + (c(Z) - x)\|^2$$
$$(\text{A.3}) = \sum_{z \in Z} \|z - x\|^2 - 2\sum_{z \in Z}(z - x) \cdot (c(Z) - x) + \sum_{z \in Z}\|c(Z) - x\|^2$$
$$(\text{def. } v()) = v(Z, x) - 2\left(\sum_{z \in Z} z - |Z|x\right) \cdot (c(Z) - x) + |Z| \|c(Z) - x\|^2$$
$$(\text{def. of } c(\cdot)) = v(Z, x) - 2|Z|(c(Z) - x) \cdot (c(Z) - x) + |Z| \|c(Z) - x\|^2$$
$$(\text{from (A.3)}) = v(Z, x) - 2|Z| \|c(Z) - x\|^2 + |Z| \|c(Z) - x\|^2$$
$$= v(Z, x) - |Z| \|c(Z) - x\|^2.$$

We thus have $v(Z, x) = v(Z) + |Z| \|c(Z) - x\|^2$ for all $x \in \mathbb{R}^d$.

(b) *Concerning the lower bound* $\min_{x \in Z} v(Z, x) \geq v(Z)$, *we consider the relaxed problem* $\min_{x \in \mathbb{R}^d} v(Z, x)$, *where we have enlarged the admissible region that was* $Z \subset \mathbb{R}^d$, *to the full space* $\mathbb{R}^d$. *Therefore the minimum x on Z is nec-*

essarily in $\mathbb{R}^d$. It follows that $\min_{x \in Z} \mathsf{v}(Z, x) \geq \min_{x \in \mathbb{R}^d} \mathsf{v}(Z, x)$. Now we calculate $\min_{x \in \mathbb{R}^d} \mathsf{v}(Z, x)$. Since the function $\mathsf{v}(Z, x)$ is strictly convex in each cluster of $x \in \mathbb{R}^d$, we set the derivative to zero:

$$\forall j \leq d \quad \frac{\partial}{\partial x_j} \sum_{z \in Z} \|z - x\|^2 = \frac{\partial}{\partial x_j} \sum_{z \in Z} (\|z\|^2 + \|x\|^2 - 2 z \cdot x)$$

$$= \sum_{z \in Z} \frac{\partial}{\partial x_j} (\|x\|^2 - 2 z \cdot x)$$

$$= \sum_{z \in Z} (2x_j - 2z_j) = |Z|x_j - \sum_{z \in Z} z_j = 0,$$

Therefore $\forall j \leq d$ $x_j = \frac{1}{|Z|} \sum_{z \in Z} z_j$ that implies that $x = \mathsf{c}(Z)$ at least. We conclude that $\min_{x \in \mathbb{R}^d} \mathsf{v}(Z, x) = \mathsf{v}(Z, \mathsf{c}(Z)) = \mathsf{v}(Z)$.

Concerning the upper bound $\min_{x \in Z} \mathsf{v}(Z, x) \leq 2\mathsf{v}(Z)$, let us notice that each term in the sum $\sum_{x \in Z} \mathsf{v}(Z, x)$ exceeds the minimum value. We thus have:

$$\sum_{x \in Z} \min_{x \in Z} \mathsf{v}(Z, x) \leq \sum_{x \in Z} \mathsf{v}(Z, x) \Rightarrow$$

$$\min_{x \in Z} \mathsf{v}(Z, x) \leq \frac{1}{|Z|} \sum_{x \in Z} \mathsf{v}(Z, x) =$$

$$from \; Eq. \, (A.5) = \frac{1}{|Z|} \sum_{x \in Z} (\mathsf{v}(Z) + |Z| \, \|\mathsf{c}(Z) - x\|^2)$$

$$= \mathsf{v}(Z) + \frac{|Z|}{|Z|} \sum_{x \in Z} \|\mathsf{c}(Z) - x\|^2$$

$$from \; def. \, of \; \mathsf{v}(Z) = \mathsf{v}(Z) + \mathsf{v}(Z) = 2\, \mathsf{v}(Z).$$

Another very concise proof for the lower/upper bounds: $\forall x \in \mathbb{R}^d$ $\mathsf{v}(Z) = \mathsf{v}(Z, x) - |Z| \, \|\mathsf{c}(Z) - x\|^2$; Since the last term is non-negative, $\mathsf{v}(Z) \leq \mathsf{v}(Z, x)$. It follows that $\mathsf{v}(z) \leq \min_{x \in Z} \mathsf{v}(Z, x)$. Upper bound: for a given value of x, that is $x = \mathsf{c}(Z)$, we have $\mathsf{v}(Z, x) = \mathsf{v}(Z) \leq 2\mathsf{v}(Z)$; this bound also holds for $\min_{x \in Z} \mathsf{v}(Z, x)$.

5. The objective function of the k-means minimizes the sum of the square intra-cluster distances for all clusters $C \in \mathcal{C}$ (with $|\mathcal{C}| = k$):

$$F(\mathcal{C}) = \sum_{C \in \mathcal{C}} \sum_{x \in C} \|x - \rho(C)\|^2, \tag{A.12}$$

where for all $C \in \mathcal{C}$, $\rho(C)$ is the prototype of cluster C. If we choose $\rho(C) = \mathsf{c}(C)$, we obtain the ordinary k-means:

$$F'(\mathcal{C}) = \sum_{C \in \mathcal{C}} v(C).$$

When considering the k-medoids, we have:

$$F''(\mathcal{C}) = \sum_{C \in \mathcal{C}} \min_{x \in C} v(C, x).$$

(a) Starting from a given configuration for the k prototypes, the two stages of Lloyd's algorithm (assignment to the closest medoid and medoid update) let reduce the k-means objective function. Convergence is therefore monotonous.

(b) The maximum number of iterations is bounded since the k-means objective function is non-negative (positive or zero). Since we never repeat a same configuration of the k-medoids, and that we have at most $\binom{n}{k}$ choices, we bound the maximum number of iterations in $O\left(\binom{n}{k}\right)$, or in $O(n^k)$ where k is a prescribed integer constant. Alternatively, we can report the Stirling number of the second kind that counts the number of partitions of n integers into k sub-sets.

(c) Let $\mathcal{C}'$ denote the optimal value of the objective function of the ordinary k-means (function F'), and $\mathcal{C}''$ the optimal value solution for the k-medoids (function F''). Then we have $F''(\mathcal{C}'') \leq 2F'(\mathcal{C}'')$ (question 4b), and from the optimality of $\mathcal{C}'$, we deduce that $F'(\mathcal{C}'') \leq F'(\mathcal{C}')$. Therefore $F''(\mathcal{C}'') \leq 2F'(\mathcal{C}')$.

Appendix B
SLURM: A Resource Manager and Job Scheduler on Clusters of Machines

It can be tedious to write manually `hostfile` configuration files for executing MPI programs on a set of interconnected machines via the `mpirun --hostfile config` command, specially when we use a large cluster of machines. Fortunately, we can use a *Task scheduler* to allocate and plan the execution of programs. SLURM[2] that is the acronym for *Simple Linux Utility for Resource Management (SLURM)* is such a utility program to manage and share resources among users. SLURM schedules tasks (jobs) to be executed on a cluster of machines. *Pending jobs* are queued jobs waiting to be executed once resources get available for them. SLURM takes care of Input/Output (I/Os), signals, etc.

Jobs are submitted by users via shell commands, and they are scheduled according to the FIFO model (First-In First-Out). Script files to launch batched jobs can also be submitted to SLURM.

From the user standpoint, the four main commands prefixed with a 's' (for 'S'LURM) are:

- `sinfo`: display general information of the system,
- `srun`: submit or initialize a job,
- `scancel`: raise a signal or cancel a job,
- `squeue`: display information of system jobs with R indicating Running state and PD PenDing state,
- `scontrol`: administrator tool to set or modify the configuration.

We recommend the online SLURM tutorial[3] for further details.

A common scenario is to organize and configure a large set of machines into a few clusters of machines. For example, the author taught the contents of this textbook to about 280 students/year using 169 machines, and organized those computers into 4 clusters, 3 of 50 machines and one cluster of 19 machines. A student logged on a

---

[2] Available online at https://computing.llnl.gov/linux/slurm/.

[3] http://slurm.schedmd.com/tutorials.html.

© Springer International Publishing Switzerland 2016
F. Nielsen, *Introduction to HPC with MPI for Data Science*, Undergraduate Topics in Computer Science, DOI 10.1007/978-3-319-21903-5

machine can display the information related to the cluster the machine belongs to by typing the `sinfo` command:

```
[malte ~]$ sinfo
PARTITION AVAIL    TIMELIMIT   NODES   STATE NODELIST
Test*            up       15:00       19     idle
allemagne,angleterre,autriche,belgique,espagne,
    finlande,france,groenland,
hollande,hongrie,irlande,islande,lituanie,malte,monaco
    ,pologne,portugal,roumanie,suede
```

We can easily execute a program called `hostname` (just reporting on the console the names of the machines used) using 5 nodes (hosts) with a maximum of two processes per node as follows:

```
[malte ~]$ srun -n 5 --ntasks-per-node=2 hostname
angleterre.polytechnique.fr
autriche.polytechnique.fr
allemagne.polytechnique.fr
allemagne.polytechnique.fr
angleterre.polytechnique.fr
```

We can also use SLURM to execute a shell command `shell.sh` that launches a MPI program `myprog` as follows:

```
[malte ~]$ cat test.sh
#!/bin/bash
LD_LIBRARY_PATH=$LD_LIBRARY_PATH:/usr/local/openmpi-1.8.3/lib/:
/usr/local/boost-1.56.0/lib/
/usr/local/openmpi-1.8.3/bin/mpirun -np 4 ./myprog

[malte ~]$ srun -p Test -n 25 --label test.sh
09: I am process 1 of 4.
09: I am process 0 of 4.
...
01: I am process 0 of 4.
01: I am process 2 of 4.
05: I am process 2 of 4.
05: I am process 3 of 4.
```

We summarize the main SLURM commands in the table below:

salloc	Resource allocation
sbatch	Give "batch" files
sbcast	Dispatch files on allocated nodes
scancel	Cancel the running "batch" file
scontrol	Control interface of SLURM
sdiag	To get the status report
sinfo	Display information related to the cluster of machines
squeue	Display the job queue
srun	Run a job
sstat	Report execution states
strigger	Manage and trigger signals
sview	Interface to view the cluster

Index

© Springer International Publishing Switzerland 2016
F. Nielsen, *Introduction to HPC with MPI for Data Science*, Undergraduate
Topics in Computer Science, DOI 10.1007/978-3-319-21903-5

Printed in the United States
By Bookmasters